CHANGING INDIAN SOCIETY

CHANGING INDIAN SOCIETY

K.V. Raman

SUMIT ENTERPRISES
New Delhi-110 002 (India)

First Published 2011

ISBN 978-81-8420-265-6

Published by:

SUMIT ENTERPRISES
4649B/21, Ansari Road, Darya Ganj
New Delhi-110 002
Phone: 011-23279353, 9810217567
E-mail: sumit_enterprises2007@yahoo.co.in

PRINTED IN INDIA

Published by Sri Lokesh Kumar for Sumit Enterprises, New Delhi-110 002, Typeset by Abhijeet Typesetters, Printed at Sachin Printers.

Preface

Chastising Indian society for failing to engage with key issues such as poverty class and caste-based reservations and to respond to the multiple crises that beset the nation, he notes how these issues are complicated by the processes of identity formations the functioning of institutions and globalisation. Indian society as a multicultural entity composed of different ethnic origins, various religions, and belonging to a variety of speech communities, and yet bonded together as a nation, sharing a common polity and economy.

India is a hierarchical society. Within Indian culture, whether in the north or the south, Hindu or Muslim, urban or village, virtually all things, people, and groups of people are ranked according to various essential qualities. If one is attuned to the theme of hierarchy in India, one can discern it everywhere. Although India is a political democracy, in daily life there is little advocacy of or adherence to notions of equality. Castes and castelike groups—those quintessential groups with which almost all Indians are associated—are ranked. Within most villages or towns, everyone knows the relative rankings of each locally represented caste, and people's behaviour toward one another is constantly shaped by this knowledge. Between the extremes of the very high and very low castes, however, there is sometimes disagreement on the exact relative ranking of castes clustered in the middle. Castes are primarily associated with Hinduism but also exist among other Indian religious groups. Muslims sometimes expressly deny that they have castes—they state that all Muslims are brothers under God—but observation of Muslim life in various parts of India reveals the existence of castelike groups and clear concern with social hierarchy. Among Indian Christians, too, differences in caste are acknowledged and maintained.

The view of modernization as offensives argues that both the developments and the altered opportunities made available by these developments are shaped and controlled by human agents. The view of modernization as offensives therefore sees it as a product of human planning and action, an active process capable of being both changed and criticized. Modernization emerged in the late 19th century and was especially popular among scholars in the mid-20th century. One foremost advocate was Harvard sociologist Talcott Parsons. The theory stressed the importance of societies being open to change and saw reactionary forces as restricting development. Maintaining tradition for tradition's sake was thought to be harmful to progress and development. Proponents of modernization lie in two camps, optimists and pessimist. The former view what a modernizer would see as a setback to the theory (events such as the Iranian Revolution or the troubles in Lebanon) as temporary setbacks, with the ability to attain "modernism" still existing. Pessimists would argue that such non-modern areas are incapable of becoming modern.

This book will be a pointer for those who are working in the field of gerontology and of immense use for researchers, planners, students, teachers and policy maker.

Contents

1

Introduction

In the social sciences, Modernization refers to a standardized evolutionary transition from a 'pre-modern' or 'traditional' to a 'modern society. The teleology of modernization is described in social evolutionism theories, existing as a template that has been generally followed by societies that have achieved modernity. Critics say it may be possible for some societies to make the transition in entirely different ways. Historians link modernization to the processes of urbanization and industrialization, as well as to the spread of education. As Kendall (2007) notes, "Urbanization accompanied modernization and the rapid process of industrialization. In sociological critical theory, modernization is linked to an overarching process of rationalisation.

Modernization theory and history have been explicitly used as guides for countries eager to develop rapidly, such as China. Indeed, modernization has been proposed as the most useful framework for World history in China, because as one of the developing countries that started late, "China's modernization has to be based on the experiences and lessons of other countries.".

Theory

According to theories of modernization, each society can in theory develop from traditionalism to modernity, and that those which have made the transition have followed similar paths. The more modern states are wealthier and more powerful, and their citizens freer and having a higher standard of living. According to the Social theorist Peter Wagner, modernization can be seen as processes, and as offensives. The former view is commonly projected by politicians and the media, and suggests that it is developments, such as new data technology or need to update traditional methods, which make modernization necessary or preferable. This view makes critique of modernization difficult, since it implies that it is these developments which control the limits of human interaction, and not vice versa.

The view of modernization as offensives argues that both the developments and the altered opportunities made available by these developments are shaped and controlled by human agents. The view of modernization as offensives therefore sees it as a product of human planning and action, an active process capable of being both changed and criticized.

Modernization emerged in the late 19th century and was especially popular among scholars in the mid-20th century. One foremost advocate was Harvard sociologist Talcott Parsons. The theory stressed the importance of societies being open to change and saw reactionary forces as restricting development.

Maintaining tradition for tradition's sake was thought to be harmful to progress and development. Proponents of modernization lie in two camps, optimists and pessimist. The former view what a modernizer would see as a setback to the theory (events such as the Iranian Revolution or the troubles in Lebanon) as temporary setbacks, with the ability to attain "modernism" still existing. Pessimists would argue that such non-modern areas are incapable of becoming modern.

IDEA OF PROGRESS

In historiography, the Idea of Progress is the theory that advances in technology, science, and social organization inevitably produce an improvement in the human condition. That is, people can become happier in terms of quality of life (social progress) through economic development (modernization), and the application of science and technology (scientific progress). The assumption is that the process will happen once people apply their reason and skills, for it is not divinely foreordained. The role of the expert is to identify hindrances that slow or neutralize progress.

Historian J. B. Bury wrote in 1920:

> *"To the minds of most people the desirable outcome of human development would be a condition of society in which all the inhabitants of the planet would enjoy a perfectly happy existence....It cannot be proved that the unknown destination towards which man is advancing is desirable. The movement may be Progress, or it may be in an undesirable direction and therefore not Progress..... The Progress of humanity belongs to the same order of ideas as Providence or personal immortality. It is true or it is false, and like them it cannot be proved either true or false. Belief in it is an act of faith."*

Sociologist Robert Nisbet finds that "No single idea has been more important than...the Idea of Progress in Western civilization for three thousand years.", and defines five "crucial premises" of Idea of Progress:

1. value of the past
2. nobility of Western civilization
3. worth of economic/technological growth
4. faith in reason and scientific/scholarly knowledge obtained through reason
5. intrinsic importance and worth of life on earth.

The Idea of Progress emerged primarily in the Enlightenment in the 18th century, although some scholars like Nisbet (1980) have traced it to ancient Christian notions. The theory of evolution in the nineteenth century made progress a necessary law of nature and gave the doctrine its first conscious scientific form. The idea was challenged by the 20th century realization that destruction, as in the two world wars, could grow out of technical progress.

Antiquity

Historian J. B. Bury argued that thought in ancient Greece was dominated by the theory of world-cycles or the doctrine of eternal return, and was steeped in a belief parallel to the Judaic "fall of man," but rather from a preceding "Golden Age" of innocence and simplicity. Time was generally regarded as the enemy of humanity which depreciates the value of the world. He credits the Epicureans with having had a potential for leading to the foundation of a theory of Progress through their materialistic acceptance of the atomism of Democritus as the explanation for a world without an intervening Deity. "For them, the earliest condition of men resembled that of the beasts, and from this primitive and miserable condition they laboriously reached the existing state of civilisation, not by external guidance or as a consequence of some initial design, but simply by the exercise of human intelligence throughout a long period."

Robert Nisbet and Gertrude Himmelfarb have attributed a notion of progress to other Greeks. Xenophanes said "The gods did not reveal to men all things in the beginning, but men through their own search find in the course of time that which is better."

Plato's Book III of *The Laws* depicts humanity's progress from a state of nature to the higher levels of culture, economy, and polity. Plato's *The Statesman* also outlines a historical account of the progress of mankind. The Roman philosopher Seneca recognized the progress of knowledge, but he did not expect from it any improvement in the world, because any advance in the arts and inventions promotes deterioration by ministering to luxury and vice.

Enlightenment

The scientific advances of the 16th and 17th centuries provided a basis for the optimistic outlook of Bacon's 'New Atlantis.' In the 17th century Bernard le Bovier de Fontenelle argued in favour of progress with respect to arts and the sciences, saying that each age has the advantage of not having to rediscover what was accomplished in preceding ages. The epistemology of John Locke provided further support and was popularized by the Encyclopedists Diderot, Holbach, and Condorcet.

Locke had a powerful influence on the American Founding Fathers

In the Enlightenment, French historian and philosopher Voltaire (1694-1778) was a major proponent. At first Voltaire's thought was informed by the Idea of Progress coupled with rationalism. His subsequent notion of the historical Idea of

Progress saw science and reason as the driving forces behind societal advancement. The first complete statement of progress is that of Turgot, in his "A Philosophical Review of the Successive Advances of the Human Mind" (1750). For Turgot progress covers not simply the arts and sciences but, on their base, the whole of culture—manner, mores, institutions, legal codes, economy, and society. [{Condorcet]] pre-dicted the disappearance of slavery, the rise of literacy, the lessening of inequalities between the sexes, reforms of prison harsh prisons and the decline of poverty.

Immanuel Kant (1724-1804) argued that progress is neither automatic nor continuous and does not measure knowledge or wealth, but is a painful and largely inadvertent passage from barbarism through civilization toward enlightened culture and the abolition of war. Kant called for education, with the education of humankind seen as a slow process whereby world history propels mankind toward peace through war, international commerce, and enlightened self-interest.

Scottish theorist Adam Ferguson (1723-1816) defined human progress as the working out of a divine plan, though he rejected predestination. The difficulties and dangers of life provided the necessary stimuli for human development, while the uniquely human ability to evaluate led to ambition and the conscious striving for excellence. But he never adequately analysed the competitive and aggressive consequences stemming from his emphasis on ambition even though he envisioned man's lot as a perpetual striving with no earthly culmination. Man found his happiness only in effort.

American Revolution

The intellectual leaders of the American Revolution—such as Benjamin Franklin, Tom Paine, Thomas Jefferson and John Adams, were immersed in Enlightenment thought and believed the Idea of Progress meant that they could reorganize the political system to the benefit of the human condition—for Americans and also, as Jefferson put it, for an "Empire of Liberty" that would benefit all mankind. Thus was born the idea of inevitable American future progress. What gave the American Revolution its widespread appeal and linked it to all subsequent political revolutions was its association with the

Idea of Progress. The most original 'New World' contribution to historical thought was the idea that history is not exhausted but that man may begin again in a new world. Besides rejecting the lessons of the past, the Jeffersonians Americanized the Idea of Progress by democratizing and vulgarizing it to include the welfare of the common man as a form of republicanism.

As Romantics deeply concerned with the past, collecting source materials and founding historical societies, the Founding Fathers were animated by clear principles. They saw man in control of his destiny, saw virtue as a distinguishing characteristic of a republic, and were concerned with happiness, progress, and prosperity. Thomas Paine, combining the spirit of rationalism and romanticism, pictured a time when America's innocence would sound like a romance, and concluded that the fall of America could mark the end of 'the noblest work of human wisdom.'

That human liberty was put on the agenda of fundamental concerns of the modern world was recognized by the revolutionaries as well as by many British commentators. Yet, within two years after the adoption of the Constitution, the American Revolution had to share the spotlight with the French Revolution. The American Revolution was eclipsed, and, in the 20th century, lost its appeal even for subject peoples involved in similar movements for self-determination. Thus, its life as a model for political revolutions was relatively short. The reason for this development lies in the fact that its concerns and preoccupations were overwhelmingly political; economic demands and social unrest remained largely peripheral. After the middle of the 19th century, all political revolutions would ultimately have to involve themselves with social questions and become revolutions of modernization.

But the American Colonies in the 1770s, in contrast to all other colonies, had been modern from the beginning. The American patriots were protecting the modernity and liberty they had already achieved, while later revolutions were fighting to obtain liberty for the first time. However, since so few modern revolutions have evinced much concern for the preservation and extension of human freedom, the American model may still come to provide a lesson for the future.

The notion that America is a highly favourable place for people seeking progress in their own lives comprises the American Dream.

SOCIAL PROGRESS

Social progress is the idea that societies can or do improve in terms of their social, political, and economic structures. The concept of social progress was introduced in the early 19th century social theories, especially those of social evolutionists like Auguste Comte and Herbert Spencer. It was present in the Enlightenment's philosophies of history.

Enlightenment

The big breakthrough to a new idea in Europe Enlightenment, when social commentators and philosophers began to realize that people *themselves* could change society and change their way of life. Instead of being made completely by gods, there was increasing room for the idea that people themselves *made their own society*-and not only that, as Giambattista Vico argued, *because* people practically made their own society, they could also fully comprehend it. This gave rise to new sciences, or proto-sciences, which claimed to provide new scientific knowledge about what society was like, and how one may change it for the better. In turn, this gave rise to progressive opinion, in contrast with conservational opinion.

The social conservationists were skeptical about panaceas for social ills. According to conservatives, attempts to radically remake society normally make things worse. Edmund Burke was the leading exponent of this, although later-day liberals like Hayek have espoused similar views. They argue that society changes organically and naturally, and that grand plans for the remaking of society, like the French Revolution, National Socialism and Communism hurt society by removing the traditional constraints on the exercise of power.

The Notion of Freedom

This new idea implied a new concept of human freedom, i.e. people independently making their own lives using their own judgment. Initially, this concept appeared rather paradoxical; thus, Jean-Jacques Rousseau wrote, "People are born free, but are everywhere in chains". A big breakthrough was the French Revolution of 1789, which inspired a lot of new philosophical thought. In the philosophy of the German thinker Hegel, history radically recasts itself as the continual development of humanity towards ever-greater freedom, continually extending the limits of freedom.

This philosophy is still religious and mystical however, insofar as Hegel sees history as culminating in the unity of God with the world, but at the same time, Hegel also affirmed and imputed a Logos or teleology to human history, and fully recognized that both evolutionary and revolutionary transformations took place in history. This was a hopeful philosophy, which in a rational way sees real progress occurring in history.

It was possible to detect human advances, as well as human regressions to an earlier state. In Hegel's view, if something existed, it was rational. If it passed out of existence, that was because it had become irrational. This contained a very important idea, however poorly expressed, namely that history was not a fluke of fate (a kismet) but that it could be *rationally understood*, at least in principle.

Marxism

Marx developed a theory of historical materialism. He describes the mid-19th century condition in the Communist Manifesto as follows:

> *"The bourgeoisie cannot exist without constantly revolutionizing the instruments of production, and thereby the relations of production, and with them the whole relations of society. Conservation of the old modes of production in unaltered form, was, on the contrary, the first condition of existence for all earlier industrial classes. Constant revolutionizing of production, uninterrupted disturbance of all social conditions, everlasting uncertainty, and agitation distinguish the bourgeois epoch from all earlier ones. All fixed, fast frozen relations, with their train of ancient and venerable prejudices and opinions, are swept away, all new-formed ones become antiquated before they can ossify. All that is solid melts into air,*

> *all which is holy is profaned, and man is at last compelled to face with sober senses his real condition of life and his relations with his kind."*

The capitalism is thought by Marx as a process of continual change, in which the growth of markets dissolve all fixities in human life. This is an almost absolute rejection of the conservative ethos, according to which nothing really changes in human life. Marxism further states that capitalism, in its quest for higher profits and new markets, will inevitably sow the seeds of its own destruction. Marxists believe that, in the future, capitalism will be replaced by socialism and eventually communism.

Modernism

> *"The reasonable man adapts himself to the world. The unreasonable man persists in trying to adapt the world to himself. Therefore, all progress depends on the unreasonable man."—George Bernard Shaw.*

Many advocates of capitalism such as Schumpeter agreed with Marx's analysis of capitalism as a process of continual change through creative destruction, but, unlike Marx, believed and hoped that capitalism could essentially go on forever.

Thus, by the beginning of the 20th century, two opposing schools of thought-Marxism and liberalism-believed in the possibility and the desirability of continual change and improvement. Marxists strongly opposed capitalism and the liberals strongly supported it, but the one concept they could both agree on was modernism.

Modernism is a trend of thought which affirms the power of human beings to make, improve and reshape their society, with the aid of scientific knowledge, technology and practical experimentation. It reaches its extreme limits with the Russian Revolution and the third Chinese revolution, inspired by Marxist ideology.

Here, people claimed such confidence in the ability to change their world for the better, which they thought that, in a relatively short time, largely illiterate peasants could begin to build a just, egalitarian and socialist order in a conscious way, armed with science and technology.

Postmodernism

"As it will be in the future, it was at the birth of Man.

There are only four things certain since Social Progress began.

That the Dog returns to his Vomit and the Sow returns to her Mire." —Rudyard Kipling.

In the postmodernist thought steadily gaining ground from the 1980s, the grandiose claims of the modernizers are steadily eroded, and the very concept of social progress is again questioned and scrutinized. In the new vision, radical modernizers like Stalin and Mao appear as totalitarian despots, whose vision of social progress is held to be totally deformed. Postmodernists question the validity of 19th century and 20th century notions of progress-both on the capitalist and the Marxist side of the spectrum.

They argue that both capitalism and Marxism over-emphasize technological achievements and material prosperity while ignoring the value of inner happiness and peace of mind. Postmodernism posits that both dystopia and utopia are one and the same, over arching grand narratives with impossible conclusions. The romanticism of our past due to present discontent has set western society into a state of nostalgia where modernism is feared. Here the past is re-presented as solution to our current problems.

Contemporary Trends

In the present time, this trend of thought about social progress leads to four main kinds of responses:

- Neo-conservatism, which returns to the old idea that nothing ever truly changes in the human condition, and the eternal values of religion. The ability of people to change anything other than themselves is vastly overrated. Here, the emphasis is on honouring a traditional way of life which proved itself as superior in the past, to which we should adhere.
- Neo-liberalism, which affirms the power and potential of change, but only on a personal, individual level. The idea that the state should be an instrument of social betterment in society as a whole is totally rejected; only

free choices made in markets can hold any promise of social progress.

- Socialism, which argues that state direction of social progress could have very important positive results; at the simplest level, would be able to help the poor by taking from the rich. This leads to the defence of public services and assets, and the case for heavy regulation of market activity.
- Various strands of new radicalism, which begin to question again the objective criteria by which we could measure human social progress. For example, labour productivity might be a criterion of social progress, but how about infant mortality? This kind of thinking rejects the political traditions of the past, and argues that a variety of criteria must be applied to assess social progress. In some cases, this leads to new charters for the moral criteria to which a society should aspire; in other cases, authentic lived experience in society with all its complexities is emphasized.

SCIENTIFIC PROGRESS

Scientific progress is the idea that science increases its problem solving ability through the application of some scientific method.

Discontinuous Model of Scientific Progress

Several Philosophers of Science have supported arguments that the progress of science is discontinuous. In that case, progress is not a continuous accumulation, but rather a revolutionary process where brand new ideas are adopted and old ideas become abandoned. Thomas Kuhn was a major proponent of this model of scientific progress, as explained in his book The Structure of Scientific Revolutions. This is especially supported by studying the incommensurability of theories. For example, consider Newtonian mechanics and relativistic mechanics. From a strict vantagepoint, in newtonian mechanics mass and energy are always conserved, where in relativistic mechanics energy and mass are always interchangeable. (Note the difference between the strict vantagepoint, and the layperson's vantagepoint that Newton's theory is applicable at low energies and low velocities relative to the velocity of light.) Because the theories are completely incompatible, scientists using one paradigm will not be able to discuss meaningfully with scientists from the other paradigm.

A discontinuous model of scientific progress may disagree with a realist's construction in the philosophy of science. This is because the intrinsic nature of the objects referred to may change wildly.

History of Science as a Model of Scientific Progress

Another model of Scientific Progress, as put forward by Richard Boyd, and others, is History of Science as a model of scientific progress. In short, methods in science are produced which are used to produce scientific theories, which then are used to produce more methods, which are then used to produce more theories and so on. Note that this does not conflict with a continuous or discontinuous model of scientific progress. This model supports realism in that scientists are always working within the same universe; their theories must be referring to real objects, because they create theories that refer to actual objects that are used later in methods to produce new theories.

A good example supporting realism is the case of the electron. It is hard to prove the existence of an electron because it is so small. However, any microscopist will tell you that he knows an electron exists, because he uses it in his electron microscope.

Origins of the Concept

Early technological and religious traditions did not concern themselves with gaining knowledge in any systematic way, and thus the concept of scientific progress would have been largely alien to them. Societies deeply invested in tradition were primarily occupied with the verbatim passing of thoughts and practises to the next generation, and did not engage in the scientific method.

Even if some esoteric traditions may have involved themselves with a rudimentary experimental method as the nucleus of their initiation, they did not overtly separate exploration from instruction. Some classical Greeks like Hippocrates did systematically gather evidence, but as a *concept* incremental increase of knowledge is first formulated in connection with the art of warfare.

Quotes on Scientific Progress

Dr. Terry Halwes wrote:

"What is required for scientific progress is mainly ordinary curiosity, ordinary awareness, ordinary learning, ordinary reasoning, and fairly ordinary communication. Of course scientists work hard to develop and use precise technical terms for many of the things they talk about, but so do lawyers and golfers and cooks."

Sir Karl Popper wrote in *The Logic of Scientific Discovery*:

The wrong view of science betrays itself in the craving to be right; for it is not his possession of knowledge, of irrefutable truth, that makes the man of science, but his persistent and recklessly critical quest for truth.

The Science Hobbyist says:

Lots of important science comes NOT from proposing hypotheses or even from performing experiments, but instead comes from unguided observation and curiosity-driven exploration: from sniffing about while learning to see what nobody else can see. Scientific discovery comes from something resembling "informed messing around," or unguided play.

PHILOSOPHICAL PROGRESS

A prominent question in metaphilosophy is the that of whether or not philosophical progress occurs, and more so, whether such progress in philosophy is even possible. It has even been disputed, most notably by Ludwig Wittgenstein, whether genuine philosophical problems actually exist. The opposite has also been claimed, most notably by Karl Popper, who held that such problems do exist, that they are solvable, and that he had actually found definite solutions to some of them.

Overview

Some philosophers believe that, unlike scientific or mathematical problems, no philosophical problem is truly solvable in the conventional sense, but rather problems in philosophy are often refined rather than solved. For example Bertrand Russell, in his 1912 book *The Problems of Philosophy* says: "Philosophy is to be studied not for the sake of any definite answers to its questions, since no definite answers can, as a rule, be known to be true, but rather for the sake of the questions themselves."

However, this is not universally accepted amongst philosophers. For example Martin Cohen, in his 1999 iconoclastic account of philosophy, *101 Philosophy Problems*, offers as the penultimate problem, the question of whether or not 'The problem with philosophy problems is that they don't have proper solutions'. He goes on to argue that there is a fundamental divide in philosophy between those who think philosophy is about *clarification* and those who think it is about recognising *complexity*.

According to Cohen, Etienne Bonnot de Condillac and Moritz Schlick illustrate this divide in views of the 'purpose of philosophy'. The former, writing in the eighteenth century, describes someone waking up from a deep sleep to find that they are in the middle of labyrinth together with some other people who are arguing over the general strategy and principles for trying to find the way out. What could appear more ridiculous says Etienne, yet that, he says, is what philosophers are doing, concluding: "It is more important to find ourselves merely where we were at first than to believe prematurely that we are out of the labyrinth."

Cohen contrasts this with the approach of the Logical Positivist movement in the interwar years of the Twentieth Century who, in the spirit of David Hume, wished to consign unanswerable questions 'to the flames'. As the 'hub' of the Logical Positivist circle, Moritz Schlick put it in an article entitled 'Unanswerable Questions' for the journal The Philosopher:

"It is very easy to ask questions the answers to which, we have the strongest reasons to believe, will never be known to any Human being. What did Plato do at eight o'clock in the morning of his fiftieth birthday? How much did Homer weigh when he wrote the first line of the Iliad? Is there a piece of silver to be found on the other side of the moon, three inches long and shaped like a fish? Obviously, men will never know the answers to these questions, however hard they may try. But at the same time, we know that they would never try very hard. These problems, they will say, are of no importance, no philosopher would worry about them, and no historian or naturalist would care whether he knew the answers or not."

Argument for Progress in Philosophy

If it is conceded that philosophical claims are a function of the sophistication of conceptual distinctions, arguments, and logical tools, and if it is conceded that there has been progress in making conceptual distinctions, progress in our sophistication about the nature of philosophical arguments, and progress in logic, then clearly there is progress in philosophy.

Those who deny progress because of lack of agreement must take stock of the fact that agreements must be relativized to those who are taking part in the discussion. And, of course, there will be degrees of sophistication. For example, someone who lacks sophistication in symbolic logic is not in a position to discuss an argument presented in symbolic form. Or, suppose that one person accuses the other of "begging the question," and the other responds: "So what?" What is the significance of lack of consensus in this instance?

Argument for Lack of Progress in Philosophy

It is often complained that philosophy has developed more slowly than the special sciences, and has not enjoyed the same sort of remarkable and definitive progress seen in chemistry or physics. It is nearly universally agreed (a remarkable feat, amongst philosophers) that this has something to do with the peculiar methods of philosophical inquiry. In particular, philosophy seems to lack the sort of developments that Thomas Kuhn called *paradigms*—achievements which, by their success, clearly determine which sort of questions are to be asked and what sort of considerations count as evidence for or against answers to those questions. However, even if it is common to hear that, there is no consensus on the issue—some philosophers, such as Marx, Sartre, and Barthes, do consider that philosophy is *historical*, i.e. in step with society, a superstructure of it. This amounts to a consideration of the contribution of philosophers of the past as obsolete, or inadequate with respect to synchronic concerns

Optimism, Pessimism, and Paradigms

But this is where the agreement ends; philosophers differ widely over the exact diagnosis of the situation, and the lesson to be taken from it. They differ, for example, over whether the lack of paradigms is an *accidental* or an *essential* feature of philosophy. We might call the former *optimists* about philosophical progress and the latter *pessimists.*

The optimists (such as the early modern philosophers George Berkeley and David Hume) typically argue that philosophy has not made much progress because philosophers have historically used methods that are unsystematic, obscure, confused, or otherwise unsuccessful; but, citing the example of the revolutionary achievements in the natural sciences during the scientific revolution, they argue that philosophers could enjoy the same sort of progress, rather than endlessly recapitulating the same obscure debates, if only philosophers can find an appropriate paradigm and a clear method for their work. The introduction to David Hume's Treatise of Human Nature is a *locus classicus* of this view; Hume subtitled his book "Being An Attempt To Introduce the Experimental Method of Reasoning Into Moral Subjects."

Pessimists, on the other hand, take the lack of progress to be an *essential* feature—arguing that philosophy *must* remain without paradigms as long as it is remains philosophy rather than something else. One way of putting the worry might be this: for something to count as a paradigm *just is* for it to be the sort of achievement that cuts off certain sorts of foundational worries about the essential nature of the subject-matter and the validity of particular methods for studying it; but these sorts of foundational worries are quintessentially *philosophical* worries. In Kant's words, human reason can say nothing about noumena, things in themselves, but only about phenomena, how things appears to us. Human understanding and thus science doesn't concern itself with the foundations of science, but only of its workings. However, in Kant's mind, this only separated dogmatism from *critique* philosophy: neither sciences nor philosophy must answer questions about noumenons, since this superate their innate capacities. That doesn't mean that it is never worthwhile to set such questions to one side—you can't make any serious progress in *physics,* for example, while you are still arguing over whether it is coherent to talk about laws of nature. But it *does* mean that whatever it is you are doing, you are, in an important respect, *ceasing* to do philosophy. If this is correct, then there is no chance of achieving progress in philosophy by adopting a paradigm—adopting a paradigm can achieve progress in *something else,* but only by making it cease to be philosophy.

Pessimists may also make a historical point about the emergence of the various natural sciences from philosophy. In the ancient and medieval world, nearly all fields of study were considered to be parts of the discipline of philosophy. (This historical reality is still reflected in the institutions of the University, where the highest degree awarded in most academic fields is still the Ph.D., or Doctor of Philosophy.) The clearest point at which the natural sciences diverged from philosophy proper just was when they adopted paradigms for research—especially the work of Galileo and Newton in mechanics. The critical step here is for the pessimist to argue that the natural sciences separated from philosophy *precisely because* they adopted a paradigm—that it was *in virtue of* that change in their direction that they began engaging in scientific rather than philosophical studies.

There seems to be a persuasive case to be made for *that* point, but even if there is the consideration is not necessarily decisive. An optimist might very well accept everything that the pessimist says about the emergence of the natural sciences—and *still* disagree with the conclusion. The argument would go something like this: it might very well be that *natural scientists* stopped doing philosophy in virtue of their adoption of a paradigm during the Scientific Revolution. But that's because they adopted *scientific* paradigms—the achievements that set the course of their research programmes were *experimental* achievements. That doesn't mean that there cannot *also* be paradigms which are specifically *philosophical* achievements. (That is, an achievement which decisively settles *certain* foundational philosophical questions for the purposes of a research programme, but which leaves other *distinctively philosophical* questions open for further inquiry, and which addresses them through *distinctively philosophical* methods.) They might even point to historical examples of seminal philosophical works which have, to some degree or another, played a similar role to paradigm achievements in the natural sciences—landmark, tradition-establishing works such as those of Plato, or Immanuel Kant's three Critiques, or the ground-breaking Analytic works of Bertrand Russell and G. E. Moore.

It seems historically unquestionable that these works have played at least *some* of the roles that Kuhn attributed to paradigms. They did create coherent traditions of research—whether Platonist, Kantian, or Analytic. It also seems that (like scientific paradigms) they achieved this by (1) convincing enough philosophers that the work had decisively settled certain philosophical problems, and (2) redirecting subsequent philosophy into energetic work on a set of specialized questions that the seminal work had left open. Kant's Critical philosophy, for example, was widely understood to put a more or less final end to the debate between rationalism and empiricism by demonstrating that the debate was based on a false alternative. A great deal of post-Kantian philosophy abandoned such debates and redirected its focus toward specific concerns that arise from within the Critiques, such as the foundations of mathematics or the possibility of an intellectual intuition.

On the other hand, it is another question whether works such as these actually live up—and whether they *could ever* live up—to *everything* that Kuhn says about scientific paradigms. Kuhn argues that the history of science is a sort of punctuated equilibrium: when a long period of "normal science" eventually stagnates, and an established paradigm can no longer hold together a coherent tradition of research, progress depends on the establishment of a new paradigm, and a scientific revolution based on this paradigm shift. Once the old paradigm breaks down and the new one is established, there seems to be no going back: the old scientific paradigm is *decisively* repudiated, and simply becomes obsolete. But does such a picture capture the history of philosophy as well as the history of science? The waxing and waning of philosophical traditions seems to be far less decisive and far more cyclical; if this doesn't cast doubt on the notion of philosophical progress *simpliciter,* it does at least tend to suggest that *lasting* progress may be an illusory goal. Similarly, although the works pointed to by optimists have had remarkable impacts in setting research programmes, it's far from clear that the specialized inquiry they inspired plays quite the same role that "normal science" plays in Kuhn's understanding of scientific progress. J. G. Fichte and Arthur Schopenhauer, for example, are sharply differing writers who focused on questions raised by Kant; but Schopenhauer's doctrine of the will or Fichte's dialectical spin on transcendental idealism could hardly be seen as examples of inquiries that close off *fundamental* questions in order to consider technical problems of *application.* At most it seems that Kant's work encouraged these later philosophers to do fundamental work in *different* areas from those that he was taken to have shown fruitless.

Would it have been Worth it, After all?

An answer to the question of whether philosophical practice is *possible,* however, is not the end of the story: it may still leave open the question of whether it is *desirable.* Those who are *optimists* about the prospect for philosophical progress have a pretty clear answer: it is, they could argue, just part of what we *mean* by "progress," that you ought to pursue it if you can get it. But the issue is somewhat trickier for pessimists. If philosophical progress is *not* possible, then there are two different lessons that could be, and have been, taken from that.

Philosophy as Worthless

On the one hand, a pessimist might take the impossibility of scientific progress in philosophy to be a sign that philosophy is a dead-end job—thus, a pessimist about philosophical progress might also be a pessimist about philosophy. The argument goes something like this: scientific progress is what makes an intellectual effort worthwhile; but there is no hope for scientific progress in philosophy; therefore there is no hope for philosophy to be worthwhile. On this view, philosophy is regarded as a sort of pseudoscience which *aspires* to scientific progress, but which (by its very nature) can never *achieve* it; and so it is best abandoned in favour of empirical scientific inquiry. Needless to say, this is not a view that most professional philosophers are particularly fond of or comfortable with, but it does seem to have been the consensus of the Vienna Circle positivists towards more or less all traditional philosophical inquiry, although not necessarily to the use of *philosophical method* to get clear on the logical structure of *empirical* questions. It is, perhaps, much more popular with professional scientists (as some of the Vienna positivists were themselves), who are inclined to think of philosophy as airy speculation that retards the serious empirical work of science.

Philosophy as Intrinsically Worthy

However, this critique of metaphysics, carried on by the first Wittgenstein, in his 1921 *Tractatus Logico-Philosophicus*, for example, has been in return criticized by philosophers, such as Heidegger in his 1927 *Being and Time*, as a form of positivism or, worse, scientism, which is accused of having decided to abandon the most important questions about humanity and the Being, under the pretext that no definitive answer can be brought to them.

Marxist Georg Lukacs would also criticize, in his book *History and Class Consciousness* (1923), the Kantian abandon of knowledge of the *concrete totality*: according to Lukacs, Kant's distinction between noumenons and phenomena lead to the abandon of the knowledge of the historical process, which could be only apprehended, in his eyes, by dialectical materialism. As marxism is essentially concerned with the historical process and the possibility of a revolution, that is of superating capitalism, marxist philosophy, from Marx and Engels to Althusser passing by Lukacs, etc., has discussed at lengths the problems of possible historical progress of philosophy and what would that mean.

Althusser, for example, considered the "epistemological break" (separating protosciences from sciences) to apply itself to philosophy itself: the discovery by Marx of a new "continent" of knowledge, History, provided the epistemological break between ancient metaphysics and modern dialectical materialism. However, if dialectical materialism was considered by Althusser as a "scientific theory", this does not mean it was permanently assured of its truth: it is a science, not a prophecy! In effect, Althusser stressed that the epistemological break was not an *event*, which could be chronologically located (in this or that book of Marx) and thus definitively separated science from ideology.

Instead, this epistemological break was a *process* that had to be endlessly renewed, thus explaining revisionist tentatives to break away from this progress and renew with the old protoscientifical (and "bourgeois") theory, which ignored the social and historical conditions which made human society what it is. Althusser's theory is interesting insofar as, contrary to Kuhn, it does not considers various paradigms to be incommensurable between themselves. In Kuhn's eyes, Ancient's sciences simply can't be compared to modern science, and they have nothing in common.

Althusser argues that this amounts to deny progress between modern sciences and ancient sciences, since the cumulative aspect of progress is ignored. However, the cumulative aspect of progress, both in philosophy and science, is not considers by Althusser as obtained "once for all": it is always a political struggle against ideology, which endlessly penetrates science and philosophy. This explains his famous word about the existence of "class struggle inside the theory" itself. Although Althusser's marxist philosophy may repels many people today, his criticisms of the notion of a "neutral science", which followed the Frankfurt School's criticisms of scientifical and technical progress, and his conception of a cumulative although discontinuous "progress" of philosophy represents one of the toughest attempt to think a cumulative progress of sciences and philosophy (both subsumed under the term of "theory") without falling into a plain scientist optimism about a "continuous and linear necessary progress". As in any marxist theory, ultimately theory is dependent on human *praxis*, and only the rebellion and continuous struggle against the dominant ideology that allows theory, whether scientific or philosophical, to be truly an objective theory.

Henceforth, one might draw the conclusion that pessimism about philosophical progress allows for a sort of *liberation* from the expectations for scientific progress, and thus for a *reasoned optimism* about philosophy. Philosophers in this camp argue that once we recognize that it makes no sense for philosophy to *make* scientific-technical progress, we ought to also realize that it makes no sense for philosophy to *aspire* to it either. In other words, philosophy is not science, and shouldn't imitate sciences. Rather than expect philosophy to prove its worth with scientific-technical progress, and then judge it worthless when it fails to, these philosophers argue that philosophical inquiry must be worthy *in its own right.*

The perceived need for philosophy to prove itself in terms of some sort of scientific-technical progress is often diagnosed as a sort of creeping scientism, and repudiated as a drastic oversimplification of our intellectual life. This *may* have been the position of Wittgenstein against the Vienna positivists—although if Wittgenstein saw any intrinsic value in philosophical inquiry he certainly didn't think that most people could profit from it. In any case, it was certainly the position of latter Wittgensteinians such as Peter Winch, as well as other contemporary philosophers such as Heidegger. The view also, its proponents argue, represents a "return" to the conception of philosophy and its value found in ancient philosophers such as Plato and Aristotle.

In *What Is Philosophy?* (1991), Deleuze and Guattari would argue that while science creates percepts and art affects, philosophy creates concepts. These concepts are *not* answers to existential questions, but a specific way of conceiving the *problem*. In other words, the accent is not, as in science, put on the answer or explanation given to a specific phenomenon, but on the way the problem itself is posed.

An illustration of this may be given by Marx's critique of political economy: *bourgeois* political economy is denounced as concerning itself with only how the capitalism system works day-to-day, but doesn't poses the problem of *how* capitalism first appeared, what are the conditions of possibility of this appearance of capitalism and, finally, what are the conditions of its dissolving. Hence, while ordinary political economy is concerned by the so-called "laws of economics", presented as universal (i.e. valid in all times and places), marxism attempts to demonstrate that these principles are only historical products of human history. A historian such as Fernand Braudel, for example, would be more interested in trying to answer the question of why capitalism appeared in Europe and not in China, exploring the historical conditions which made capitalism possible, than describing the "laws of economics".

Philosophy as Instrumentally Worthy

Nor do these alternatives exhaust the possibilities: one might agree with the optimists that philosophical inquiry *has* value, but agree with the pessimists that philosophical inquiry must justify itself in terms of scientific-technical progress to have any value. This may seem to conflict with the shared premise between progress-pessimists that there is no progress in philosophy, but the trick here is to argue that *philosophical* progress is not the only sort of progress to which philosophical inquiry might contribute. Philosophy is seen as being justified by progress—but not by progress in *philosophy*, but rather in providing *useful tools* for making progress in *other fields*.

Since this view values philosophy as a means to an end rather than as an end in itself, we might call it "instrumental optimism" about philosophy, as opposed to the "intrinsic optimism" already discussed. On this view, philosophy is seen neither as a sort of pseudoscience, nor as something *radically distinct* from the sciences, but rather as a sort of *incubator for new sciences* — protosciences. While the intrinsic optimists draw on Plato and Aristotle's writings on the value of philosophical inquiry, the instrumental optimists can draw on another aspect of the ancients' work: specifically, Aristotle was concerned both about "physics" (and biology) and "metaphysics". He didn't really make any distinction between these two fields. Actually, the name "meta-physics" was given by later scholars who meant by this word: what is "beyond" or "after" the study of "nature" (*phusis*-physics).

Thus, "philosophy" ("love of wisdom" in Greek) at that time included both "physics" and "metaphysics". Instrumental optimists thus argue this non-distinction between physics and metaphysics, and point out the historical role that the Ancient's philosophical works played in the development of the natural sciences, and then later the social sciences. From this history instrumental optimists might urge that speculative philosophy can have value as a place for proposing new sciences and new research programmes within the sciences, as well as a critical location for exposing and clearing away confusions that obstruct progress in the natural sciences. Philosophy, then, is seen as a sort of midwife: she does not give birth to any progress of her own, but proves her worth by making it possible for others to bring *their* progress into the world. Thus, whereas the value of mechanics or biology or psychology is taken to be *internal* to the practice (i.e., judged in terms of the progress of *mechanical, biological,* or *psychological* achievements), the value of *philosophy* is taken to be *external* (i.e., judged in terms of its effects on achievements in other fields, such as mechanics, biology, and psychology). This view is congenial to the conception of philosophy, most famously propounded by John Locke, as a sort of intellectual "underlabourer" to the sciences. It is also a view endorsed in various articles by Hilary Putnam, and may be the most popular view amongst contemporary Analytic philosophers—especially those with a naturalistic bent.

Instrumental optimism is, of course, not without its own difficulties. For example, there's hardly any reason to deny the truth of what the instrumental optimists say about the historical relationship between what some philosophers did and what natural scientists do today. But that doesn't necessarily mean that the ancients philosophers were doing *philosophy* when they did work that contributed to natural science. Of course, they might have *called* what they were doing "philosophy." But if so, that just means that they meant something more expansive by the word than what we mean by it today, and we might think that there are perfectly good reasons for sticking to the narrower conception of philosophical method. Moreover, whatever the status of their works that eventually contributed to natural science, and whatever the value of those contributions it's very difficult to make a case that the *philosophical* value is best captured by its contribution to scientific posterity. (Is the lasting value of Aristotle's work better exhibited by his Physics or by his Metaphysics? By his reflections on horse's teeth or on the good life for rational beings?)

Critics of this conception of philosophy as being essentially an epistemology (or philosophy of science) dedicated to exploring psychic or ideological blocks which prevent scientifics from making specific hypothesis (such as in Gaston Bachelard's theory) argue that this only reverse the hierarchy between philosophy and science. Instead of philosophy being located on top of the pyramid of knowledge, as in Hegel's *Phenomenology of Spirit*, it becomes a simple tool for rationalism and sciences. This view has been criticized by certain philosophers, such as

Deleuze or Michel Foucault, who declared that Thought couldn't be identified to rationalism, and that irrationalism wasn't to be considered as the contrary of thought (i.e. as madness, which, as Foucault demonstrated, is the product of a historical conception and disciplinary technologies of power). Deleuze, for example, argued that thought, which could take the form of philosophy, arts or sciences, basically *created* new possibilities of thought and life, and therefore new modes of existence. This liberty of thought was, in the eyes of these French philosophers, the only real "use" of philosophy-although Deleuze mocked the utilitarian view which would assigned to philosophy a specific "use", which could, in his mind, only be ideologically assigned. This joins a critique of science often made, first of all by the Frankfurt School: scientific research only tries to resolve certain problems and exclude others. For example, tropical diseases are not subject to much research, as it is not considerated profitable by the pharmaceutical industry. On the other side, fat or sex-issues are considered much more important, thus allowing for the huge investments necessary to the invention of Viagra. Henceforth, saying something is "useful" only extends the problem to the criteria of this "usefulness": science is often said "useful" because it has "practical effects", which "philosophy" doesn't seems to have. However, is science that ignores tropical diseases in order to concentrate itself on Viagra really is useful? Does it helps to have, as in Aristotle's views, a "good life"? This explains why Deleuze rejected the definition of philosophy as something "useful", and preferred it to be an "opening of possibles", something which made new possible worlds possible.

Nor, of course, does accepting the instrumental value of philosophy for other fields require one to abandon the view that philosophy *also* has *intrinsic* worth, nor the view that its intrinsic worth should be the primary reason to pursue philosophical inquiry. Some things are valued both for themselves and for their consequences; if the instrumental optimist wants (as some of them surely *do*) to insist not only on accepting the instrumental worth of philosophy, but also of accepting *nothing but* its instrumental worth, then she must *support* the stronger claim that philosophy could *only* have value in virtue of its contribution to scientific-technical progress in *some* field or another. But, if philosophy is like a mother-lode for the nascent sciences, so too like a godmother, philosophy has traditions which can guide her godchildren past ethical and moral quagmires, into which they might stray, to the detriment of their progress.

MODERN TRANSFORMATIONS

The process of modernization in India, well under way during the British colonial period (1757-1947), has brought with it major changes in the organizational forms of all religions. The missionary societies that came with the British in the early nineteenth century imported, along with modern concepts of print media and propaganda, an ideology of intellectual competition and religious conversion. Instead of the customary interpretation of rituals and texts along received sectarian lines, Indian religious leaders began devising intellectual syntheses that could encompass the varied beliefs and practices of their traditions within a framework that could withstand Christian arguments.

One of the most important reactions was the Arya Samaj (Arya Society), founded in 1875 by Swami Dayananda (1824-83), which went back to the Vedas as the ultimate revealed source of truth and attempted to purge Hinduism of more recent accretions that had no basis in the scriptures. Originally active in Punjab, this small society still works to purify Hindu rituals, converts tribal people, and runs centers throughout India. Other responses include the Ramakrishna order of renunciants established by Swami Vivekananda (1863-1902), which set forth a unifying philosophy that followed the Vedanta teacher Shankara and other teachers by accepting all paths as ultimately leading toward union with the undifferentiated *brahman*. One of the primary goals of the Ramakrishna movement has been to educate Hindus about their own scriptures; the movement also runs book stores and study centres in all major cities. Both of these paths are directly modelled on the institutional and intellectual forms used by European missionaries and religious leaders.

During the 1930s and 1940s, again responding to institutional models from Europe, the more activist Rashtriya Swayamsevak Sangh (RSS—National Volunteer Organisation) emerged to protect Hinduism. The RSS had been founded in 1925 by Keshav Baliram Hedgewar (1889-1944), a native of Maharashtra who was concerned that Hinduism was in danger of extinction from its external foes and needed a strong, militant force of devotees to protect it. Members believe that the Indian nation is the divine mother to whom the citizen devotes mind and body through *karma-yoga* , or disciplined service. Training consists of daily early morning meetings at which the saffron, white, and green Indian flag and the swallow-tailed, red-ocher RSS banner are raised as rows of members salute silently. There are then group drills in gymnastic exercises, sports, discussions of patriotic themes from a primarily Hindu viewpoint, group singing of nationalist songs, and a final assembly with saluting. Throughout India in the early 1990s, there were cells (*shakha*) of fifty to 100 members from all walks of life (the RSS rejects class differences) who were devoted to the nation. Although it has attracted hundreds of thousands of members from all over India, the RSS has never projected itself as a political party, always remaining a national club that is ready to send its members to trouble spots for the defense of the nation and the national culture, embodied in Hinduism. The Jana Sangh, established in 1951, was the RSS's political arm until it joined the Janata Party in 1977 and its membership split away in 1980 to form the BJP.

Another activist organization is the Vishwa Hindu Parishad (VHP—World Hindu Council), founded in 1964. The VHP runs schools, medical centres, hostels, orphanages, and mass movements to support Hinduism wherever it is perceived as threatened. This ultraconservative organization played a role in the extensive agitation for the demolition of a mosque in Ayodhya, leading to the destruction of the structure during a huge demonstration in 1992. As a result of the VHP's complicity in the affair, the Ministry of Home Affairs imposed a two-year ban on the Vishwa Hindu Parishad under the Unlawful Activities Act. When the ban expired in December 1994, the government reimposed it for two additional years.

The spread of Hindu "communal" (that is, religious) sentiment parallels a similar rise in religious chauvinism and "fundamentalist" ideologies among religious minorities, including Muslims and Sikhs. Against this background of agitation, the periodic outbreak of communal riots in urban areas throughout India contributes to an atmosphere of religious tension that has been a hallmark of the national political scene during the twentieth century. Hindu-Muslim riots, especially in North India, reached a peak during the partition of India in 1947 and periodically escalated in urban areas in the early 1990s. This strife typically involves low-income groups from both communities in struggles over land, jobs, or local resources that coalesced around a religious focus after seemingly trivial incidents polarized the two communities. In practice, although members of other religious communities are the victims of violence, rioters are rarely motivated by religious instructors, although fundamentalist agitators are often implicated. The situation in North India became complicated during the 1980s by Sikh terrorism connected with the crisis in Punjab, the widespread anti-Sikh riots after Prime Minister Indira Gandhi's assassination in November 1984 by her Sikh bodyguards, and a series of terrorist or counterterrorist actions lasting into the 1990s. In all of these cases, many observers believe that religion has appeared as a cover for political and economic struggles.

The perception that one's religion is in danger receives periodic reinforcement from the phenomenon of public mass religious conversion that receives coverage from the news media. Many of these events feature groups of Scheduled Caste members who attempt to escape social disabilities through conversion to alternative religions, usually Islam, Buddhism, or Christianity. These occasions attract the attention of fundamentalist organizations from all sides and heighten public consciousness of religious divisions. The most conspicuous movement of this sort occurred during the 1950s during the mass conversions of Mahars to Buddhism. In the early 1980s, the primary example was the conversion of Dalits to Islam in Meenakshipuram, Tamil Nadu, an event that resulted in considerable discussion in the media and an escalation of agitation in South India. Meanwhile, conversions to Christianity among tribal groups continue, with growing opposition from Hindu revivalist organizations.

Alongside the more publicized violent outbreaks, there have been major nonviolent changes, as new sectarian movements continue to grow and as established movements change. For example, the Radhasoami Satsang movement of North India, which includes adherents in Punjab and Uttar Pradesh, encompasses yogic ideas on the relationship between humans and the universe, the *bhakti* saint tradition including select Sikh influences, and the veneration of the enlightened guru. The dominant tendency of these new religions, following the example of the great teachers of the past that was reiterated by Mahatma Gandhi and most modern gurus, remains nonviolence to all living beings and acceptance of the remarkable diversity of Indian religion.

THEMES IN INDIAN SOCIETY

India is a hierarchical society. Within Indian culture, whether in the north or the south, Hindu or Muslim, urban or village, virtually all things, people, and groups of people are ranked according to various essential qualities. If one is attuned to the theme of hierarchy in India, one can discern it everywhere. Although India is a political democracy, in daily life there is little advocacy of or adherence to notions of equality.

Castes and castelike groups—those quintessential groups with which almost all Indians are associated—are ranked. Within most villages or towns, everyone knows the relative rankings of each locally represented caste, and people's behaviour toward one another is constantly shaped by this knowledge. Between the extremes of the very high and very low castes, however, there is sometimes disagreement on the exact relative ranking of castes clustered in the middle.

Castes are primarily associated with Hinduism but also exist among other Indian religious groups. Muslims sometimes expressly deny that they have castes—they state that all Muslims are brothers under God—but observation of Muslim life in various parts of India reveals the existence of castelike groups and clear concern with social hierarchy. Among Indian Christians, too, differences in caste are acknowledged and maintained.

Throughout India, individuals are also ranked according to their wealth and power. For example, there are "big men" (*bare admi*, in Hindi) and "little men" (*chhote admi*) everywhere. "Big men" sit confidently on chairs, while "little men" come before them to make requests, either standing or crouching down on their haunches, certainly not presuming to sit beside a man of high status as an equal. Even men of nearly equal status who might share a string cot to sit on take their places carefully—the higher-ranking man at the head of the cot, the lower-ranking man at the foot.

Within families and kinship groupings, there are many distinctions of hierarchy. Men outrank women of the same or similar age, and senior relatives outrank junior relatives. Several other kinship relations involve formal respect. For example, in northern India, a daughter-in-law of a household shows deference to a daughter of a household. Even among young siblings in a household, there is constant acknowledgment of age differences: younger siblings never address an older sibling by name, but rather by respectful terms for elder brother or elder sister. However, an older sibling may address the younger by name.

Even in a business or academic setting, where colleagues may not openly espouse traditional observance of caste or class ranking behaviour, they may set up fictive kinship relations, addressing one another by kinship terms reflecting family or village-style hierarchy. For example, a younger colleague might respectfully address an older colleague as *chachaji* (respected father's younger brother), gracefully acknowledging the superior position of the older colleague.

PURITY AND POLLUTION

Many status differences in Indian society are expressed in terms of ritual purity and pollution. Notions of purity and pollution are extremely complex and vary greatly among different castes, religious groups, and regions. However, broadly speaking, high status is associated with purity and low status with pollution. Some kinds of purity are inherent, or inborn; for example, gold is purer than copper by its very nature, and, similarly, a member of a high-ranking Brahman, or priestly, caste is born with more inherent purity than a member of a low-ranking Sweeper (Mehtar, in Hindi) caste. Unless the Brahman defiles himself in some extraordinary way, throughout his life he will always be purer than a Sweeper. Other kinds of purity are more transitory—a Brahman who has just taken a bath is more ritually pure than a Brahman who has not bathed for a day. This situation could easily reverse itself temporarily, depending on bath schedules, participation in polluting activities, or contact with temporarily polluting substances.

Purity is associated with ritual cleanliness—daily bathing in flowing water, dressing in properly laundered clothes of approved materials, eating only the foods appropriate for one's caste, refraining from physical contact with people of lower rank, and avoiding involvement with ritually impure substances. The latter include body wastes and excretions, most especially those of another adult person. Contact with the products of death or violence are typically polluting and threatening to ritual purity.

During her menstrual period, a woman is considered polluted and refrains from cooking, worshiping, or touching anyone older than an infant. In much of the south, a woman spends this time "sitting outside," resting in an isolated room or shed. During her period, a Muslim woman does not touch the Quran. At the end of the period, purity is restored with a complete bath. Pollution also attaches to birth, both for the mother and the infant's close kin, and to death, for close relatives of the deceased.

Members of the highest priestly castes, the Brahmans, are generally vegetarians (although some Bengali and Maharashtrian Brahmans eat fish) and avoid eating meat, the product of violence and death. High-ranking Warrior castes (Kshatriyas), however, typically consume nonvegetarian diets, considered appropriate for their traditions of valour and physical strength. A Brahman born of proper Brahman parents retains his inherent purity if he bathes and dresses himself properly, adheres to a vegetarian diet, eats meals prepared only by persons of appropriate rank, and keeps his person away from the bodily exuviae of others (except for necessary contact with the secretions of family infants and small children).

If a Brahman happens to come into bodily contact with a polluting substance, he can remove this pollution by bathing and changing his clothing. However, if he were to eat meat or commit other transgressions of the rigid dietary codes of his particular caste, he would be considered more deeply polluted and would have to undergo various purifying rites and payment of fines imposed by his caste council in order to restore his inherent purity.

In sharp contrast to the purity of a Brahman, a Sweeper born of Sweeper parents is considered to be born inherently polluted. The touch of his body is polluting to those higher on the caste hierarchy than he, and they will shrink from his touch, whether or not he has bathed recently. Sweepers are associated with the traditional occupation of cleaning human feces from latrines and sweeping public lanes of all kinds of dirt. Traditionally, Sweepers remove these polluting materials in baskets carried atop the head and dumped out in a garbage pile at the edge of the village or neighbourhood. The involvement of Sweepers with such filth accords with their low-status position at the bottom of the Hindu caste hierarchy, even as their services allow high-status people, such as Brahmans, to maintain their ritual purity.

Members of the Leatherworker (Chamar) caste are ascribed a very low status consonant with their association with the caste occupation of skinning dead animals and tanning the leather. Butchers (Khatiks, in Hindi), who kill and cut up the bodies of animals, also rank low on the caste hierarchy because of their association with violence and death. However, castes associated with ruling and warfare—and the killing and deaths of human beings—are typically accorded high rank on the caste hierarchy. In these instances, political power and wealth outrank association with violence as the key determinant of caste rank.

Maintenance of purity is associated with the intake of food and drink, not only in terms of the nature of the food itself, but also in terms of who has prepared it or touched it. This requirement is especially true for Hindus, but other religious groups hold to these principles to varying degrees. Generally, a person risks pollution—and lowering his own status—if he accepts beverages or cooked foods from the hands of people of lower caste status than his own. His status will remain intact if he accepts food or beverages from people of higher caste rank. Usually, for an observant Hindu of any but the very lowest castes to accept cooked food from a Muslim or Christian is regarded as highly polluting. In a clear example of pollution associated with dining, a Brahman who consumed a drink of water and a meal of wheat bread with boiled vegetables from the hands of a Sweeper would immediately become polluted and could expect social rejection by his caste fellows. From that moment, fellow Brahmans following traditional pollution rules would refuse food touched by him and would abstain from the usual social interaction with him. He would not be welcome inside Brahman homes—most especially in the ritually pure kitchens—nor would he or his close relatives be considered eligible marriage partners for other Brahmans.

Generally, the acceptance of water and ordinary foods cooked in water from members of lower-ranking castes incurs the greatest pollution. In North India, such foods are known as *kaccha khana*, as contrasted with fine foods cooked in butter or oils, which are known as *pakka khana* . Fine foods can be accepted from members of a few castes slightly lower than one's own. Local hierarchies differ on the specific details of these rules. Completely raw foods, such as uncooked grains, fresh unpeeled bananas, mangoes, and uncooked vegetables can be accepted by anyone from anyone else, regardless of relative status. Toasted or parched foods, such as roasted peanuts, can also be accepted from anyone without ritual or social repercussions. (Thus, a Brahman may accept gifts of grain from lower-caste patrons for eventual preparation by members of his own caste, or he may purchase and consume roasted peanuts or tangerines from street vendors of unknown caste without worry.)

Water served from an earthen pot may be accepted only from the hands of someone of higher or equal caste ranking, but water served from a brass pot may be accepted even from someone slightly lower on the caste scale. Exceptions to this rule are members of the Waterbearer (Bhoi, in Hindi) caste, who are employed to carry water from wells to the homes of the prosperous and from whose hands members of all castes may drink water without becoming polluted, even though Waterbearers are not ranked high on the caste scale.

These and a great many other traditional rules pertaining to purity and pollution constantly impinge upon interaction between people of different castes and ranks in India. Although to the non-Indian these rules may seem irrational and bizarre, to most of the people of India they are a ubiquitous and accepted part of life. Thinking about and following purity and pollution rules make it necessary for people to be constantly aware of differences in status. With every drink of water, with every meal, and with every contact with another person, people must ratify the social hierarchy of which they are a part and within which their every act is carried out. The fact that expressions of social status are intricately bound up with events that happen to everyone every day—eating, drinking, bathing, touching, talking—and that transgressions of these rules, whether deliberate or accidental, are seen as having immediately polluting effects on the person of the transgressor, means that every ordinary act of human life serves as a constant reminder of the importance of hierarchy in Indian society.

There are many Indians, particularly among the educated urban elite, who do not follow traditional purity and pollution practices. Dining in each others' homes and in restaurants is common among well-educated people of diverse backgrounds, particularly when they belong to the same economic class. For these people, guarding the family's earthen water pot from inadvertent touch by a low-ranking servant is not the concern it is for a more traditional villager. However, even among those people whose words and actions denigrate traditional purity rules, there is often a reluctance to completely abolish consciousness of purity and pollution from their thinking. It is surely rare for a Sweeper, however well-educated, to invite a Brahman to dinner in his home and have his invitation unselfconsciously accepted. It is less rare, however, for educated urban colleagues of vastly different caste and religious heritage to enjoy a cup of tea together. Some high-caste liberals pride themselves on being free of "casteism" and seek to accept food from the hands of very low-caste people, or even deliberately set out to marry someone from a significantly lower caste or a different religion. Thus, even as they deny it, these progressives affirm the continuing significance of traditional rules of purity, pollution, and hierarchy in Indian society.

SOCIAL INTERDEPENDENCE

One of the great themes pervading Indian life is social interdependence. People are born into groups—families, clans, subcastes, castes, and religious communities—and live with a constant sense of being part of and inseparable from these groups. A corollary is the notion that everything a person does properly involves interaction with other people. A person's greatest dread, perhaps, is the possibility of being left alone, without social support, to face the necessary challenges of life. This sense of interdependence is extended into the theological realm: the very shape of a person's life is seen as being greatly influenced by divine beings with whom an ongoing relationship must be maintained.

Social interaction is regarded as being of the highest priority, and social bonds are expected to be long lasting. Even economic activities that might in Western culture involve impersonal interactions are in India deeply imbedded in a social nexus. All social interaction involves constant attention to hierarchy, respect, honour, the feelings of others, rights and obligations, hospitality, and gifts of food, clothing, and other desirable items. Finely tuned rules of etiquette help facilitate each individual's many social relationships.

Western visitors to India are sometimes startled to find that important government and business officials have left their posts—often for many days at a time—to attend a cousin's wedding or participate in religious activities in a distant part of the country. "He is out of station and will be back in a week or two," the absent official's officemates blandly explain to the frustrated visitor. What is going on is not laziness or hedonistic recreation, but is the official's proper recognition of his need to continually maintain his social ties with relatives, caste fellows, other associates, and God. Without being enmeshed in such ties throughout life, a person cannot hope to maintain long-term efficacy in either economic or social endeavours. Social bonds with relatives must be reinforced at family events or at rites crucial to the religious community. If this is not done, people who could offer vital support in many phases of life would be alienated.

In every activity, there is an assumption that social ties can help a person and that their absence can bring failure. Seldom do people carry out even the simplest task on their own. From birth onward, a child learns that his "fate" has been "written" by divine forces and that his life will be shaped by a plan decided by more powerful beings. When a small child eats, his mother puts the mouthfuls of food into his mouth with her own hand. When a boy climbs a tree to pluck mangoes, another stands below with a basket to receive them. When a girl fetches water from the well in pots on her head, someone at her home helps her unload the pots. When a farmer stacks sheaves of grain onto his bullock cart, he stands atop the cart, catching the sheaves tossed up to him by his son.

A student applying to a college hopes that he has an influential relative or family friend who can put in a good word for him with the director of admissions. At the age of marriage, a young person expects that parents will take care of finding the appropriate bride or groom and arranging all the formalities. At the birth of a child, the new mother is assured that the child's kin will help her attend to the infant's needs. A businessman seeking to arrange a contract relies not only on his own abilities but also on the assistance of well-connected friends and relatives to help finalize the deal. And finally, when facing death, a person is confident that offspring and other relatives will carry out the appropriate funeral rites, including a commemorative feast when, through gifts of clothing and food, continuing social ties are reaffirmed by all in attendance.

2

Indian Population Profile and Social Demography

The demographics of India are remarkably diverse. India's population of approximately 1. 17 billion people (estimate for July, 2009) consists of more than one-sixth of the world's population. India has more than two thousand ethnic groups, and every major religion is represented, as are four major families of languages (Indo-European, Dravidian, Austro-Asiatic and Tibeto-Burman languages) as well as a language isolate (the Nihali language spoken in parts of Maharashtra). Further complexity is lent by the great variation that occurs across this population on social parameters such as income and education. Only the continent of Africa exceeds the linguistic, genetic and cultural diversity of the nation of India.

Salient Features

India occupies 2. 4% of the world's land area and supports over 17. 5% of the world's population. India has more arable land area than any country except the United States, and more water area than any country except Canada and the United States. Indian life revolves mostly around agriculture and allied activities in small villages, where the overwhelming majority of Indians live. As per the 2001 census, 72. 2% of the population lives in about 638, 000 villages and the remaining 27. 8% lives in more than 5, 100 towns and over 380 urban agglomerations.

Religious Demographics

India contains the majority of the world's Zoroastrians, Sikhs, Hindus, Jains and Bahai. India is also home to the third-largest Muslim population in the world after Indonesia and Pakistan.

Religious majorities vary greatly by state. Jammu and Kashmir and Lakshadweep are Muslim majority states; Nâgaland, Mizoram and Meghalaya are Christian majority; Punjab is mostly Sikh; It is to be noted that while participants in the Indian census may choose to not declare their religion, there is no mechanism for a person to indicate that he/she does not adhere to any religion. Due to this limitation in the Indian census process, the data for persons not affiliated with any religion may not be accurate.

Table 1: 2001 Religious Data Composition

Religious Composition	*Population*	*(%)*
Hindus	827, 578, 868	80. 5%
Muslims	138, 188, 240	13. 4%
Christians	24, 080, 016	2. 3%
Sikhs	19, 215, 730	1. 9%
Buddhists	7, 955, 207	0. 8%
Jains	4, 225, 053	0. 4%
Other Religions & Persuasions	6, 639, 626	0. 6%
Religion not stated	727, 588	0. 1%
Total	1, 028, 610, 328	100. 0%

N. B. "Total" excludes Mao-Maram, Paomata and Purul subdivisions of Senapati District of Manipur state.

The table below summarizes the findings of the 2001 census with regards to religion in India:

1. All figures in %.
2. *Others* including Bahais, Jews, and Parsis.
3. Tribal Animists (and non religious) are grouped under Others after 1926 (1931 census onwards)

Linguistic Demographics

43% of the Hindus speak Hindi while the rest speak Bangla, Telugu, Marathi, Tamil, Gujarati, Kannada, Assamese and other languages. Almost 45% of the Muslims speak Urdu while the rest speak Bangla, Hindi, Kashmiri, Malayalam, Telugu, Tamil, Gujarati, Assamese and other languages. About one-third of the Christians speak Malayalam, one-sixth speak Tamil while the rest speak a variety of languages. In total, there are 1, 652 languages and dialects spoken in India.

CIA World Factbook Demographic Statistics

The following demographic statistics are from the CIA World Factbook, unless otherwise indicated.

Total Population

1, 166, 079, 217 (July 2009 est. CIA) 1, 028. 7 million (2001 Census final figures, March 1 enumeration and estimated 124, 000 in areas of Manipur that could not be covered in the enumeration)

Rural Population;

72. 2%, male: 381, 668, 992, female: 360, 948, 755 (2001 Census).

Urban Population

Age structure;

0–14 years: 30.8%,

male: 188, 208, 196, female: 171, 356, 024

15–64 years: 64. 3%,

male: 386, 432, 921, female: 364, 215, 759

65+ years: 4. 9%,

male: 27, 258, 259, female: 30, 031, 289 (2007 est.)

Median age; 25. 1 years.

Population growth rate;

1. 548% (2009 est.).

Birth rate; 21. 76 births/1, 000 population (2009 est.).

*Death rate;*6. 4 deaths/1, 000 population (2009 est.).

Literacy rate; 79. 9%

Percent of the population under the poverty line;

22% (2006 est.).

*Unemployment Rate;*7. 8%.

Net migration rate;

-0. 05 migrant(s)/1, 000 population (2007 est.).

Sex ratio;

At birth: 1. 12 male(s)/female

Under 15 years: 1. 098 male(s)/female

15–64 years: 1. 061 male(s)/female

65 years and over: 0. 908 male(s)/female

Total population: 1. 064 male(s)/female (2006 est.).

Infant mortality rate

Total: 30. 15 deaths/1, 000 live births (2009 est.) male: 34. 61 deaths/1, 000 live births female: 25. 17 deaths/1, 000 live births.

Life expectancy at birth;

Total population: 69. 89 years

Male: 67. 46 years

Female: 72. 61 years (2007 est.).

Total fertility rate; 2. 72 children born/woman (2009 est.) The TFR (Total number of children born per women) according to Religion in 2001 was :

Hindus — 2. 0

Muslims — 2. 4

Sikhs — 1. 6

Christians — 2. 1

Buddhists — 2. 1

Jains — 1. 4

Animists and Others — 2. 99

Tribals — 3. 16 Scheduled Castes — 2. 89

Religions; Hindu 80. 5% Muslim 13. 4% Christian 2. 3% Sikh 1. 8% Buddhists 0. 8% Jains 0. 4% others 0. 7% unspecified 0. 1% (2001 Census).

Scheduled Castes and Tribes; Scheduled Castes: 16. 2% (2001 Census) Scheduled Tribes: 8. 2% (2001 Census).

Languages: There are 216 languages with more than 10, 000 native speakers in India. The largest of these is Hindi with some 337 million (the second largest being Bangla with some 207 million). 22 languages are recognized as official languages. In India, there are 1, 652 languages and dialects in total.

Population Growth

- According to 2001 final census India's total population has crossed 1, 027, 015, 247 out of which 531, 277, 078 are males and females are 495, 738, 169.
- Of this number, 157, 863, 145 are children up to the age of six years out of which 81, 911, 041 are males and 75, 952, 104 are females.
- India's landscape is just 2. 4% of the total world area whereas its population is nearly 16. 7% of the world population.
- The population of India which at the turn of the 20th century was around 238. 4 million increased to reach 1, 027million at the dawn of the 21st century.
- As per census 2001 the sex-ratio has gone up from 927 in 1991 to 933 in 2001.
- The literacy rate increased from 52. 21% to 65. 38%. For males it has increased to 75. 85% and for females 54. 16%. The gap in male-female literacy rates has decreased from 24. 84% points to 21. 70% points in 2001.
- The density of population has increased in all states and UTs between 1991 and 2001. Population density increased from 274 in 1991 to 324 persons per sq. km in 2001. West Bengal is the most densely populated state 904 followed by Bihar 880 and Kerala 819.
- The percentage of urban population of total population has increased from 25. 7% in 1991 to 27. 8% in 2001.
- The number of cities having a population of more than one million increased from 23 in 1991 to 35 in 2001. Population-wise UP is at the top followed by Maharashtra, Bihar and West-Bengal and so on.
- The crude death rate in India has declined from 25. 1 in 1951 to 9. 8 in 1991 and to 8. 7 in 1999 while the crude birth rate declined from 40. 8 in 1951 to 29. 5 in 1991 and to 26. 1 in 1999. The child mortality rate stands at 23. 9 (0-4 years per 1000 children).
- The decadal growth rate in 1991-2001 was lowest in Kerala (9. 42%) and highest in Nagaland (64. 41%). The sex-ratio declined in the age-group 0-6 years from 945

to 927. **Kerala** has the highest (1058) sex-ratio while Haryana has the lowest (861).

- The life expectancy for males is 62 years and for females it is 63 years.

COMPONENTS OF POPULATION GROWTH

The age and sex composition of a population affects its social life in many ways. Changes in age composition are due mainly to changes in birthrates and are presently increasing the proportion of aged and reducing the proportion of children in many countries. Migration is affected by the push given to people by unsatisfactory conditions at home by the pull of attractive opportunities elsewhere and by the channels or means through which they are able to migrate.

Sex Composition: The small family norm together with a desire for a male child has further distorted a sex ratio against the girl-child. The sex ratio has steadily declined: From 972 (for every 1000 boys) in 1901 to 927 in 1991. The latest census shows a slight overall improvement in the sex ratio to 933. Unfortunately, this is offset by a worsening of the sex ratio of children up to the age of six. The sex ratio for children up to the age of six has gone down from 962 girls per 1000 boys in 1981, to 945 in 1991, to 927 in 2001. The sharpest declines in sex ratio for the child population are reported from Himachal Pradesh, Punjab, Haryana, Gujarat, Uttaranchal, Maharashtra and Chandigarh, where abortions of female fetuses are known to be widely practised.

Population Density: Defined as the number of persons per sq km the population density of India in 2001 was 324 per sq km. West Bengal is still the most thickly populated state with a population density of 903 in 2001. Bihar (880) is now the second highest densely populated state pushing Kerala to the third place.

Age Composition: The current age distribution of Indian population is little more than 31. 7 percent are under the age of 15 years (male 173, 869, 856; female 164, 003, 915); 63. 5 percent are between 15 and 64 (male 349, 785, 804; female 326, 289, 402), and 4. 8 percent are over the age of 60 (male 25, 885, 725; female 25, 235, 905). The Indian Planning Commission's Technical Group on Population Projections predicted in the

National Population Policy (2000) that India's population would be 1. 012 billion in March 2001, going up to 1. 179 billion and 1. 264 billion in March 2011 and 2016 respectively.

Morality: According to 2001 census Seventy-two out of every 1, 000 babies born die before their first birthday. Seven percent (72/1, 000) of newborn infants perish within a year of birth, because of low birth weight, pre-maturity, malnutrition, diarrhea diseases, acute respiratory infections and malnutrition. Compare this to the IMRs in Sri Lanka (18/1, 000) and China (41/1, 000 Moreover, in India, there are more female deaths (rural or urban areas) in the age group of 0-14 than elsewhere. Although the IMR has decreased from 146 per 1000 births in 1951 to 72 per 1000 births (1997) and the sex differentials are narrowing, there are wide inter-state differences.

Measurements of Mortality

" Crude Death Rate " Birth Rate " Infant Mortality Rate.

Factors for the Low Death Rate

" Health-care services " Vaccinations and control of epidemics " Reduction in the occurrence of famines and droughts.

Theories of Demography

Malthus: The essay on the principle of population an important work of Malthus is a landmark in the history of population studies. The theme of the Essay was mainly to argue that the tendency of the population to grow faster in relation to its means of subsistence has led to human misery and placed several obstacles in the path of human progress. In 1803, Malthus published the second edition of his essay, a much expanded and changed edition which can't really be called a re print of the 1797 essay, for in the new edition the emphasis was more on arguments against the poor laws than on country arguments against the opinions of Condorcet and Godwin.

Neo-Maltusian theory: Neo-Malthusians maintain that although the gloomy predictions of Malthus may have been pre-mature they are basically correct. According to Anti Malthusians' world's resources are adequate for a much larger population. Exploitation not over population is the basic cause of world hunger.

Demographic Transition Theory

Two different interpretations have been given for this theory. One by Frank Notestein says that every country passes through three stages of population growth; 1. High birth rate and high death rate ii. High birth rate and low death rate (population explosion) iii. Low birth rate and low death rate. In western nations the desire for high standard of living led to the reductions in the birthrate. These nations are approaching a new equilibrium with both birthrates and death rates quite low and little population growth. This is explained by the theory of demographic transition-the theory that industrial and commercial development first cuts the death rate but creates a desire for smaller families and eventually cuts the birthrate.

The other theory is given by C. P Blacker. There are five phrases in this theory.

i. High stationary phase marked by high fertility and mortality rate.
ii. Early expanding phase marked by high fertility and high but declining mortality.
iii. Late Expanding phase with declining fertility but mortality declining more rapidly.
iv. Low stationary phase with low fertility and equally low mortality.
v. Declining phase with low mortality, low fertility and an excess of deaths over births.

Optimum Population Theory

According to Canan the propounder of this theory population must grow upto certain desired level after which further growth is harmful. The two important principles of this theory are:

1. When there is an increase in population than the ratio between the total population and the working population remains almost constant.
2. When at a point of time the population of a country increases the natural resources capital and technical know how do not change with the result that after sometime the law of diminishing returns begins to operate. This law provides that for maximum production all the sources of production should be combined in that

proper ratio than it shall not be possible to have maximum production.

Population Policy

A policy is a plan of action, statement of aims and ideals especially one made by a government, a political party, a business company etc. Population policy is an effort to affect the size, structure and distribution or characteristics of population. In its broader range it includes efforts to regulate economic and social conditions which are likely to have demographic consequences.

National Population Policy

The immediate objective of this new policy is to address the unmet needs of contraception, health infrastructure, health personnel and to provide integrated service delivery for basic reproductive and child health care. The medium term objective is to bring the total fertility rated to replacement level by 2010. The long term objective is to achieve a stable population by 2045. In pursuance of these objectives 14 National Socio-Demogragraphic goals are formulated to be achieved by 2010. The important goals are:

1. Making school education compulsory and to reduce the drop-outs.
2. Reduce infant-mortality rate to 30 per 1000 live births.
3. Reduce maternal mortality rate to below 100 per 100000 live births.
4. Promote delayed marriage.
5. Achieve 80% institutional deliveries.
6. Prevent and control communicable diseases.
7. Promote vigorously the small family norm to achieve replacement levels of Total Fertility Rate.

The policy speaks about the formation of National Commission of Population under the chairmanship of the Prime-Minister to monitor and implement population policy and to guide planning implementations.

The policy also suggests some promotional and motivational measures to promote adoption of the small family norm. The main features of the policy are:

1. Reward panchayats and Zila Parishads for promoting small family norms.
2. Incentives to adopt two child norms.
3. Couples below poverty line, having sterilization with not more than two living children will be eligible for health insurance plan.
4. Strengthening abortion facility scheme.

POPULATION DYNAMICS

Structure and Dynamics

Population of India. Although India occupies only 2. 4% of the world's land area, it supports over 15% of the world's population. Only China has a larger population. Almost 40% of Indians are younger than 15 years of age. About 70% of the people live in more than 550, 000 villages, and the remainder in more than 200 towns and cities. Over thousands of years of its history, India has been invaded from the Iranian plateau, Central Asia, Arabia, Afghanistan, and the West; Indian people and culture have absorbed and changed these influences to produce a remarkable racial and cultural synthesis. Religion, caste, and language are major determinants of social and political organization in India today. The government has recognized 18 languages as official; Hindi is the most widely spoken. Although 83% of the people are Hindu, India also is the home of more than 120 million Muslims—one of the world's largest Muslim populations. The population also includes Christians, Sikhs, Jains, Buddhists, and Parsis. The caste system reflects Indian occupational and religiously defined hierarchies. Traditionally, there are four broad categories of castes (varnas), including a category of outcastes, earlier called "untouchables" but now commonly referred to as "dalits." Within these broad categories there are thousands of castes and subcastes, whose relative status varies from region to region. Despite economic modernization and laws countering discrimination against the lower end of the class structure, the caste system remains an important source of social identification for most Hindus and a potent factor in the political life of the country.

India Population: The 1991 final census count gave India a total population of 846, 302, 688. However, estimates of

India's population vary widely. According to the Population Division of the United Nations Department of International Economic and Social Affairs, the population had already reached 866 million in 1991. The Population Division of the United Nations Economic and Social Commission for Asia and the Pacific (ESCAP) projected 896. 5 million by mid-1993 with a 1. 9 percent annual growth rate. The United States Bureau of the Census, assuming an annual population growth rate of 1. 8 percent, put India's population in July 1995 at 936, 545, 814. These higher projections merit attention in light of the fact that the Planning Commission had estimated a figure of 844 million for 1991 while preparing the Eighth Five-Year Plan (FY 1992-96).

India accounts for some 2. 4 percent of the world's landmass but is home to about 16 percent of the global population. The magnitude of the annual increase in population can be seen in the fact that India adds almost the total population of Australia or Sri Lanka every year. A 1992 study of India's population notes that India has more people than all of Africa and also more than North America and South America together. Between 1947 and 1991, India's population more than doubled.

Throughout the twentieth century, India has been in the midst of a demographic transition. At the beginning of the century, endemic disease, periodic epidemics, and famines kept the death rate high enough to balance out the high birth rate. Between 1911 and 1920, the birth and death rates were virtually equal—about forty-eight births and forty-eight deaths per 1, 000 population.

The increasing impact of curative and preventive medicine (especially mass inoculations) brought a steady decline in the death rate. By the mid-1990s, the estimated birth rate had fallen to twenty-eight per 1, 000, and the estimated death rate had fallen to ten per 1, 000. Clearly, the future configuration of India's population (indeed the future of India itself) depends on what happens to the birth rate. Even the most optimistic projections do not suggest that the birth rate could drop below twenty per 1, 000 before the year 2000. India's population is likely to exceed the 1 billion mark before the 2001 census.

The upward population in India spiral began in the 1920s and is reflected in intercensal growth increments. South Asia's population increased roughly 5 percent between 1901 and 1911 and actually declined slightly in the next decade. Population increased some 10 percent in the period from 1921 to 1931 and 13 to 14 percent in the 1930s and 1940s. Between 1951 and 1961, the population rose 21.5 percent. Between 1961 and 1971, the country's population increased by 24.8 percent. Thereafter a slight slowing of the increase was experienced: from 1971 to 1981, the population increased by 24.7 percent, and from 1981 to 1991, by 23.9 percent.

Population in India density has risen concomitantly with the massive increases in population. In 1901 India counted some seventy-seven persons per square kilometer; in 1981 there were 216 persons per square kilometer; by 1991 there were 267 persons per square kilometer—up almost 25 percent from the 1981 population density. India's average population density is higher than that of any other nation of comparable size. The highest densities are not only in heavily urbanized regions but also in areas that are mostly agricultural.

Population of India growth in the years between 1950 and 1970 centred on areas of new irrigation projects, areas subject to refugee resettlement, and regions of urban expansion. Areas where population did not increase at a rate approaching the national average were those facing the most severe economic hardships, overpopulated rural areas, and regions with low levels of urbanization.

The 1991 census, which was carried out under the direction of the Registrar General and Census Commissioner of India (part of the Ministry of Home Affairs), in keeping with the previous two censuses, used the term *urban agglomerations*. An urban agglomeration forms a continuous urban spread and consists of a city or town and its urban outgrowth outside the statutory limits. Or, an urban agglomerate may be two or more adjoining cities or towns and their outgrowths. A university campus or military base located on the outskirts of a city or town, which often increases the actual urban area of that city or town, is an example of an urban agglomeration. In India urban agglomerations with a population of 1 million or more—there were twenty-four in 1991—are referred to as metropolitan areas. Places with a population of 100, 000 or more are termed "cities" as compared with "towns, " which have a population of less than 100, 000. Including the metropolitan areas, there were 299 urban agglomerations with more than 100, 000 population in 1991. These large urban agglomerations are designated as Class I urban units. There were five other classes of urban agglomerations, towns, and villages based on the size of their populations: Class II (50, 000 to 99, 999), Class III (20, 000 to 49, 999), Class IV (10, 000 to 19, 999), Class V (5, 000 to 9, 999), and Class VI (villages of less than 5, 000.

The results of the 1991 census revealed that around 221 million, or 26. 1 percent, of Indian's population lived in urban areas. Of this total, about 138 million people, or 16 percent, lived in the 299 urban agglomerations. In 1991 the twenty-four metropolitan cities accounted for 51 percent of India's total population living in Class I urban centres, with Bombay and Calcutta the largest at 12. 6 million and 10. 9 million, respectively.

In the early 1990s, growth was the most dramatic in the cities of central and southern India. About twenty cities in those two regions experienced a growth rate of more than 100 percent between 1981 and 1991. Areas subject to an influx of refugees also experienced noticeable demographic changes. Refugees from Bangladesh, Burma, and Sri Lanka contributed substantially to population growth in the regions in which they settled. Less dramatic population increases occurred in areas where Tibetan refugee settlements were founded after the Chinese annexation of Tibet in the 1950s.

The majority of districts had urban populations ranging on average from 15 to 40 percent in 1991. According to the 1991 census, urban clusters predominated in the upper part of the Indo-Gangetic Plain; in the Punjab and Haryana plains, and in part of western Uttar Pradesh. The lower part of the Indo-Gangetic Plain in southeastern Bihar, southern West Bengal, and northern Orissa also experienced increased urbanization. Similar increases occurred in the western coastal state of Gujarat and the union territory of Daman and Diu. In the Central Highlands in Madhya Pradesh and Maharashtra, urbanization was most noticeable in the river basins and adjacent plateau regions of the Mahanadi, Narmada, and Tapti rivers. The coastal plains and river deltas of the east and west coasts also showed increased levels of urbanization. The hilly, inaccessible regions of the Peninsular Plateau, the northeast, and the Himalayas remain sparsely settled. As a general rule, the lower the population density and the more remote the region, the more likely it is to count a substantial portion of tribal people among its population. Urbanization in some sparsely settled regions is more developed than would seem warranted at first glance at their limited natural resources. Areas of western India that were formerly princely states (in Gujarat and the desert regions of Rajasthan) have substantial urban centres that originated as political-administrative centres and since independence have continued to exercise hegemony over their hinterlands.

The vast majority of Indians, nearly 625 million, or 73. 9 percent, in 1991 lived in what are called villages of less than 5, 000 people or in scattered hamlets and other rural settlements. The states with proportionately the greatest rural populations in 1991 were the states of Assam (88. 9 percent), Sikkim (90. 9 percent) and Himachal Pradesh (91. 3 percent), and the tiny union territory of Dadra and Nagar Haveli (91. 5 percent). Those with the smallest rural populations proportionately were the states of Gujarat (65. 5 percent), Maharashtra (61. 3 percent), Goa (58. 9 percent), and Mizoram (53. 9 percent). Most of the other states and the union territory of the Andaman and Nicobar Islands were near the national average.

Two other categories of India's population that are closely scrutinized by the national census are the Scheduled Castes and Scheduled Tribes. The greatest concentrations of Scheduled Caste members in 1991 lived in the states of Andhra Pradesh (10. 5 million, or nearly 16 percent of the state's population), Tamil Nadu (10. 7 million, or 19 percent), Bihar (12. 5 million, or 14 percent), West Bengal (16 million, or 24 percent), and Uttar Pradesh (29. 3 million, or 21 percent). Together, these and other Scheduled Caste members comprised about 139 million people, or more than 16 percent of the total population of India. Scheduled Tribe members represented only 8 percent of the total population (about 68 million).

They were found in 1991 in the greatest numbers in Orissa (7 million, or 23 percent of the state's population), Maharashtra (7. 3 million, or 9 percent), and Madhya Pradesh (15. 3 million, or 23 percent). In proportion, however, the populations of states in the northeast had the greatest concentrations of Scheduled

Tribe members. For example, 31 percent of the population of Tripura, 34 percent of Manipur, 64 percent of Arunachal Pradesh, 86 percent of Meghalaya, 88 percent of Nagaland, and 95 percent of Mizoram were Scheduled Tribe members. Other heavy concentrations were found in Dadra and Nagar Haveli, 79 percent of which was composed of Scheduled Tribe members, and Lakshadweep, with 94 percent of its population being Scheduled Tribe members.

DEMOGRAPHICS OF INDIA

This population is remarkably diverse; it has more than two thousand ethnic groups, and every major religion is represented, as are four major families of languages (Indo-European, Dravidian, Austro-Asiatic and Tibeto-Burman languages) as well as two language isolates (Nihali and the Burushaski language spoken in disputed parts of Jammu & Kashmir). Further complexity is lent by the great variation that occurs across this population on social parameters such as income and education. These factors render the task of comprehensively detailing the Demographics of India prohibitive; some important indices are available, nevertheless.

SALIENT FEATURES

Although India occupies only 2.4% of the world's land area, it supports over 16% of the world's population. Currently it is the second most populous nation on Earth, though if current trends persist, India will replace China as the most populous nation in less than 40 years. Almost 40% of Indians are younger than 15 years of age. More than 70% of the people live in more than 550,000 villages, and the remainder in more than 200 towns and cities.

Over thousands of years of its history, India has had invasions and migrations from the Middle East, Central Asia and the West, as well as migrations from Tibet and southern China; Indian people and culture have absorbed and changed these influences to produce a remarkable racial and cultural synthesis. Religion, caste, and language are major determinants of social and political organization in India today. The government has recognized 22 languages as official; Hindi is the most widely spoken. India also has the second largest number of English speakers in the world, after the US, with over 60 million people speaking English in India. Many millions more have a rudimentary knowledge of English. Although 82.0% of the people are Hindus, India is also home to the second-largest Muslim population in the world (13.1%). India also contains the majority of the world's Zoroastrians (0.01%), Sikhs (1.94%) and Jains (0.40%). Other religious groups include Christians (2.3%), Buddhists (0.76%), Jews and Bahais. The caste system reflects Indian occupational and socio-religiously defined hierarchies. Traditionally, there are four broad categories of castes (varnas), including a category of outcastes, earlier called "untouchables" but now commonly referred to as "dalits." Within these broad categories there are thousands of castes and subcastes, called jatis, whose relative status varies from region to region. Despite economic modernization and laws countering discrimination against the lower end of the class structure, the caste system remains an important source of social identification for most Hindus and many non-Hindus as well, thus making it a potent factor in the political life of the country.

CENSUS

The most recent census of India was performed in 2001. It was the 14th census in an unbroken series, and the 6th after independence in 1947 (except for Assam which did not figure in the 1981 census). Eight censuses were performed under the British Raj, the first one was carried out throughout the 1860s and completed in 1871. After this, there has been one census every decade. The 2001 census was conducted in two phases, the first being Housenumbering and Houselisting operations, carried out in May 2000, and the second being population enumeration, carried out from February 9 to 28, 2001.

The reference time for the census is 1 March, 2001. The houseless population was enumerated on 28 February. A revisional round was undertaken 1 to 5 March 2001 to account for mutations between the time of visit in February and 1 March. The total population calculated for 1 March 2001 was 1,027,015,247, making the 2001 census the first to count more than a billion Indians. The population had risen by 21.34% compared to the 1991 total. The female population had increased by 0.3 percentage points to 48.4%. Maharashtra has the largest urban agglomeration while Delhi is the most urbanised market at over 93%.

KEY DATA

Population: 1,128,000,000 (July 2006 est.); 1,027,000,000 (2001 Census)

Rural Population: 742,617,747 (72.2%)

Male: 381,668,992,

Female: 360,948,755 (2001 Census)

Table: Population History

Year	*Total Population*
1960	443,000,000
1970	553,000,000
1980	684,000,000
1990	838,141,000
2000	1,004,591,054
2005	1,095,054,669
2007	1,129,866,154
2010	1,184,000,000
2020	1,364,000,000
2030	1,532,000,000
2040	1,684,000,000
2050	1,807,000,000

Table: Population Projections (in millions)

Year	*Under 15*	*15-64*	*65+*	*Total*
2000	361	604	45	1010
2005	368	673	51	1093
2010	370	747	58	1175
2015	372	819	65	1256
2020	373	882	76	1331

Source: Based on P.N. Mari Bhat, "Indian Demographic Scenarion 2025", Institute of Economic Growth, New Delhi, Discussion Paper No. 27/2001.

Urban: Age structure:

0-14 years: 30.8% (male 173,478,760/female 163,852,827)

15-64 years: 64.3% (male 363,876,219/female 340,181,764)

65 years and over: 4.9% (male 27,258,020/female 26,704,405) (2006 est.)

The average age of Indians is 26 years.

Population Growth Rate: 1.38% (2006 est.)

Birth Rate: 22.01 births/1,000 population (2006 est.)

Death Rate: 8.18 deaths/1,000 population (2006 est.)

Literacy Rate: 79.9%

Percent of the population under the poverty line: 22% (2006 est.)

Unemployment Rate: 9.2%

Sex Ratio:

At Birth: 1.05 male(s)/female

Under 15 Years: 1.06 male(s)/female

15-64 Years: 1.07 male(s)/female

65 Years and Over: 1.02 male(s)/female

Total Population: 1.06 male(s)/female (2006 est.)

Infant Mortality Rate:

Total: 54.63 deaths/1,000 live births female: 55.18 deaths/ 1,000 live births (2006 est.) male: 54.05 deaths/1,000 live births

Life Expectancy at Birth:

Total Population: 64.71 years

Male: 63.9 years

Female: 65.57 years (2006 est.)

Total Fertility Rate: 2.73 children born/woman (2006 est.) The TFR (Totalnumber of children born per women) according to Religion in 2001 was:

Hindus-2.27, Muslims-3.06, Sikhs-1.86, X'ians-2.06, Budhists-2.29, Jains-1.50, Animists and Others-2.99, Tribals-3.16, Scheduled Castes-2.89.

Nationality:

Noun: Indian(s)

Adjective: Indian

Religions:

Hindu 82%, Muslim 12.20%, Christian 2.31%, Sikh 2.00%, Buddhists 0.77%, Jains 0.41 %,

Others or not stated 0.76% (2001 Census)

Scheduled Castes and Tribes: Scheduled Castes: 16.2% (2001 Census) Scheduled Tribes: 8.2% (2001 Census)

Languages: There are 216 languages with more than 10,000 native speakers in India. The largest of these by far is Hindi with some 337 million (the second largest being Telugu with some 80 million). 22 languages are recognized as "official languages". In India, there are 1,652 languages and dialects in total.

RELIGIOUS BREAKDOWN

Censuses were conducted in India in ancient times with examples such as Kautilya's Arthashastra which describes the collection of population statistics for taxation. The British census in 1871 was the first conducted in modern times in India.

1. All figures in %.
2. Gender Ratio*: no of females/1000 males
3. Others includes Jews, Parsis and Bahais
4. Tribal Animists (and non religious) are grouped under Others after 1926 (1931 census onwards)

Table: Census Information for 2006

Composition	Hindus	Muslims	Christians	Sikhs	Buddhists	Jains	Others
% total of population 2001	81.50	12.70	2.31	2.00	0.77	0.41	0.76
10-Yr Growth % (est '91-'01)	20.3	36.0	22.6	18.2	24.5	26	NA
Gender ratio* (avg. 944)	935	936	1009	893	953	950	992
Literacy rate (avg. 79.9)	75.1	69.1	90.3	79.4	82.7	100.0	49.6
Work Participation Rate	40	31.3	40	37.7	40	32.9	NA
Rural gender ratio	944	953	1001	895	958	937	995
Urban gender ratio	894	907	1026	886	944	941	966
Child gender ratio (0-6 yrs)	925	950	964	786	942	870	927

However, some unofficial estimates claim a higher figure of Muslim population supposedly discounted in Censuses. For instance, in an interview with a well circulated newspaper of India The Hindu Justice K.M. Yusuf, a retired Judge from Calcutta High Court and Chairman of West Bengal Minority Commission, says that the real percentage of Muslims in India is at least 20%. On the other hand, some believe that Muslim population figures are exaggerated due to various reasons. For instance, As per Syed Shahabuddin, a diplomat-turned-politician, a Muslim scholar and one of the members in the All India Muslim Personal Law Board, both Hindu and Muslim 'spokesmen', speaking for their respective communities amplify and exaggerate the Muslim population in India, the first, to convince their followers about the rising 'Islamic menace', a threat to the country and at least to its Hindu character, the second, to raise the morale of a politically deprived, educationally backward, economically poor and socially vilified, frustrated community.

POPULATION PROJECTIONS

The Registrar General and Census Commissioner of India (both positions are held by the same person) oversees an ongoing intercensal effort to help maintain accurate annual estimates of population. The projection method used in the mid-1980s to predict the 1991 population, which was accurate enough to come within 3 million (843 million) of the official, final census count in 1991 (846 million), was based on the Sample Registration System. The system employed birth and death rates from each of the twenty-five states, six union territories, and one national capital territory plus statistical data on effective contraceptive use. Assuming a 1.7 percent error rate, India's projection for 1991 was close to those made by the World Bank and the UN.

Projections of future population growth prepared by the Registrar General, assuming the highest level of fertility, show decreasing growth rates: 1.8 percent by 2001, 1.3 percent by 2011, and 0.9 percent by 2021. These rates of growth, however, will put India's population above 1.0 billion in 2001, at 1.2 billion in 2011, and at 1.3 billion in 2021. ESCAP projections published in 1993 were close to those made by India: nearly

1.2 billion by 2010, still considerably less than the 2010 population projection for China of 1.4 billion. In 1992 the Washington-based Population Reference Bureau had a similar projection to ESCAP's for India's population in 2010 and projected nearly 1.4 billion by 2025 (nearly the same as projected for 2025 by the United Nations Department of International Economic and Social Affairs). According to other UN projections, India's population may stabilize at around 1.7 billion by 2060.

Such projections also show an increasingly aging population, with 76 million (8 percent of the population) age sixty and above in 2001, 102 million (9 percent) in 2011, and 137 million (11 percent) in 2021. These figures coincide closely with those estimated by the United States Bureau of the Census, which also projected that whereas the median age was twenty-two in 1992, it was expected to increase to twenty-nine by 2020, placing the median age in India well above all of its South Asian neighbours except Sri Lanka.

POPULATION AND FAMILY PLANNING POLICY

Population growth has long been a concern of the government, and India has a lengthy history of explicit population policy. In the 1950s, the government began, in a modest way, one of the earliest national, government-sponsored family planning efforts in the developing world. The annual population growth rate in the previous decade (1941 to 1951) had been below 1.3 percent, and government planners optimistically believed that the population would continue to grow at roughly the same rate.

Implicitly, the government believed that India could repeat the experience of the developed nations where industrialization and a rise in the standard of living had been accompanied by a drop in the population growth rate. In the 1950s, existing hospitals and health care facilities made birth control information available, but there was no aggressive effort to encourage the use of contraceptives and limitation of family size. By the late 1960s, many policy makers believed that the high rate of population growth was the greatest obstacle to economic development. The government began a massive program to lower the birth rate from forty-one per 1,000 to a target of twenty to twenty-five per 1,000 by the mid-1970s. The

National Population Policy adopted in 1976 reflected the growing consensus among policy makers that family planning would enjoy only limited success unless it was part of an integrated program aimed at improving the general welfare of the population. The policy makers assumed that excessive family size was part and parcel of poverty and had to be dealt with as integral to a general development strategy. Education about the population problem became part of school curriculum under the Fifth Five-Year Plan (FY 1974-78). Cases of government-enforced sterilization made many question the propriety of state-sponsored birth control measures, however.

During the 1980s, an increased number of family planning programs were implemented through the state governments with financial assistance from the central government. In rural areas, the programs were further extended through a network of primary health centres and subcenters. By 1991, India had more than 150,000 public health facilities through which family planning programs were offered. Four special family planning projects were implemented under the Seventh Five-Year Plan (FY 1985-89). One was the All-India Hospitals Post-partum Programme at district- and subdistrict-level hospitals. Another program involved the reorganization of primary health care facilities in urban slum areas, while another project reserved a specified number of hospital beds for tubal ligature operations. The final program called for the renovation or remodelling of intrauterine device (IUD) rooms in rural family welfare centres attached to primary health care facilities.

Despite these developments in promoting family planning, the 1991 census results showed that India continued to have one of the most rapidly growing populations in the world. Between 1981 and 1991, the annual rate of population growth was estimated at about 2 percent. The crude birth rate in 1992 was thirty per 1,000, only a small change over the 1981 level of thirty-four per 1,000. However, some demographers credit this slight lowering of the 1981-91 population growth rate to moderate successes of the family planning program. In FY 1986, the number of reproductive-age couples was 132.6 million, of whom only 37.5 percent were estimated to be protected effectively by some form of contraception. A goal of the seventh plan was to achieve an effective couple protection rate of 42 percent, requiring an annual increase of 2 percent in effective use of contraceptives.

The heavy centralization of India's family planning programs often prevents due consideration from being given to regional differences. Centralization is encouraged to a large extent by reliance on central government funding. As a result, many of the goals and assumptions of national population control programs do not correspond exactly with local attitudes toward birth control. At the Jamkhed Project in Maharashtra, which has been in operation since the late 1970s and covers approximately 175 villages, the local project directors noted that it required three to four years of education through direct contact with a couple for the idea of family planning to gain acceptance. Such a timetable was not compatible with targets. However, much was learned about policy and practice from the Jamkhed Project. The successful use of women's clubs as a means of involving women in community-wide family planning activities impressed the state government to the degree that it set about organizing such clubs in every village in the state. The project also serves as a pilot to test ideas that the government wants to incorporate into its programs. Government medical staff members have been sent to Jamkhed for training, and the government has proposed that the project assume the task of selecting and training government health workers for an area of 2.5 million people.

Another important family planning program is the Project for Community Action in Family Planning. Located in Karnataka, the project operates in 154 project villages and 255 control villages. All project villages are of sufficient size to have a health subcenter, although this advantage is offset by the fact that those villages are the most distant from the area's primary health centres. As at Jamkhed, the project is much assisted by local voluntary groups, such as the women's clubs. The local voluntary groups either provide or secure sites suitable as distribution depots for condoms and birth control pills and also make arrangements for the operation of sterilization camps. Data provided by the Project for Community Action in Family Planning show that important achievements have been realized in the field of population control. By the mid-1980s, for example, 43 percent of couples were using family planning, a full 14 percent above the state average. The project has significantly improved the status of women, involving them and empowering them to bring about change in their communities. This contribution is important because of the way in which the deeply entrenched inferior status of women in many communities in India negates official efforts to decrease the fertility rate.

Studies have found that most couples in fact regard family planning positively. However, the common fertility pattern in India diverges from the two-child family that policy makers hold as ideal. Women continue to marry young; in the mid-1990s, they average just over eighteen years of age at marriage. When women choose to be sterilized, financial inducements, although helpful, are not the principal incentives. On average, those accepting sterilization already have four living children, of whom two are sons.

The strong preference for sons is a deeply held cultural ideal based on economic roots. Sons not only assist with farm labour as they are growing up (as do daughters) but they provide labour in times of illness and unemployment and serve as their parents' only security in old age. Surveys done by the New Delhi Operations Research Group in 1991 indicated that as many as 72 percent of rural parents continue to have children until at least two sons are born; the preference for more than one son among urban parents was tabulated at 53 percent. Once these goals have been achieved, birth control may be used or, especially in agricultural areas, it may not if additional child labour, later adult labour for the family, is deemed desirable.

A significant result of this eagerness for sons is that the Indian population has a deficiency of females. Slightly higher female infant mortality rates (seventy-nine per 1,000 versus seventy-eight per 1,000 for males) can be attributed to poor health care, abortions of female fetuses, and female infanticide. Human rights activists have estimated that there are at least 10,000 cases of female infanticide annually throughout India.

The cost of theoretically illegal dowries and the loss of daughters to their in-laws' families are further disincentives for some parents to have daughters. Sons, of course continue to carry on the family line. The 1991 census revealed that the national sex ratio had declined from 934 females to 1,000 males in 1981 to 927 to 1,000 in 1991. In only one state—Kerala, a state with low fertility and mortality rates and the nation's highest literacy—did females exceed males. The census found, however, that female life expectancy at birth had for the first time exceeded that for males. India's high infant mortality and elevated mortality in early childhood remain significant stumbling blocks to population control. India's fertility rate is decreasing, however, and, at 3.4 in 1994, it is lower than those of its immediate neighbours (Bangladesh had a rate of 4.5 and Pakistan had 6.7). The rate is projected to decrease to 3.0 by 2000, 2.6 by 2010, and 2.3 by 2020.

During the 1960s, 1970s, and 1980s, the growth rate had formed a sort of plateau. Some states, such as Kerala, Tamil Nadu, and, to a lesser extent, Punjab, Maharashtra, and Karnataka, had made progress in lowering their growth rates, but most did not. Under such conditions, India's population may not stabilize until 2060.

FACTS ABOUT INDIA

The Indus Valley civilization, one of the oldest in the world, dates back at least 5,000 years. Aryan tribes from the northwest infiltrated onto Indian lands about 1500 B.C.; their merger with the earlier Dravidian inhabitants created the classical Indian culture. Arab incursions starting in the 8th century and Turkish in the 12th were followed by those of European traders, beginning in the late 15th century.

By the 19th century, Britain had assumed political control of virtually all Indian lands. Indian armed forces in the British army played a vital role in both World Wars. Nonviolent resistance to British colonialism led by Mohandas GANDHI and Jawaharlal NEHRU brought independence in 1947. The subcontinent was divided into the secular state of India and the smaller Muslim state of Pakistan. A third war between the two countries in 1971 resulted in East Pakistan becoming the separate nation of Bangladesh. Despite impressive gains in economic investment and output, India faces pressing problems such as the ongoing dispute with Pakistan over Kashmir, massive overpopulation, environmental degradation, extensive poverty, and ethnic and religious strife.

GEOGRAPHY OF INDIA

Location: Southern Asia, bordering the Arabian Sea and the Bay of Bengal, between Burma and Pakistan

Coordinates: 20 00 N, 77 00 E

Area:

Total: 3,287,590 sq km

Land: 2,973,190 sq km

Water: 314,400 sq km

Area comparative: slightly more than one-third the size of the US.

Land boundaries:

Total: 14,103 km

Border countries: Bangladesh 4,053 km, Bhutan 605 km, Burma 1,463 km, China 3,380 km, Nepal 1,690 km, Pakistan 2,912 km

Coastline: 7,000 km

Maritime claims:

Contiguous zone: 24 NM

Territorial sea: 12 NM

Continental shelf: 200 NM or to the edge of the continental margin

Exclusive economic zone: 200 NM

Climate: varies from tropical monsoon in south to temperate in north

Terrain: upland plain (Deccan Plateau) in south, flat to rolling plain along the Ganges, deserts in west, Himalayas in north

Elevation extremes:

Lowest point: Indian Ocean 0 m

Highest point: Kanchenjunga 8,598 m

Natural resources: coal (fourth-largest reserves in the world), iron ore, manganese, mica, bauxite, titanium ore, chromite, natural gas, diamonds, petroleum, limestone, arable land

Natural hazards: droughts; flash floods, as well as widespread and destructive flooding from monsoonal rains; severe thunderstorms; earthquakes

Environment current issues: deforestation; soil erosion; overgrazing; desertification; air pollution from industrial effluents and vehicle emissions; water pollution from raw sewage and runoff of agricultural pesticides; tap water is not potable throughout the country; huge and growing population is overstraining natural resources

Geography - note: dominates South Asian subcontinent; near important Indian Ocean trade routes

POPULATION OF INDIA

Population: 1,129,866,154 (July 2007 est.)

Age structure:

0-14 years: 30.8% (male 173,478,760/female 163,852,827)

15-64 years: 64.3% (male 363,876,219/female 340,181,764)

65 years and over: 4.9% (male 27,258,020/female 26,704,405)

Median age: 24.9 years

Growth rate: 1.38%

Infant mortality: 54.63 deaths/1,000 live births

Life expectancy at birth: total population: 64.71 years

Male: 63.9 years

Female: 65.57 years

Fertility rate: 2.73 children born/woman

Nationality:

Noun: Indian(s)

Adjective: Indian

Ethnic groups: Indo-Aryan 72%, Dravidian 25%, Mongoloid and other 3%

Religions: Hindu 80.5%, Muslim 13.4%, Christian 2.3%, Sikh 1.9%, other 1.8%, unspecified 0.1%

Languages: English enjoys associate status but is the most important language for national, political, and commercial communication; Hindi is the national language and primary tongue of 30% of the people; there are 14 other official languages:

Bengali, Telugu, Marathi, Tamil, Urdu, Gujarati, Malayalam, Kannada, Oriya, Punjabi, Assamese, Kashmiri, Sindhi, and Sanskrit; Hindustani is a popular variant of Hindi/Urdu spoken widely throughout northern India but is not an official language

Literacy: definition: age 15 and over can read and write.

Total : 59.5%

Male: 70.2%

Female: 48.3%

GOVERNMENT

Country name: conventional long form: Republic of India

Government type: federal republic

Capital: New Delhi

Administrative divisions: 28 states and 7 union territories*; Andaman and Nicobar Islands*, Andhra Pradesh, Arunachal Pradesh, Assam, Bihar, Chandigarh*, Chhattisgarh, Dadra and Nagar Haveli*, Daman and Diu*, Delhi*, Goa, Gujarat, Haryana, Himachal Pradesh, Jammu and Kashmir, Jharkhand, Karnataka, Kerala, Lakshadweep*, Madhya Pradesh, Maharashtra, Manipur, Meghalaya, Mizoram, Nagaland, Orissa, Pondicherry*, Punjab, Rajasthan, Sikkim, Tamil Nadu, Tripura, Uttaranchal, Uttar Pradesh, West Bengal

Independence: 15 August 1947 (from UK)

National holiday: Republic Day, 26 January (1950)

Constitution: 26 January 1950

Legal system: based on English common law; limited judicial review of legislative acts; accepts compulsory ICJ jurisdiction, with reservations

Suffrage: 18 years of age; universal

Executive branch: chief of state: President A.P.J. Abdul KALAM; Vice President Bhairon Singh SHEKHAWAT

Head of government: Prime Minister Manmohan SINGH

Cabinet: Cabinet appointed by the president on the recommendation of the prime minister

Elections: president elected by an electoral college consisting of elected members of both houses of Parliament and the legislatures of the states for a five-year term (no term limits);

vice president elected by both houses of Parliament for a five-year term; prime minister chosen by parliamentary members of the majority party following legislative elections.

Legislative branch: bicameral Parliament or Sansad consists of the Council of States or Rajya Sabha (a body consisting of not more than 250 members, up to 12 of whom are appointed by the president, the remainder are chosen by the elected members of the state and territorial assemblies; members serve six-year terms) and the People's Assembly or Lok Sabha (545 seats; 543 elected by popular vote, 2 appointed by the president; members serve five-year terms).

Judicial branch: Supreme Court (one chief justice and 25 associate justices are appointed by the president and remain in office until they reach the age of 65 or are removed for "proved misbehaviour")

3

Tribes and Modernization in India

INTRODUCTION

After discussing social structure and religion of the tribal societies in India, we now examine the impact of the process of modernisation on them. Before proceeding to discuss the tribal societies of India in relation to modernisation process extreme heterogeneity, being placed at different levels of social and economic development. Each one has reacted differently to the forces of modernisation. Some have become devastated as they came into contact with highly developed societies. In contrast, there are some who have richly benefited from the gains of modernisation. Because of differential impact the tribals have received, it is hazardous to generalise, although some of the basic trends of modernisation and change may be conveniently outlined. To give an idea of differing impacts of modernisation, we shall first describe the heterogeneous character of the tribal societies and see how in anthropology a tribe is conceptualised in relation to its contacts with other tribal and non-tribal groups. Secondly, we will give some case studies to show the nature of modernisation in the tribal groups from different parts of India. Then we will discuss different aspects of modernisation in relation to the tribal societies.

SCHEDULED TRIBES IN INDIA

Scheduled Tribes in India constitute, according to 1981 Census, 8 per cent of the total population, divided into 427 communities, and inhabiting almost all the regions and parts of India. By 1991 they were 8.10 per cent of the total population (Census of India, 1991) with 533 communities of which 75 were said to be primitive tribes. They widely differ in their demographic and cultural characteristics. The Great Andamanese number only in two digits the Toda are in three digits; Hill Miri (Arunachal Pradesh) are in four digits; there are Chenchu in five digits; Saora constitute a population of six digits; the Gond are more than 4 million, and so are the Santal and Bhil. Santal, Gond, Bhil and Munda are plough-cultivators; Rabari (Gujarat) are pastoralists; Chenchu are hunters and food-gatherers; Maler (Rajmahal Hills) are shifting cultivators like some of the tribes of the North-East. The large, plough-cultivating tribes are not different from the peasants. They are politically conscious, aware of their rights, and their level of modernisation and development is relatively high. They have come to be known as *haldar* (owner of the plough), *Kisan* (peasant), *Kashtkar* (tiller of the land) in different areas. They have also responded to modern education. In independent India, they have started taking advantage of the policy of reservation. Similarly, the tribes of the North-East have modernised by seeking advantages of the educational institutions.

But such is not the situation with a large number of other tribes especially what are called 'minor' ones. Some of them, especially the tribes of Andaman Islands (Jarawa, Onge, Great Andamanese, Shompen, and Sentinel) and Toda, are facing the problem of declining numbers and extinction. During the Fifth Five-Year Plan, it was felt that the benefits of state-sponsored modernisation and development activities were being chiefly monopolised by the big tribes, thus the gulf between them and the other smaller tribes was widening. The need was to have special schemes for them. From the list of Scheduled Tribes, the communities which were educationally and socially backward and nearly isolated, surviving at a pre-agricultural level, and had a declining or near-constant population, were separately placed in a list of Primitive Tribes. There were 72 such communities in India in 1981. In the year 2003, 75 communities were termed as primitive. The degree of modernisation amongst them is low. As their number has been less, with people living in dispersed villages, most of these tribes have not been able to form 'associations' that could exercise pressure on the state or central government. Some of them have 'associations' but they are concerned with social reforms rather than acting as effective pressure groups.

Contacts of the Tribal Societies with other Tribal and Non-tribal Social Groups

In anthropology, a tribe was conceptualised as a relatively isolated or semi-isolated community. Such a community had its own cultural system being defined by self-sufficiency, political autonomy, a well-demarcated territory, a common dialect, folklore and deities. It had a sense of belongingness to the same group. The geographic and cultural isolation of a tribe, thus defined, had implications for methodology. A tribe could be studied in itself without necessarily referring to other exterior social units. If a tribe was 'whole society' the peasant constituted 'part-society' with 'part-culture'. Such a neat formulation of 'tribe' as juxtaposed to 'peasant' was an ideal representation, far from both historical and contemporary reality.

A large number of examples were offered to show that a tribe was never completely isolated. It entered into a set of relationship with its neighbouring communities, tribals as well as non-tribals. The relationship in some cases was of intense hostility, punctuated with cases of periodic raids (as was the case with the tribes of Naga Hills). Or some economic exchanges obtained between independent tribes, a classical example of which was described by Mandelbaum from the tribes of Nilgiri Hills. Notwithstanding these relations between independent tribes, each one of them was a cultural whole, if not a cultural isolate.

And moreover, the inter-tribal relations did not contribute to vast magnitudes of acculturative changes. In spite of sharing the same geographic and ecological zones, each tribe maintained its own identity and cultural patterns. For example, in several tribal villages of Ranchi, Oraon and Munda live together. They may have faith in the local holy men. For instance, the holy man (Baba) of Kamre village (Ranchi district) was 'worshipped' by both Oraon and Munda. But the historic facts of living together and several cross-cutting ties did not mitigate the inter-tribal cultural and linguistic differences: Oraon speak Kurukh which is Dravidian while Munda belong to the Austro-

Asiatic branch of linguistic groups in India. Besides the inter-tribal relations, the tribal settlements close to caste Hindu villages had exchange relations on the pattern of *jajmani* with other patron and occupational castes. As a result, some of the tribal communities came to call themselves *Adivasi jati*. Once they entered into service relations with other jati, they also started incorporating certain Hindu deities and the elements of Hindu cosmology. Gradually, the little tradition of the tribals became a part of the great tradition of the Hindus. But such an absorption of the tribals in the caste system, as Bose (1971) has described it, did not signal the beginning of their modernisation, which actually began when they came in contact with the wider world? the world that had already undergone qualitative changes because of the colonial rule.

The Tribals and the British Policy

The British policy towards the tribals had two major elements. Firstly, it favoured isolation of the tribal areas from the mainstream (Bhowmick 1980; Chaudhuri 1982). Thus was given the concept of 'excluded' and/or 'partially excluded areas'. Because the British tribal policy was political and colonial, the British administrators feared, that if these tribals (bow-and-arrow armed tribals were often labelled as militant, unruly and *junglee*) were to have contact with the mainstream of Indian society, the freedom movements would gain further strength. In this background it seemed logical to them to isolate, administratively and politically, the regions that had predominantly tribal populations.

Secondly, at the level of reform, the British administration was interested in 'civilising' these people. In an ethno-centric assessment, the tribals were viewed at par with stage of bestiality.

The classical theory of evolution, which had gripped academic attention in late nineties and early twenties, had treated the 'contemporary primitives' as the remnants or survivals of the early stages of humanity, savagery and barbarism. In the words of Sir E.B. Tylor, these people inhabiting the hilly or forested terrain with sparse population and difficult communication were 'social fossils'; a study or whom would illuminate the prehistoric phases of human existence.

The intellectual climate about the historical and evolutionary place of these 'primitives' considerably influenced the political action. Missionaries were sent to some of the difficult areas inhabited by these people. Animism, as the tribal religion was often characterised, was replaced by one or the other denomination of Christianity. Schools were opened up, and obviously English was opted as the main language of instruction. Along with came the Western medical system, which slowly started exorcising the traditional practices of cure. Styles of life and ways of behaviour began changing. And they became very conspicuous in dress patterns, especially of men.

The Westernisation of tribals had begun. Here, two things need to be mentioned. Not all tribes were subjected to the efforts of modernisation. There were many which continued to survive in their traditional modes till India's Independence. Secondly, the decision of the Administration to admit missionaries in some areas to open schools there was conditioned by strategic factors. Chotanagpur plateau and the North-Eastern India were the main candidates for the mission activities and concomitant modernisation. In these cases, as well as in others, Christianity was the sole vehicle of modernisation. The neo-converts not only became a part of the Great Tradition of Christianity, but were also linked to the Great Tradition of the Western culture, English language, Western dress, mannerism and medicines, being ineluctable components of the rulers, culture, flourished as far superior and 'advanced' to the local culture. The fate of traditional material culture and styles of living was decided: they were to be 'preserved' as museum specimens.

And this evaluation – the tribal culture must be 'museumified' lest it disappear with the onslaught of modernity – promoted the classical ethnographic studies. In them, the way they were changing was not attended to. The attempt was to record as meticulously as possible the tradition, or better the dying tradition of the people. These studies served another purpose. They provided the administrators with the cultural background of the people they were going to rule. Detailed accounts of the local customary laws were written so that the administration of people and arbitration of their inter-personal conflicts could be done very much in terms of their laws and rules of conflict settlement. Along with this, attempts were made to synthesise the customary and the modern laws. In all these efforts, the focus was on modernising the tribals. But the colonial experience elsewhere had taught the protagonists that were the people to be detached from their tradition almost completely, there would be a backlash of modernisation and breakdown of its agencies. In the next section we discuss actual cases of the impact of modernisation on selected tribal groups of India.

CASE-STUDIES TO EXAMINE THE IMPACT OF MODERNIZATION

Modernisation is a process of spreading the values, institutions and technical aspects of 'modern society'. To highlight different responses to the forces of modernisation we give you five case studies of the tribal groups from different parts of India.

The Baiga Tribe of Madhya Pradesh

The Baiga tribe of Madhya Pradesh is famous in anthropological literature because it was in its context that Elwin (1938: 511-521) suggested one of the first, most controversial approaches to the tribal problem. According to him, since the genesis of tribal problem lay in their contact with the non-tribal exploiters, the tribes (and in this case, the Baiga) should be isolated in a 'tribal reserve area', where the entry of non-tribals, missionaries, landlords and other exploiting elements should be completely prohibited. Though Elwin later withdrew his advice of isolating the tribals, the positive consequences of isolation, fostered by geographical factors and strongly supported by the Administration, have been noticed in some hill tribes, the most outstanding being the Apa Tani of Arunachal Pradesh, a case we shall discuss after that of the Baiga. Having a population of 1,76,934 individuals (according to Census 1971), the Baiga, one of the six Primitive Tribes of Madhya Pradesh, are mainly concentrated in the districts of Mandla, Shahdol, Sidhi, Balaghat, Bilaspur and Surguja. According to a Tribal Research Institute (Bhopal) Report (1986: 5) they are 'one of the most backward tribes of the state', with the percentage of literacy among them being 4.51.

The Baiga used to practice shifting cultivation *(bewar)* till quite recently. They have now been advised (or 'forced') to give it up. Only inside the Baiga-Chak reservation, which has fifty-two villages, in Mandla district, that they are permitted to pursue *bewar*-cultivation in a restricted manner. Though mentally adjusting to the new requirements of plough cultivation now, they are nostalgic about their past when they used to grow twelve varieties of grain through *bewar*. The Baiga term Bewar refers to tilling of the land by the axe.

Their cultural system has not undergone any perceptible changes. Traditionally, the males used to keep tangled hair, almost resembling a bun, on the occiput region of their head. Now, except for a couple of educated people, this cultural trait is still valued. Similarly, the women were tattooed on every part of the body, including forehead. Even now this custom prevails. The Baiga had been famous as shaman *(gunia)*. The shamanistic lore has not weakened over time. Marriage rules are strictly adhered to. The inter-personal conflicts are resolved in the village by the intervention of their council. As a matter of fact, the details of their culture as documented by Elwin in his field work from 1932 till 1939 are not very different from the facts collected by a contemporary ethnographer.

The headquarters of Baiga Chak is called *Charha*. There is a dispensary having a resident doctor, a pharmacist and a nurse. Only a negligible number of the Baiga attend the dispensary when they are ill. Their faith in shamanistic healing *(gunia)* is unshakable.

It has primary, middle and secondary schools. But there are very few Baiga children attending the schools as compared to the Gond. As one moves to higher classes, the number of the Baiga further declines. Dropout rate amongst them is much higher than among other communities. There are only two Baiga teachers in the whole region. The following photograph, taken by Dr. Surinder Nath, is from Baiga Chak, Mandla District, Madhya Pradesh. Hero two Baiga teachers, in shirt and trousers, are convincing an illiterate Baiga about the importance of modern education inspiring him to send his children to the school.

A couple of changes may be noticed in their economic life. As said earlier, the plough-hating Baiga (for them, ploughing amounted to 'tearing the mother earth's breasts') have taken up settled cultivation. Some of them work as agricultural labourers with the Gond. They also work on the jobs provided by the forest department like, wage labourers for making the forest wall, working in the ropemaking factory, in jobs of plantation, etc. In spite of all this, they have maintained aloofness in behaviour, mixing less with the Gond and other communities. Even today, it is not uncommon to see the Baiga running away to seek shelter in dense forests when they encounter non-tribal cosmopolitan people coming to their hamlets.

Apa Tani and other Tribes of the North-East

Apa Tani, numbering about 15000, live in the high lands of Subansiri district of Arunachal Pradesh. For a very long time, they maintained a self-contained social order, which was uninfluenced by outside power. Though they had developed an efficient system of rice cultivation, they did not have the knowledge of plough and wheel, and their cattle were not used for traction, carriage, or milking. They used to produce a surplus of grain for barter with neighbouring tribes. Their economy was non-monetised. Besides speaking their own language and a few languages of their neighbours, they did not know any other national language or any other language of wider communication. Knowledge of Assamese could have helped them in communicating with the wider world. In view of the Apa Tani's geographical and cultural isolation, it may be assumed that they would have greater obstacles in the path of their development and modernisation compared to the tribes of Central India, like the Gond, who have been in touch with advanced and modern societies. But this has not been so.

Apa Tani have made tremendous progress in the direction of modernisation. Despite the literacy rate of 14.04 per cent in Arunachal Pradesh (Census 1981), they have done extremely well in seeking modern education. By the beginning of 1980, there were forty-five Apa Tani with university degrees. Many of them were studying in the universities of Guwahati, Dibrugarh, Shillong and even Delhi. Most of these University graduates had entered government employment, out of which in 1978, there were no less than fifteen serving in gazetted and

342 in non-gazetted posts. Furer-Haimendorf (1982: 296-297), who had been studying these people from 1944, in his field work in the early 1980s, found some fully qualified doctors and a pilot officer in the Indian Air Force amongst them.

The gains of this development are cumulative? over generations even more Apa Tani will take advantage of modern education, entering bureaucratic jobs. With these changes, however, the Apa Tani have been able to keep their cultural identity intact. There have been negligible changes in their religious and ritual life. Furer-Haimendorf (1982: 299) says that in traditional ritual practices, "even the most educated participate with undiminished dedication". Similarly, their marriage rules and family life have undergone fewer changes.

For Furer-Haimendorf, this has been a case of rapid modernisation in material, technological and social life, without the loss of distinct ethnic identity. In their modernisation, geographic isolation protected by the governmental measures of not allowing the outsiders to take advantages of the local resources and opportunities, has been the crucial factor. Furer-Haimendorf writes, "One of the causes of the rapid economic and educational development of the Apa Tani is their freedom from oppression and exploitation by more advanced communities."

The North-East India, beyond the present-day Assam, was always protected from the entry of the outsiders by the Inner Line Policy. Even today, Indians from other states have to seek Inner Line permit to enter certain states of the North-East like Nagaland, Mizoram, Arunachal Pradesh etc. The outsiders are not permitted to establish their own business enterprises. In the model of indigenous development, only the locals are eligible for obtaining contracts of developmental works and business. Thus, the North-East was saved from the uneven, even devastating, influences of cultural contact as in Central India, where the outsiders played havoc with the local resources. They usurped the land of the tribals, the proud owners who were reduced to the state of serfdom. In addition to the Inner Line Policy, Christian missions played a responsible role in modernising the people, especially in Nagaland and Mizo hills, Khasi and Jaintia hills, and NEFA (Sema 1986). Modern educational institutions were introduced. English became the language of instruction. Western dress and culture came along (Furer Haimendorf 1976).

But these missions did not uproot the people from their traditional moorings. The local tribal languages were not replaced by English. They were treated with respect. Each one came to have its own script, with Roman alphabet along with accent marks. For facilitating an exogenous religion, Christianity in this context, to reach grass-root levels, the religious scriptures and holy books, regulating the daily life of the people, were translated (and subsequently published) in local languages. Dictionaries of the local languages were compiled (for example, the English-Khasi Dictionary by V. Nissor Singh was published in 1906). Gradually, the local people were trained to take up the role of religious functionaries. With this, the effects of modernisation were visible in all aspects of the society.

We saw in the case of the Apa Tani that in spite of developments and modernisation, they have been able to retain their distinct cultural identity. And such can be said about other tribes of the North-East. The Naga, for example, are one of the modernised tribes of India. But this exterior facade of modem values, dress and mannerism has not mitigated their sentiments of belonging to the same society, the Naga (Horam 1977: 94-108). In these cases, one may notice continuity in change; modernisation has not diluted the traditional bonds of social cohesion.

Rabari

The Rabari are a lesser studied community, spreading from Western Rajasthan to the Kutch region of Gujarat. Their settlements (locally called *dhani*) are also found in some villages of Haryana, Punjab and Uttar Pradesh. Numbering more than 400,000 members, these people have been differently designated in the states of their predominance for the grant of preferential treatment, in Gujarat, they are one of the Scheduled Tribes while in Rajasthan they are included in the lists of other Backward Classes (OBCs) and the Semi-nomadic Tribes. Some confusion also entails from their nomenclature: in Gujarat, they call themselves Rabari (or Rahbari) while in Rajasthan, the term used is Raika. The Rabari are pastoralists. They domesticate camels, sheep, cows, buffaloes and goats. As the grazing areas have drastically reduced, and the areas they have been traditionally inhabiting have a harsh climate with a measely rainfall, these people are constrained to migrate with their flocks to other regions rich in fodder (Saizman 1986: 49-61). They have permanent villages, which for the most part of the year are inhabited by the women, old, and infirm people, as the men are away with their cattle.

At one time, the Rabari of Western Raiasthan were patronised by the princely lineages. They looked after the imperial camels, took them out for grazing, looked after their diseases, trained them for various tasks, and more important, these camel-riding Rabari were entrusted with the job of carrying confidential mail from one part to the other. Once these imperial lineages declined, and the importance of camel reduced, there was a subsequent decline in the position of the Rabari.

Actually, the term Raika used for the Rabari was an occupational one: it designated a 'camel riding messenger'. Living in hamlets which were outside the main boundary of the village and leading an isolated existence, the Rabari were less affected by the development plans. Only in recent years, they have started taking advantage of modern education. Some of the Rabari have taken up teaching profession. The other educated people are working in government offices, police, camel and sheep breeding farms, and private and public sector. And the Raika teachers and other professionals are making every effort to inspire the new generation to take education as an important source of mobility. The Rabari of Gujarat have changed much more than their counterparts in Rajasthan. In Gujarat, they identified themselves with the dominant pastoral caste, the Bharawad, and were able to enter milk-cooperatives as dairymen, thus their economic status improved. There was a Rajya Sabha M.P. from the Rabari of Gujarat. For taking up the issues of their community, the Rabari have founded an Association, and it publishes some periodicals titled *Gopalbandhu* (from Gujarat) and *Raika Jagriti* (from Haryana). They provide a forum where the problems of their community are identified and the efforts to modernise it are discussed.

Toda

The Toda are well known in anthropological literature for

having been pastoralists with a 'sacred complex of buffalos'; for paractising fraternal polyandry where the fatherhood of a child was established through a ritual ceremony called 'bow-andarrow'; and for participating in a complex network of economic, social and ritual relationships with three other groups of Nilgiri Hills, Kota, Badaga and Kurumba (Mandelbaum 1970). Though the Toda society is still rooted in tradition, it "at the same time is branching out into modernity" (Walker 1986: 286).

The symbiotic relations between the Toda and other Nilgiri communities were initially based on an exchange of services. Now each economy has replaced barter exchanges. The network of relations among the Toda has become open. They now have social and business relations with other immigrants from surrounding plains and beyond. Their contacts with a great many government agencies like Nilgiri Collectorate, Agricultural Department, Veterinary, Health and Medical Offices, Police Department etc., have increased. Further the Toda hamlets-especially those close to Ootacamund-attract tourists and travellers from various parts of the world. These contacts along with a number of others that the Toda have with other communities and immigrants have influenced the spread of modernity among them.

One of the changes that modernisation has brought in small communities, which at one time were relatively isolated, pertains to the domain of religion. Once their isolation was broken, they developed contact with communities that preserved the great tradition of a religion. The Toda, as an example of this process of change, have become oriented to South Indian Hinduism. In the markets of Ootacamund, which they frequent quite regularly, they hear of the religious merit of pilgrimages to the Hindu shrines in the Nilgiris and far beyond. Pictorial representations of Hindu gods and goddesses have found an honourable place in many Toda households. This fact of their drawing closer to popular Hinduism has not shown a decline in their indigenous rituals. The modern Toda, Walker (1986: 288) writes, has accepted the "efficacy of two parallel ritual systems: his own and that of popular South Indian Hinduism".

Education has been, as is the case with other tribal societies, another factor of change. But compared to market and temple, the schools took longer time to bring about desired effects. In the Indian context, modernisation, has reinforced both English and the regional language. In Kohima district, for example, both English and Angami are equally strong; in Meghalaya, both English and Khasi have been developed, similarly among the Toda, Tamil and English have been equally accepted. Having been educated in Tamil and English, some of the Toda have taken up white-collar occupation, unheard of by their ancestors.

Santal Tribe in Transition

Through the Santal case, we would try to explicitly show various steps in the process of modernisation of a tribe. A summary of this case may be presented at the outset.

i) The first exposure of the Santal to exogenously introduced changes was when the outsiders? money lenders, *zamindars*, missionaries? started encroaching upon their area. Their land was forcibly annexed by some of them, and the Santal were subjugated to the state of serfdom.

ii) Against such an exploitative and oppressive state, the Santal Uprising (also called Santal Rebellion) 1855-1857 took place, and was brutally crushed.

iii) The building of steel mill and company city at Jamshedpur had an important bearing on the Santal, where both the educated and illiterate could find suitable work.

iv) Having close interaction with caste Hindus, the Santal, especially of upper classes, imbibed Hindu religion, caste practices, and claimed the status of Kshatriya.

v) As a result of the revival movement, mainly to save the Santal from a steady loss of land, exploitative and oppressive interests of the outsiders, the Santal leaders rejected the Hindu model.

vi) With Jharkhanda Party, the Santal acquired an important political organ for mobilising their interests.

vii) Industrialisation especially in Jamshedpur had important consequences: the Santal became aware of new sources of upward mobility; importance of education was realised, and the political path of raising one's status became clear to them. In other words, industrialisation and education were crucial to the modernisation of the Santal.

Here we will examine under the following six sub-headings various changes in the life of the Santal tribals.

Rejection of Hinduism and the Reference Groups of Upper Castes

All this is rooted in the revivalistic movement, which began in mid-nineteenth century. Despite little political cohesion among the Santal. There is considerable cultural similarity, thanks to the revivalistic movement, and a strong feeling that the Santal are different from the Hindus. The Sanskritic values emulated by the Santal, when they were attracted to Kshatriya or Brahmin model, are being given up under the tremendous impact of the cultural identity movement. Jharkhanda movement's role has been crucial in this regard. Martin Orans' (1965: 108) observation is worth quoting here: "Once I saw a young party activist who had grown up in the Jharkhanda movement persuading an older Santal with a few years of education that he must take up beef-eating again if he wished to preserve the Santal caste". The rejection of Hinduism or Hindu identity and the most sacred Hindu element (sacredness of cow being one) is not only for returning to the chaste Santal identity, it is also because their exploiters? money lenders, land lords, etc. who were all Hindus.

Santal Uprising: 1855-1857

The first event to take the Santal on the inroads of a conscious cultural identity was their uprising of 1855-1857. On 30th June 1855, a massive rally of Santal, over ten thousand, protested against their exploitation and oppression. The rally, led by Sidho and Kano, took an oath to end the oppressive rule of the British, *Zamindars*, and money lenders, and it decided to set up an independent *Santali Raj*. The money lenders and *zamindars* had flocked into the Santali areas, the legal procedures and financial institutions they imposed were patronised by the colonial government. The crops of the Santal were forcibly seized, the interest charged on loans varied from fifty to five hundred per cent. Once the complaints of people fell on deaf ear, they decided to rise in arms. It is estimated that fifteen to twenty-five thousand Santal were killed in this uprising. The courage of the Santal against the oppressive rule is still commemorated in the local folk songs and traditions.

There have also been other revolts in which the cultural identity of the Santal was reasserted. In 1917, the Santal of Mayurbhanj revolted against their recruitment to serve in Egypt during the First World War.

Influence of Christianity

For a very long time, the Santal had been living with the non-tribals. The latter became prosperous by fleecing the Santal of their land and property. Those of the upper classes took over to Sanskritic practices? like worship of Hindu deities, abstaining from eating beef, offering liquor on festive occasion, observance of the norms of purity and pollution? so that they could be identified with higher *varna* categories. But the Hindu model was essentially traditionalistic. Sanskritisation offered ritual mobility in the caste system. It did not provide them an opportunity to modernise.

Christianity was a prime mover initiating modern changes among the Santal. In their area, Scandinavian and American Missions made efforts to convert the local people. These missionaries as elsewhere in India opened educational institutions preparing people to enter new occupations. Christianity gave the people a readymade great tradition. The institutions like hospital and school that came with the missions introduced them to the wider world, beyond the interaction they had within themselves and with other non-tribals. Notwithstanding the introduction of the Santal to modernity through the missions their identity was eroded because of Christianity. If their immediate exploiters were Hindus, those who patronised these cases of exploitation were Christians. Thus, any movement for a reassertion of the cultural identity required a rejection of both Hindu and Christian models of change.

Impact of Industrialisation

The installation of industries in Santal dominated areas was another very important factor of change and modernisation.

These industries provided jobs to both educated and illiterate and offered a new source of mobility. Moreover, these industries were free from one or another religious domination. They promoted caste-free and class-free occupation. A large number of Santal found jobs in them. These industries, having recruited local tribals, provided an opportunity to the people to further cement their traditional linkages: in fact, these industries were the 'world of kinsmen'. Santal identity was further strengthened by the tribal-workers.

Cultural Identity and Political Action

The articulation of cultural identity into political term was facilitated once the Jharkhanda Party was founded. This Party demanded creation of a tribal state. For the Santal in the industrial belt, most of the traditional customs and practices have been weakened, but the tribal identity is reinforced through Jharkhanda movement remains primary. The Santal in the city are akin to other city dwellers. They too have individualism and aspirations of social mobility. The ethnic ties as expressed politically continue to exist. With modernisation, they are not weakening. Every Santal feels attached to *Ol Chiki,* the Sarna *Dharm*, the parables of mythological origin, and to Jharkhanda Party. At the same time, he aspires to take up modern education, a good job which opens avenues for upward mobility. Having discussed the Santal tribe in transition, let us now also review, in general, different aspects of modernisation in relation to the tribal societies in India.

DIFFERENT ASPECTS OF MODERNIZATION IN RELATION TO THE TRIBAL SOCIETIES

The cases, discussed in section 28.3, are chosen from different parts of India. They amply demonstrate that modernisation in the tribes can be traced back to their contact with the agencies spreading the values of modernity like opennetworks, achievement, competition, equality, caste-and class-free occupations, etc. The entry of missionaries in some areas (as in the North-East) initiated modernisation. Incorporation of a community into milk-cooperatives (as in Gujarat) created situations bringing the local people in contact with developed sections of the society. Encroachment of commercial frontiers and modern markets has contributed a lot to the modernisation of tribals. In some parts of India, especially, the central, installation of heavy industries and creation of urban centres were instrumental in spreading modernity. Let us examine the two factors of change, namely, industrialisation and education.

Industrialisation

During the last four decades and particularly during the Plan periods, there has been an acceleration of mining and manufacturing industries. Forest resources have been gradually exploited, leading eventually to deforestation, in the hilly and forested belts of tribal India. Most of these industries came to be established in or around tribal areas because they were rich in mineral and other resources. Close to these industries grew small towns housing mainly the industrial workers. As the exploitation of mineral and forest resources was chiefly confined to Assam, Bihar, Madhya Pradesh and Orissa, there was a rapid increase of urban population in these states. Demographer Bose (1962: 26) writes that with a concentration of industries in these states, there was a relative shift of urban population from Indo-Gangetic plain to the hilly and plateau areas which offered new industrial and natural resources.

It was not only industrialisation that was responsible for the migration ? promoted by 'pull', 'push', or 'forced' factors ? of tribals from their homesteads but also other economic institutions. In certain states like Assam and of South India, tea, coffee and rubber estates were formed. The tribals were dispossessed of their land, and were made to work as plantation labourers (Jain 1988). Out-migration from Chotanagpur plateau and other neighbouring regions occurred phenomenally to these estates. The tribes were forcibly migrated to other countries, like the Kol who were sent to Mauritius as labourers. Kondha of Orissa were taken to Mesopotamia to serve in World War I. A large number of Bhil were recruited for military service (Pathy 1986: 74).

Industrialisation in the tribal areas offered new jobs. But the tribals, unskilled in initial stages. could only get the jobs at the lower rungs. At one time owners of land were now depressed into the class of industrial proletariat. This happened because of a number of factors. Firstly, their land had been usurped by the nontribal *Zamindars* in many areas, and they were looking for some alternatives. Secondly, installation of big industrial and developmental projects in tribal zones required the displacement of the native population, often to unknown areas (Vidyarthi 1968: 13-29, Fernandes 1998). In these cases of uprooting local tribals and non-tribals were equally affected, but as the tribals outnumbered the nontribals in these areas, they suffered the maximum. Finally, as a result of over exploitation of forest resources by the outsiders, the tribal economics, which is to a large extent were forest-based, dwindled. Thus, a combination of local impoverishment and availability of new opportunities sent these tribals to seek jobs in heavy industries, tea plantations, construction sites, etc.

These tribals now-turned labourers have changed a lot. The traditional dresses have been replaced by those that came with modernity. Their occupational structure has changed, and it has important implications. A sense of mobility is gradually instilled in the community. Mobility becomes inter-generational as the children of tribal workers aspire to do better in life than their parents, by taking hold of opportunities offered by modernity.

In this process, some of the traditional institutions weaken. For example, in his study of tribals working in Bokaro Steel Plant, Vidyarthi (1968: 21), says that their village institutions like the '*jajmani* system', the cycle of festivals and rituals, the caste-affiliations etc., have completely been disintegrated, and all round depression and despair seems to have affected the life of the uprooted villages. This, however, does not mean that there is also a subsequent decline in the feeling of oneness amongst the tribals in a new setup. Industrialisation has fostered a new sense of solidarity between the co-workers. Once there already exist ethnic and social ties between the tribals, the relations in the industry cement them further. Trade unions on the lines of tribal-workers crystallise (Bhowmik 1982: 461-473). The feeling of ethnicity becomes strong and they begin exerting pressure on the state and the centre.

Education

Having been exposed to industrialisation for almost four decades, having migrated to various industrial towns, and having imbibed the spirit of upward mobility, the tribals have realised the importance of modern education. The missionaries have played an outstanding role in spreading Western education. The Government is also committed to the idea that one of the avenues to speedy development is education. For diversifying the tribals to different occupations, they must be educationally equipped to face the challenges. Besides the fact that education promotes social mobility and enhances the ability of the people to think about their amelioration, it can save them from being exploited by money lenders who have been taking advantage of the illiterate tribals by forging and tempering with the promissory notes.

According to Census 1981, literacy rate in India was 36.23 per cent; among the Scheduled Castes and Scheduled Tribes, it was 21.38 and 16.33 per cent respectively. The North-Eastern states had done exceptionally well: the highest literacy is in Mizoram (59.63 per cent), followed by Nagaland (40.31 per cent), Manipur (39.74 per cent), and Meghalaya (31.55 per cent). The literacy rates in India in 1991 and 2001 were 52.21 and 63.38 percent respectively. As per the 1991 Census the literacy rates of Scheduled Castes and Scheduled Tribes were 37.41 and 29.60 percent respectively. The literacy rate of the tribals in 1991 was 23.63 per cent. This is lower than not only of the general population figures but also of the SC population figures. The litracy rate of the rural tribal women was recorded in 1991 to be 12.74, which was the lowest of all social groups in India. Literacy rate for STs was lowest in Andhra Pradesh (17.16 percent) and highest was in Mizoram (82 percent).

Ashram schools, especially meant for tribal children living in remote and isolated villages, have been opened up. While a separate school for each tribal hamlet is not feasible, the nearest regular school? for all children with no specification? is too far away, for them to attend it and return home the same day. That is why the Ashram schools are residential, providing free board and lodging to the pupils. In terms of their curriculum, they are supposed to impart craft-based education, thus linking learning with productive activities. Once the students finish the school, they are sufficiently prepared to take up any of the craft-based occupations. In this way, diversification of tribals in different jobs is expected to result.

But the evaluative studies of these schools speak otherwise. The curriculum is more tilted towards literacy-based education. Half-hearted attempts are made to impart craft-oriented education. And the specific character of Ashram schools is relegated to the background. They start resembling the regular schools. A study of the patterns of tribal education in India raises two important issues. The dropout rate of the tribal children is very high, and as one moves to secondary and higher levels, this rate increases exponentially. According to Census 1981, the dropout rate in primary, middle and secondary stages was 75 per cent (boys 71.57, girls 78.43), 84.99 per cent and 91.65 per cent respectively. Secondly, the number of tribal students reaching professional and university courses is very low. Writing about the Gond of Andhra Pradesh, Furer-Haimendorf (1982: 130) concludes that, "in thirty-six years of tribal education only five Gond and two Pradhan have been awarded university degrees". The representation of tribals in professional courses, according to the figures of 1978-79, given in the Report of the Commissioner for Scheduled Castes and Scheduled Tribes, 1986-88 (Twentyeighth Report: 522-523) it is clear that very few tribal students reach post-graduate courses in professional disciplines. Therefore, their distribution in higher professional positions is almost negligible.

This Report shows also that the Scheduled Tribes have done well as compared to the Scheduled Castes. But, the figures from North-Eastern Hill University (NEHU), Shillong, a central university, have in fact tilted the graph in favour of the Scheduled Tribes. In this University, there are five Professors, nine Readers, forty-six Lecturers, and five Research Associates from various tribal communities. Thus all the five Professors and all the nine readers in central universities are from NEHU. Out of a total of 50 Scheduled Tribe Lecturers, 46 are from this university. When we take the figures from NEHU, thinking that Meghalaya is predominantly a tribal state with Khasi and Garo having a long tradition of education, we find that in none of the teaching and research positions does the percentage of Scheduled Tribes reach fifty. There are only 10.20 per cent Professors, 10.71 per cent Readers, 31.72 per cent Lecturers and 45.45 per cent Research Associates from tribal communities in NEHU. In other words, even in tribal states the non-tribals are holding a majority of the higher positions. Some tribes like Meena of Rajasthan have been quite successful. A large number of them have taken up jobs in administration (Civil Services), private sector, financial institutions and colleges.

Certainly there has been an increase in tribal literacy. But the number of students continuing to stay in schools till higher classes and then entering the portals of college is very low. Dropout rate, as said earlier, is very high, and for girls, it is much higher. In mixed areas, where small tribes live with larger ones, the dropout rate among the former is higher. In the schools of Baiga Chak, we saw that the Baiga students generally failed to stay in schools after the primary, while the Gond continued to study till higher classes. Education is one of the crucial factors of modernisation, but when the tribals fail to seek its advantages, the degree of modernity, mobility and diversification of occupations among them is sharply reduced.

There are several reasons accounting for high dropout rate. The curriculum in most cases is not relevant to the conditions in which the tribals live. They find education a kind of onerous burden. Low standard of teaching and facilities in tribal schools is another factor. It has also been found that teachers in these schools are generally from non-tribal communities and they take posting in tribal areas as a kind of punishment. Thus, they are able to evince little interest. Domestic duties of the tribal children, especially the girls, are another factor. From young age, they are entrusted with household chores, fetching water to looking after the younger brothers and sisters. Absence of feedback from the family, inspiring the children to take their study seriously, is an important factor. The economic status of tribal households, in most cases, cannot afford to keep the children as consuming, rather than producing members for a long time.

In some cases, the medium of instruction poses grave problems. If the Kond are taught in Oriya instead of their own dialect, they may find learning an uphill task (Mahapatra, 1984: 376). Moreover, the objectives of educational departments in imparting teaching to students are not clear. Their chief interest lies in raising literacy, rather than making education a productive activity, guaranteeing social mobility and ameliorating the local people in their traditional milieu.

Adverse Effects of Modernity

The aim of modernisation is to bring the society on the path of progress, to diversify its occupational structure, to provide the people with efficient technology which vouchsafes higher production, to give them avenues of social mobility and to bring them on par with other developed sections of the society. But the results are not encouraging in all cases. With an introduction of development plans, some societies have found themselves disintegrated. Modernity has given rise to adverse effects. Take the case of industrialisation. As we saw earlier, the establishment of heavy industries, construction of dams and launching of development plans in tribal zones has necessitated displacement of the local population. Thousands of tribal families were displaced from their traditional habitats. Compensation was supposed to be provided to them in terms of money and alternative land, but not all of them got an alternative place to live.

The report of the Commissioner for Scheduled Castes and Scheduled Tribes for 1962-1963 informed that in Ranchi district of Bihar, 14,461 tribal families were displaced from an area of 62,494 acres, and only 3,479 of them were allotted alternative land. The compensation provided to them in cash was recklessly spent. The tribals not fully conversant with cash economy squandered the money on various attractions that were available in nearby industrial towns. Soon their funds had depleted. With their land gone for developmental activities and left with no training, equipment or aptitude for skilled or semi-skilled jobs, they had no option but to enter the town as unskilled labourers, taking up various 'marginal jobs' of domestic servants, rickshaw pullers, vendors, hawkers, etc. They could enter the industrial sector at the lowest level, and their chances of moving up were meagre as they remained untrained for industrial jobs requiring technical know-how. Eventually they were proletarianised. Furer-Haimendorf (1982: 321) writes, "....in the streets of Ranchi one can still see Munda and Oraon rickshaw-pullers who not long ago were independent cultivators tilling their own land".

Contact situations with the outsiders have been equally detrimental. Destruction of the forests as a consequence of felling of trees for industrial purposes has threatened the small communities of hunters and food-gatherers. Modern diseases unknown to tribals have been introduced with the entry of outsiders in tribal areas. The tribal population in Andaman Islands has greatly declined because of high mortality rate. Measles and influenza, the killer diseases for those who had not developed any resistance to them, played havoc with the Andaman tribals.

Similarly, at the time of Independence, the Toda population had fallen to under 500. The chief cause of their decline was the prevalence of venereal diseases (Walker 1986: 283). In most cases, depopulation of a tribe was mainly because of rapid ecological changes that created imbalances in their habitats. For new schemes, either of medical treatment or development, the people were not fully prepared to accept them. Hence, they reacted in a lukewarm manner to all those institutions that could have changed and modernised them. Modernisation created economic disparities in various sections of the society. Those who could take advantages of new economic and educational frontiers were able to better their lot, while a large sections of the tribals, not adequately prepared to deal with new challenges, gradually depressed into poorer sections of the society. Against economic and social disparities, they have raised a collective voice. Modernisation, in other words, has given rise to a new consciousness amongst the people. The already existing solidarity between them has become strengthened.

Tribal Movements

In the latter half of the last century, the tribals, especially in central India, had reacted against their exploiters. These movements were directed towards freeing their land from all those who exploited them economically and culturally. At the same time, each of these movements put emphasis on revitalisation of their culture, their traditional culture which was swayed under the impact of the outsiders. The Tana Bhagat movement, for example, derived its name from the ritual of 'expelling from the Oraon land foreign spirits, nefarious powers and ghosts', borrowed from the Munda. Along with this, they also sought to drive away the 'evil powers of modern innovations' like steam boat, motor car, bicycle, etc. These modern innovations that were being introduced into their land were seen as the means of exploitation. Exorcising the 'ghost of modernity', they desired to revert to their original religion, the *Kurukh Dharma* (Roy 1915). The charismatic leaders of Oraon, Santal and Munda were believed to free the people not only from the webs of evil supernatural powers, but also from the 'iron clutches' of the nontribal exploiters and oppressors. Another such movement occurred in 1922 among the tribals of South Gujarat where under supernatural command of the female goddess, Devi, they stopped consuming liquor, and later on it took nationalist turn (Hardiman 1987).

The rebellion of 1855-1857 was a great event in history of the Santal. This event is still remembered in their folk songs and talks. It was an attempt to recover the tribal land, which was steadily lost to the outsiders, and to wipe out the nontribals from their territory. In the Santal myths of the nineteenth century, there was a description of the ancient days of independence and glory, and all this was swept away once the outsiders with modern weaponry started infiltrating into their areas. Martin Orans (1965: 35) writes, "The Santal are thus pictured as independent, powerful and constituted exactly in the image of an ideal Hindu Kingdom". The movement had the aim of reverting to their traditional religion *Sarna Dharam*, and social structure.

As a response to modernity, and the fact that traditional institutions of the people disintegrate under its impact, there have been conscious attempts to revive traditional ways of living. Cultural identity is cemented, because it can be instrumental in achieving political goals. Consciously the tribals have tried to introspect into their cultures to single out and eradicate their 'evil customs and practices'. For regulating the behaviour of people, so that the feeling of collectivity remains intact, rules have been collectively arrived at. Nonconformity to any one of them may call for an imposition of fine. Modernity has made people conscious of their culture. For example, the Sahariya of Morena district (Madhya Pradesh) have founded their association called *Adivasi Jati Sudhar Sangha*. For 'purifying' their people, it has identified twelve principles like regular bath, education for the children, abstaining from eating 'dirty' animals (like swine, sambur, etc.), respect for the educated people, etc. Similarly, the Rabari have formed *Akhil Bhartiya Rawari Rayaka Samaj Mahasabha,* where measures for uplifting the community and eradicating its evils have been collectively arrived at. In the same way, one of the major aims of the Toda Uplift Society is "to strive for the eradication of bad habits", and by 'bad habits' they mean "polyandry, wife-capture, drunkenness and the excessive sacrifice of buffaloes at funeral ceremonies".

These tribal associations serve two purposes. They endeavour their best to keep the whole group united. For such a unity, the traditional styles of living, except those, which are 'bad' cannot be given up. They must be revived. Such a unity is needed for demanding better deal from the government. The ethnic interests of the tribals, thus, merge with political demands for separate states and are voiced and sustained.

One of the best studied cases is of Jharkhanda movement. The Jharkhanda Party, founded by Jai Pal Singh, an Oxford educated Christian of the Munda tribe, demanded carving out of a new state, spreading from Palamau in Bihar to Keonjhar in Orissa and from Surguja in Madhya Pradesh to Midnapur in West Bengal, of the Indian union of which tribal people would be numerically dominant. The basic issues behind this movement were land and forest alienation, training and job deprivation due to influx of the outsiders, cultural submergence, and imbalanced development. As you already know, Jharkhand has now achieved the status of a state. Coming to the North-East, the Bodo and the Naga movements are good examples of how ethnic identity takes up political route for realising their interests. Uneven development and modernisation, concentration of gains in some areas and their non-dispersal to the others, and urban-oriented models of growth are the chief causes in all these separatist movements.

INDIAN TRIBAL SOCIETY

According to Oxford Dictionary "A tribe is a group of people in a primitive or barbarious stage of development acknowledging the authority of a chief and usually regarding themselves as having a common ancestor. D. N Majumdar defines tribe as a social group with territorial affiliation, endogamous with no specialization of functions ruled by tribal officers hereditary or otherwise, united in language or dialect recognizing social distance with other tribes or castes. According to Ralph Linton tribe is a group of bands occupying a contiguous territory or territories and having a feeling of unity deriving from numerous similarities in a culture, frequent contacts and a certain community of interests.

L. M Lewis believes that tribal societies are small in scale are restricted in the spatial and temporal range of their social, legal and political relations and possess a morality, a religion and world view of corresponding dimensions. Characteristically too tribal languages are unwritten and hence the extent of communication both in time and space is inevitably narrow. At the same time tribal societies exhibit a remarkable economy of design and have a compactness and self-sufficiency lacking in modern society. T. B Naik has given the following features of tribes in Indian context:-

- A tribe should have least functional interdependence within the community.
- It should be economically backward (i.e. primitive means of exploiting natural resources, tribal economy should be at an underdeveloped stage and it should have multifarious economic pursuits).
- There should be a comparative geographical isolation of its people.
- They should have a common dialect.
- Tribes should be politically organized and community panchayat should be influential.
- A tribe should have customary laws.

Naik argues that for a community to be a tribe it should possess all the above mentioned characteristics and a very high level of acculturation with outside society debars it from being a tribe. Thus term usually denotes a social group bound together by kin and duty and associated with a particular territory.

Characteristics of Indian Tribes

Mandelbaum mentions the following characteristics of Indian tribes:-

- Kinship as an instrument of social bonds.
- A lack of hierarchy among men and groups.

- Absence of strong, complex, formal organization.
- Communitarian basis of land holding.
- Segmentary character.
- Little value on surplus accumulation on the use of capital and on market trading
- Lack of distinction between form and substance of religion
- A distinct psychological bent for enjoying life.

Geographical Location of Tribes

Geographical location of tribes: Tribals in India originate from five language families, i.e. Andamanese, Austro-Asiatic, Dravidian, and Tibeto-Burman. It is also important to point out that those tribals who belong to different language families live in distinct geographic settings. For example, in South Orissa there are languages that originate from the Central Dravidian family, Austro-Asiatic (Munda) family and the Indo-Aryan. In the Jharkhand area, languages are from the Indo-Aryan, North Dravidian and Austro-Asiatic. Tribals in India live in the following five territories.

1. The Himalayan belt: (Assam, Meghalaya, Arunachal Pradesh, Nagaland, Manipur, Mizoram, Tripura, hills of Uttar Pradesh and Himachal Pradesh)
2. Central India: Bihar, West Bengal, Orissa, and Madhya Pradesh. 55% of the total tribal population of India lives in this belt.
3. Western India: Rajasthan, Maharashtra, Gujarat, Goa, Dadra and Nagar Haveli.
4. The Dravidian region: Karnataka, Andhra Pradesh, Kerala and Tamil Nadu.
5. Andaman, Nicobar and Lakshadweep islands.

Tribal-Caste Continuum

Anthropologists have differed on the question relating to tribe and caste. According to Ghurye tribal people are backward Hindus differing only in degrees from the other segments of Hindu society. Elwin argued for the recognition of separate social and cultural identity of tribal people. Government of India gives tacit recognition to this identity of keeping alive under constitution sanction their lists of Scheduled Tribe. According to Andre Beteille there are certain commonly observed differences between tribes and castes. The tribes are relatively isolated as to the castes. They are world within itself having few externalities. Tribes speak a variety of dialects which separates them from non tribes. They follow their own religion and practices which are not common in Hinduism. Language is a criterion of difference as tribes speak their local dialect for example Mundas and Oraons of Chota Nagpur speak different dialects but Bhumij have lost their tribal dialect and speak dominant language of the area.

According to N. K Bose there are many similarities in customs between tribes and castes and they are interdependent. Marriage within the clan is forbidden both in the tribe as well as in the caste. Both generally don't encourage marriage outside the group. According to Herbert Risley the convention of endogamy is not rigidly enforced in the tribe where as such is the case in a tribe. But this view is not acceptable since the law of endogamy is enforced with extreme rigidity in some tribes.

Max Weber writes in Social Structure that when an Indian tribe loses its territorial significance it assumes the form of an Indian caste. In this way the tribe is a local group whereas caste is a social group. According to D. N Majumdar the tribe looks upon Hindu ritualism as foreign and extra-religious even though indulging in it and the in the worship of God and Goddess where as in the caste these are necessary part of the religion.

In caste individuals generally pursue their own definite occupations because functions are divided under the caste system. In the tribe individuals can indulge in whatever profession they prefer as there is no fixed relation between them and occupation. According to Bailey tribe and caste should be viewed as continuum. He seeks to make distinction not in terms of totality of behaviour but in more limited way in relation to the political economic system. Briefly Bailey's argument is that a caste society is hierarchical while a tribal society is segmentary and egalitarian. But in contemporary India both caste and tribe are being merged into a different system which is neither one nor the other.

The tribes in India have been influenced by certain traditions of the communities around them. Major neighbouring community in all the areas has always been Hindus. As a result from the very period there have been several points of contact between the Hindus of the area and tribal communities living within it. The nature and extent of contact the pattern of mutual participation and characteristics of revitalization movements have been different in different parts of India. The ethnographic records establish that the contacts varied from semi-isolation to complete assimilation. The numerous castes among Hindus have emerged out of the tribal stratums. The recent studies of tribes of Himalayan western and middle India have left no doubt that some of the tribes are Hinduized to the extent that they have been assimilated with the different castes at different levels in the caste system.

The study of two major Central Himalayan tribes Tharu and Khasa reveal that though they have a tribal matrix and continue to practice certain distinctive tribal customs they have been accepted as Kshatriya. Their culture have been modelled on the ways of living of the Rajputs and Brahmins of the neighbor plain areas. With their fast adoption of the Hindu names and establishment of social connections with the Rajputs and Brahmins of the plains. They declare themselves as Rajputs and with Brahmins constitute the apex of the social order. With the long and continuous contacts with the regional Hindu castes the tribals of Kharwars has long been assimilated as Rajput castes. There are numerous other tribes which have undergone selective acculturation and have added selected traits or features of the regional Hindus to their respective traditional cultures. In this practice of acculturation most of them failed to occupy any rank in the castes hierarchy while few of them were integrated into the lower strata of the Hindu social system.

Exploitation and Unrest of the Tribes

For ages tribals are considered primitive segment of Indian society. They lived in forests and hills without any contact with civilizations. During British rule they consolidated their position and their political aspirations and administrative needs necessitated to open up the entire country. The British introduced the system of landownership and revenue. Annual tax was trebled which was beyond the paying capacity of tribal cultivators. Many nontribals began to settle in the tribal areas offering credit facilities. Initially it provided relief to tribals but gradually the system became exploitative. Over the years the tribal population faced all types of exploitation. This aroused the tribal leaders to mobilize the tribals and start agitations.

Thus it is the cumulative result of a number of factors.

- Indifference from administrators and bureaucracy in dealing with tribal grievances.
- Harsh and unfriendly forest laws and regulations.
- Lack of legislation to prevent the passing of tribal land into the hands of non-tribals.
- Lack of credit facilities.
- Ineffective government measures to rehabilitate tribal population.
- Delay in implementation of recommendations of different committee
- Discrimination in implementation of reform measures.

Problems of Tribal Communities

Land Alienation: The history of land alienation among the tribes began during British colonialism in India when the British interfered in the tribal region for the purpose of exploiting the tribal natural resources. Coupled with this tribal lands were occupied by moneylenders, zamindars and traders by advancing them loans etc. Opening of mines in the heart of tribal habitat and even a few factories provided wage labour as well as opportunities for factory employment. But this brought increasing destitution and displacement. After the British came to power, the Forest policy of the British Government was more inclined towards commercial considerations rather than human. Some forests were declared as reserved ones where only authorized contractors were allowed to cut the timber and the forest-dwellers were kept isolated deliberately within their habitat without any effort to ameliorate their economic and educational standards. The expansion of railway in India heavily devastated the forest resources in India. The Government started reserving teak, Sal and deodar forests for the manufacture of railway sleepers.

Forest land and its resources provide the best means of livelihood for the tribal people and many tribes including the women engage in agriculture, food gathering and hunting they are heavily dependent on the products of the forest. Therefore when outsiders exploit the tribe's land and its resources the natural life cycle of tribal ecology and tribal life is greatly disturbed.

Poverty and Indebtedness

Majority tribes live under poverty line. The tribes follow many simple occupations based on simple technology. Most of the occupation falls into the primary occupations such as hunting, gathering, and agriculture. The technology they use for these purposes belong to the most primitive kind. There is no profit and surplus making in such economy. Hence there per capita income is very meager much lesser than the Indian average. Most of them live under abject poverty and are in debt in the hands of local moneylenders and Zamindars. In order to repay the debt they often mortgage or sell their land to the moneylenders. Indebtedness is almost inevitable since heavy interest is to be paid to these moneylenders.

Health and Nutrition

In many parts of India tribal population suffers from chronic infections and diseases out of which water borne diseases are life threatening. They also suffer from deficiency diseases. The Himalayan tribes suffer from goiter due to lack of iodine. Leprosy and tuberculosis are also common among them. Infant mortality was found to be very high among some of the tribes. Malnutrition is common and has affected the general health of the tribal children as it lowers the ability to resist infection, leads to chronic illness and sometimes leads to brain impairment. The ecological imbalance like cutting of trees have increased the distances between villages and the forest areas thus forcing tribal women to walk longer distances in search of forest produce and firewood.

Education

Educationally the tribal population is at different levels of development but overall the formal education has made very little impact on tribal groups. Earlier Government had no direct programme for their education. But in the subsequent years the reservation policy has made some changes. There are many reasons for low level of education among the tribal people: Formal education is not considered necessary to discharge their social obligations. Superstitions and myths play an important role in rejecting education. Most tribes live in abject poverty. It is not easy for them to send their children to schools, as they are considered extra helping hands. The formal schools do not hold any special interest for the children. Most of the tribes are located in interior and remote areas where teachers would not like to go from outside.

Cultural Problems

Due to contact with other cultures, the tribal culture is undergoing a revolutionary change. Due to influence of Christian missionaries the problem of bilingualism has developed which led to indifference towards tribal language. The tribal people are imitating western culture in different aspects of their social life and leaving their own culture. It has led to degeneration of tribal life and tribal arts such as dance, music and different types of craft.

TRIBAL DEVELOPMENT EFFORTS AFTER INDEPENDENCE

The sources of funds made available are;

1. State Plan
2. Special Central Assistance
3. Sectoral Programmes of Central Ministries/Departments
4. Institutional Finance.

The State Governments are required to quantify the funds from State Plan for tribal area development in proportion to percentage of tribal population in the states.

Construction of the Hostels for Tribal students

Construction, Maintenance expense is to be borne by the State Governments/Union Territories. The rates for construction of the hostels are fixed which are different for the plains and the hills. It has been represented by various States that these rates are not workable any more in view of the escalation of prices of building materials and long distance involved particularly for the hilly areas. It is, therefore, proposed to revise the norms and to adopt the State PWD schedule of rates as in the case of construction of Ashram Schools. During 1990-91 to 1992-93, the amount of Rs. 8. 64 crores has been released to the States/Union under various stages of completion. The scheme envisages setting up of vocational training institutes in inner tribal areas away from the district headquarters to impart training in various courses relevant to the areas.

The tribal youth would be given training in three trades of his or her choice, the course in each trade having duration of four months. The trainee is to be attached at the end of one month training to master craftsman for a period of three months to learn his skills by practical experience. At the end of 15 months, the trainee will emerge as a multi-skilled person who can exploit existing employment potentials to his/her best advantage. This is a Central Sector Scheme where the construction and maintenance costs are fully borne by the Central Government. It is implemented through the State Governments.

Grant-in-Aid to State Tribal development Cooperative Corporation and others

This is a Central Sector Scheme, with 100% grant, available to the state Tribal Development Cooperative Corporation (STDCCs) and other similar corporations of State engaged in collection and trading of minor forest produce (MFP) through tribals Grants under the Scheme are provided to strengthen the Share Capital of Corporations, construction of Warehouses, establishment of processing industries of MFPs etc. to ensure high profitability of the corporation so as to enable them to pay remunerative prices for MFPs to the tribals.

Price Support to Trifed

The Ministry provides Grants-in-aid to its corporation, TRIFED to set off losses on account of fluctuations in prices of MFPs being marketed by it for ensuring remunerative prices to tribal engaged in collection of MFPs either directly or through STDCCs and other such Cooperative Societies. Investment in Share Capital of Trifed The Ministry is the largest shareholder of TRIFED with over 99% contribution in its Share Capital.

Under this Scheme, the Ministry provides funds to TRIFED as its contribution in the Share Capital.

Village Grain Banks

This Scheme provides Grants for establishment of Village Grain Banks to prevent deaths of STs specially children in remote and backward tribal villages facing or likely to face starvation and also to improve nutritional standards. The Scheme provides funds for building storage facility, procurement of Weights & Measures and for the purchase of initial stock of one quintal of food grain of local variety for each family. A Committee under Chairmanship of village Headman runs the Grain Bank thus established.

Grant-In-Aid to Voluntary Organizations

As many as 27 types of projects with focus on tribal education, literacy, medical & health care, vocational training in agriculture, horticulture, craftsmanship etc., are being supported by the Ministry under this Scheme through registered Non-Governmental Organizations.

Research and Training

Under the Scheme "Research & Training" the Ministry provides financial assistance under Grants to Tribal Research Institutes on 50:50 sharing basis; for conducting Research & Evaluation Studies, Seminars, and Workshops etc. Award of Research Fellowship to Tribal Students on 100% basis registered in Indian Universities. Supporting projects of All-India or Inter-State nature on 100% basis to NGOs/Universities etc. for conducting research on tribal matters, Travel Grants and for Publication of Books on tribals.

Development of Primitive Tribal Groups

Under this Scheme cent per-cent assistance is provided to NGOs and other institutions for under-taking projects on development of PTGs on activities mainly focusing on their food security literacy, agriculture technology up gradation, etc.

Post Matric Scholarships, Overseas Scholarships and Book Banks

The post-matric scholarship Scheme provides financial assistance to all ST students for pursuance of post-matric studies in recognized institutions within India. The Scheme provides for 100% assistance from the Ministry to State Governments and UT Administrations implementing the Scheme, over and above their respective committed liabilities. The Ministry also gives financial assistance for setting up Book-Banks in institutions running professional courses like Medicine, Engineering, Law, Agriculture, Veterinary, Chartered Accountancy, Business Management, and Bio-Sciences. Annually, Ministry provides financial assistance to 9 meritorious ST students for Post-graduate, Doctoral and Post-Doctoral studies in foreign universities/institutions of repute.

Up gradation of Merit and Coaching

These Schemes provide 100% central assistance to State/ UT Administrations. The up gradation of merit Scheme is for arranging coaching classes in reputed colleges for developing competence among ST students for their better performance in competitive examinations conducted by various universities institutes for admission to Medical and Engineering courses while the Scheme for coaching is for conducting Pre-Examination Coaching for tribal students for various examinations conducted by UPSC, SSC, Banking Services Recruitment Boards etc.

Tribal Advisory Council (Tac)

Eight states having scheduled areas, namely, Andhra Pradesh, Bihar (now Bihar & Chhatisgarh), Gujarat, Himachal Pradesh, Maharashtra, Madhya Pradesh (now Madhya Pradesh and Chhatisgarh), Orissa & Rajasthan and two non-scheduled area states, namely, Tamil Nadu and West Bengal have constituted tacs. The TAC consists of not more than twenty-five members of whom as many as three-fourth members are scheduled tribe representatives of the state legislative assembly. The governor of the state may refer matters concerning to administration of welfare of tribals to the TAC for recommendations. The ministry issues guidelines for TAC. As per latest guidelines the TAC should meet at least twice a year and discuss the issues concerning tribal interests and making appropriate recommendation for protection of tribal interests.

Point 11(b) of 20-point Programme

The point 11 (b) of 20-point programme is to provide

economic assistance to the scheduled tribe families to enable them to rise above poverty line. The ST families are assisted through various schemes implemented by departments of agriculture, rural development, horticulture, animal husbandry, sericulture, forestry, small & cottage industries, etc. The ministry fixes the targets for 22-states/ut s and also monitors the progress of achievements on monthly basis. The officers of the ministry inspected more than 75 projects in the states of Andhra Pradesh, Assam, Manipur, Meghalaya, Orissa, West Bengal, Jharkhand, Maharashtra and Madhya Pradesh.

TRIBAL STRUGGLES

Numerous uprisings of the tribals have taken place beginning with the one in Bihar in 1772 followed by many revolts in Andhra Pradesh, Andaman and Nicobar Islands, Arunchal Pradesh, Assam, Mizoram and Nagaland. The important tribes involved in revolt in the 19th century were Mizos (1810), Kols (1795&1831), Mundas (1889), Daflas (1875), Khasi and Garo (1829), Kacharis (1839), Santhals (1853), Muria Gonds (1886), Nagas (1844 & 1879) and Konds (1817). After independence the tribal struggle may be classified into three groups:

- Struggles due to exploitation of the outsiders.
- Struggles due to economic deprivations
- Struggle due to separatist tendencies.

The tribal movements may also be classified on the basis of their orientation into four types:

- Movements seeking political autonomy and formation of separate state.
- Agrarian movement
- Forest-based movements
- Socio-religious movements.

Most of the tribal movements were result of oppression and discrimination, neglect and backwardness and apathy of government towards tribal problems.

Tana Bhagat Movement

In the Tana Bhagat movement an attempt was made to emulate the way of life of the Hindu higher castes. It emerged among the Oraon of Chotanagpur; Bihar. It tried to raise the status of its members in the eyes of the surrounding Hindu society and was characterized by a large scale incorporation of Hindu belief-practices into its ideology.

Birsa Munda Movement

During the second half of the 19th century the whole of Chotanagpur underwent a tremendous change. The old Munda system of Khuntakatti tenure gave way to a new and alien system of exploitation by the landlords known as Jagirdar and Thikadar. In 1895 Birsa Munda of Chalkad started a movement. In him the Munda found the embodiment of their aspiration. He gave them leadership, a religion and a code of life. He held before them the prospect of Munda Raj in place of foreign rule.

TRIBAL POLICY-ISOLATION, ASSIMILATION AND INTEGRATION

Historical Perspective-Isolation

The coexistence of fundamentally different culture patterns and styles of living has always been a characteristic feature of the Indian stage. Unlike most parts of the world, in India, the arrival of new immigrants and the spread of their way of life did not necessarily cause the disappearance of earlier and materially less advanced ethnic groups.

The old and the new co-existed. Such a consequence was partly due to the great size of the sub-continent and dearth of communications. More important than this was an attitude basic to Indian ideology, which accepted variety of cultural forms as natural and immutable, and did not consider their assimilation to one dominant pattern in any way desirable. This does not mean, however, that none of the tribes ever became incorporated in the systems of hierarchically ranked castes. Wherever economic necessity or encroachment of their habitant by advanced communities led to continued inter-action between tribes and Hindus, cultural distinctions were blurred, and what had once been self-contained and more or less independent tribes gradually acquired the status of castes.

In many cases they entered caste systems at the lowest rung of the ladder. Some untouchable castes of Southern India, such as the Cherumans and the Panyers of Kerala, were undoubtedly at one time independent tribes, and in their physical characteristics they still resemble neighbouring tribal groups, which have remained outside the Hindu society. There are some exceptions, such as the Meitheis of Assam who achieved a position comparable to that of Kshatriyas. Tribes who retained their tribal identity and resisted inclusion within the Hindu fold fared on the whole better than the assimilated groups and were not treated as untouchables, even if they indulged in such low-caste practices as eating beef. Thus the Raj Gond princes sacrificed and ate cows without thereby debasing their status in the eyes of their Hindu neighbours, who recognized their social and cultural separateness and did not insist on conformity to Hindu patterns of behaviour.

This respect for the tribal way of life prevailed as long as contacts between tribes and Hindu populations of open plains were of a casual nature. The tribal people, though considered strange and dangerous, were taken for granted as part of the world of hills and forests, and a more or less frictionless co-existence was possible, because there was no population pressure and the advanced communities did not feel any urge to impose their own values on people placed clearly outside the spheres of Hindu civilization.

This position remained unchanged during the Muslim period. Now and then a military campaign extending for a short spell into the wilds of tribal country would bring the inhabitants temporarily to the notice of princes and chroniclers, but for long period the hill men and forest-dwellers were left to themselves. Under British rule, however, a new situation arose. The extension of a centralized administration over areas, which previously were outside the effective control of princely rulers, deprived many aboriginal tribes of their autonomy. Though British administrators had no intention of interfering with tribesmen's rights and traditional manner of living, the very process of establishment of law and order in outlying areas exposed the tribes to the pressure of more advanced populations. Thus in areas which had previously been virtually un-administered and hence unsafe for outsiders who did not enjoy the confidence and goodwill of the tribal inhabitants, traders and money-lenders could now establish themselves under the protection of the British administration and in many cases they were followed by settlers who succeeded in acquiring large stretches of tribes' land. Administrative officers who did not understand tribal system of land tenure introduced uniform methods of revenue collection. But these had the un-intended effect of facilitating the alienation of tribal land to members of advanced populations. Though it is unlikely that British officials actively favoured the latter at the expense of primitive tribesmen, little was done to stem the rapid erosion of tribal rights to land.

In many areas tribals unable to resist the gradual alienation of their ancestral land, either withdrew further into hills and tracts of marginal land, or accepted the economic status of tenants or agricultural labourers on the land their forefathers had owned. There were some tribes, however, who rebelled against an administration, which allowed outsiders to deprive them of their land. In the Chhota Nagpur and the Santhal pargansas such rebellions of desperate tribesmen recurred throughout the nineteenth century, and there were minor risings in the Agency tracts of Madras and in some of the districts of Bombay inhabited by Bhils. Thus the Santhals are believed to have lost about 10, 000 men in their rebellion of 1855. None of these insurrections were aimed primarily at the British administration, but they were a reaction to their exploitation and oppression by Hindu landlords and money-lenders who had established themselves in tribal areas and were sheltered by a Government which had instituted a system of land settlement and administration of justice favoring the advanced communities at the expense of simple and illiterate tribes. In some cases these rebellions led to official inquiries and to legislative enactments aimed at protecting tribes' right to their land. Seen in historical perspective it appears that land alienation laws had, on the whole, only a palliative effect. In most areas encroachment on land held by tribes continued even in the face of protective legislation.

Assimilation of Tribals

Acceptance or denial of the necessity for assimilation with Hindu society is ultimately a question of values. In the past, Hindu society had been tolerant of groups that would not conform to the standards set by the higher castes. True, such groups were denied equal ritual status; but no efforts were made to deflect them from their chosen style of living. In recent years this attitude has changed. Perhaps it is the influence of the Western belief in universal values which has encouraged a spirit of intolerance vis-a-vis cultural and social divergences. Yet India is not only a multilingual and multiracial country, but is also multi-cultural. And as long as Muslims, Christians, and Parsis are free to follow their traditional way of life, it would seem only fair that the culture and the social order of tribes however distinct from that of the majority community should also be respected. Assimilation, of course, will occur automatically and inevitably where small tribal groups are enclosed within numerically stronger Hindu populations. In other areas, however, and particularly all along India's northern and north-eastern frontier live vigorous tribal populations which resist assimilation as well as inclusion within Hindu caste system.

Democratic Decentralization and Tribals

With the introduction of a system of democratic decentralization to take the place of paternalism characteristic of traditional form of Indian government, a new element has entered the relations between tribes and the more advanced majority communities. The ability to vote in general elections for the Parliament in Delhi and the Legislative Assembly of their respective States did not make much difference to tribals, because they did not understand the implication of the franchise, but the local elections aroused their interest to a much greater extent.

The very fact, that some of the most powerful people of the district approached the poorest villagers for their votes and tried to gain their confidence, convinced them of a fundamental change. The very idea that they could choose their representatives was novel. At first, tribals only voted, for non-tribals, for very few were sufficiently educated to stand for election. Even in areas with a preponderance of tribals, the elected representatives were often non-tribes and abused their powers by exploiting those who had voted for them. But as time passed and the tribes gained experience, they have become shrewder in the choice of their representatives.

The Government of India has adopted a policy of integration of tribals with the mainstream aiming at developing a creative adjustment between the tribes and non tribes leading to a responsible partnership.

By adopting the policy of integration or progressive acculturation the Government has laid the foundation for the uninhibited march of the tribals towards equality, upward mobility, and economic viability and assured proximity to the national mainstream.

The constitution has committed the nation to two courses of action in respect of scheduled tribes:

- Giving protection to their distinctive way of life
- Protecting them from social injustice and all forms of exploitation and discrimination and bringing them at par with the rest of the nation so that they may be integrated with the national life.

Thus by the Constitution Order 1950 issued by the President of India in exercise of powers conferred by Clause (i) of Article 342 of the Constitution of India 255 tribes in 17 states were declared to be scheduled tribes. Besides enjoying the rights that all citizens and minorities have the member of the Scheduled Tribes have been provided with special safeguards as follows:

Protective Safeguards

- Educational safeguards-Article 15(4) and 29
- Safeguards for employment-Articles 16(4), 320(4) and 333
- Economic safeguards-Article 19
- Abolition of bonded labour-Article 23
- Protection from social injustice and all forms of exploitation-Article 46

Political Safeguards

- Reservation of seats for ST in Lok Sabha and Assemblies-Article 330, 332, 164
- Appointment of Minister in charge of Tribal welfare
- Special provisions in respect of Nagaland, Assam and Manipur-Articles-371(A), 371(B) and 371

Developmental Safeguards

- Promoting the educational and economic interests of the Scheduled Tribes-Articles 46
- Grants from Central Government to the states for welfare of Scheduled Tribes and raising the level of administration of Scheduled Areas-Article 75.

Following the reorganization of states, the list of STs was modified by the Scheduled Castes and Tribes List (Modification) order, 1956 on the recommendations of the Backward Classes Commission. In the revised list 414 tribes were declared STs. Since the revision of the list in 1956 there have been several proposals for fresh inclusions and deletion from the lists of the SC and STs

Characteristics of Tribal Society

The tribe inhabits and remains within definite and common topography. The members of a tribe possess a consciousness of mutual unity. The members of a tribe speak a common language. The members generally marry into their own group but now due to increased contact with outsiders there are instances of tribal marring outside as well. The tribes believe in ties of blood relationship between its members. They have faith in their having descended from a common, real or mythical, ancestor and hence believe in blood relationships with other members. Tribes follow their own political organization which maintains harmony. Religion is of great importance in the tribe. The tribal political and social organization is based on religion because they are granted religious sanctity and recognition.

Tribal Practices

- Joking relationships prevails in Matrilineal Hopi, Matrilineal Trobriand Islanders, Oraons and Baigas
- Group marriage prevail among Marquesans and Todas
- Couvade is practiced mainly in Khasi, Toda, Ho and Oraon
- Teknonymy in Khasis
- Ultimogeniture in Khasis
- Uxorilocal in Garos

- Matrilineal societies are present among Moplahs, Hopi, Nayars
- Polyandry practices tribes are-Todas, Ladaki Botas and Nayars
- Polygamy is found among Eskimo tribes, Crows of North America
- Levirate marriages are found in Ahirs in Haryana, Kodagus of Mysore and Jats and Gujars of UP.

PROFILES OF SOME OF THE SELECTED INDIAN TRIBES

Bhils

- Constitute the largest tribal group in India.
- Found mainly in Madhya Pradesh (Jhabua, Dhar, Kahnwa) and east Gujarat.
- Martial race; primarily agriculturalist.
- Badwas are witch finder, Pujaro are priests and Kotwal are drummers, Tadni is village headman.
- Generally endogamous
- Practice polygamy also.

Gonds

- Second largest tribal group in India.
- Dravidian background
- Found mainly in Madhya Pradesh
- Some of the tribal groups are Bastai, Marias, Murias, Prajas, Bhatras
- Dependent mainly on agriculture, cattle rearing second main occupation.
- Divided into exogamous sects or clans.
- Speak Gondi dialect.
- Lineage is traced through male lines.

Santhals

- Third largest tribal group in India believed to be of Pre-Aryan origin.
- Mainly in Santhal Paraganas of Bihar, West Bengal etc.
- Speak Santhali language.

- Naik is the village priest, Gorait is the messenger, Jogmanjhi is the headmentribal council is Parganait.
- Singlonga or Sun God is the main deity.

Todas

- Found mainly in Nilgiri Hills of South India.
- Classic example of polyandry.
- Call themselves Tora
- Badaga, Kota, Kurumbaand Irula tribes
- The word Toda is derived from Tundra, name of sacred tree of Topdas.
- Divided into two moieties called Taratharal and Teivaloil. These are endogamous units. All the sacred herd and cattle are owned by Tartharal thus they occupy a higher status.
- The clans are divided into families locally known as Kudupeli.
- Fraternal polyandry found.
- Divorce freely allowed.
- Todas have classificatory type of kinship calling many relatives or friends by some designation.
- Females have low status.
- People are governed by council of five elders called as Naim. Three members of this council come from Tarthar clans, two from Teivali clans and one from Badagas.
- Two of the main deities are Teikirizi and On.

Chenchu

- Mainly found in Andhra Pradesh on the river Krishna.
- They are mostly settled cultivators and very much influenced by neighbouring plains people.
- They speak dialect of Dravidian origin.
- Now they have started living in semi-permanent huts.
- They are divided into exogamous clans and have animal totems.
- Divorce is common.
- Chenchus have traditional leader Peddamanshi.
- Bhaivov and Garelamaisama are popular local deities.

Khasis

- One of the matriarchial tribes of world.
- Have a rich economy influenced by industrialization and urbanization.
- They are mainly in Jaintia hills of Assam.
- Divided into four main sub-groups-Khynrian, Pnar, War and Bhoi.
- They speak a dialect that belongs to the Mon-Khmer branch of Austric family.
- Each of the sub-tribes is divided into a number of clans known as Kurs.
- Marriage within the clan is prohibited.
- Khasis are characterized by matrilineal descent.
- The clan is further sub-divided into sub class known as kpoh (composed of descendents of one grandmother.

INDIAN TRIBAL WOMEN

The tribal people of India have been in contact with other people, that is the urban society, for a very long time and have been greatly influenced by them. The degree of influence is proportional to the intermingling with outsiders. Tribes-people like the Gond, Bhil, and Halbi almost live like Hindus do in the outside world. But there are still a few tribes in the Bastar district of the state of Madhya Pradesh, which are totally unaffected by any developmental program.

The tribals of the Bastar district are mostly confined to Narayanpur tahsil (county) where their population is as low as twenty people per square kilometer, as per the 1975 census. They live in small villages consisting of not more than twenty-thirty houses. Their everyday activities are very well coordinated and inter-linked. Irrespective of one's gender, every person has a vital role to play in the welfare of the community.

Tribal Women in the Bastar District

The typical day of a tribal Housewife: She rises early in the morning, fetches water from a distant spring, prepares a breakfast of "paje" (pulp) for the family, brews "landra" (a liquor) for the adults, cleans the house, cooks the other meals, accompanies her husband to the forest, and gathers fruits, leaves and firewood while the husband hunts. During the monsoon season, she assists in all agricultural activity and this includes hard labour. She can cover forty to fifty kilometers in a day, can carry a heavy-load on her head through difficult mountains and can go without food for an entire day! How many of us would even try to do that? Most of us crib when we have to keep a fast for one day!

Material wealth and riches are not the indices of happiness-this is very well portrayed by a tribal woman. Compared to modern women a tribal woman has very little wealth of her own or of her family. A typical tribal woman has just a piece of coarse cloth to cover her womanhood. She is very fond of ornaments, yet has just one or two strings of red, blue or white beads. In addition, she may have some bangles, earrings and necklaces made of cheap metal. She is always very cheerful and light-hearted, often laughing and joking with members of her family or with the neighbours. She is truthful and honest. She never denies any offence she might have committed and willingly faces the consequences. Even though she lives in sheer poverty, has less than the minimum standard of living, even though she is constantly struggling to keep her and her family happy and living, a tribal woman's light heartedness is amazing and is something to learn and admire by the urban women of the society.

Women power: Its all seen and heard in the urban society or as to say, the so called, "Hindu" society of this country, that women can never be equal to men. They are always considered subordinate to men and they are the weak and delicate species! One might have to change their opinion and admire a tribal woman even more when they get to know about her status in a tribe. The tribal woman fondles her man like she would a child, loves him like immensely, keeps him company like a companion would and works with him like an equal partner. While she will do everything for him, she will never be his subordinate. She has gained this status by sheer hard work and not by being demanding. There is nothing she will not or cannot do. She even attends to the funerals of her near and dear ones, something so called `refined` Hindus do not allow for a woman. The tribal woman also assists in erecting a memorial for the dead.

What is considered as a special joyful moment in any traditional Hindu family in the country? Well, the birth of a son! But this is not the case in the tribals in India, as girls and boys are both considered equal. In most of the so-called "modern" Indian families, women are susceptible to undergo an abortion as soon as they come to know that the fetus is that of a girl child. Women undergo number of pregnancies just because they want a boy and not a female child. Well, modern women should and must learn something from the tribal society regarding this. A tribal woman declares her pregnancy with pride and does not welcome her husband till she is willing to conceive again. Delivery is without the assistance of a midwife and mother herself cuts the umbilical chord. The mother nurses the baby with her milk, carries it everywhere in a piece of old cloth hanging from her shoulder. She puts her child to sleep in a bamboo cradle. Older sisters attend to their younger siblings.

THE GHOTUL TRIBE

The normal daily life: Ghotul, coming from the special institution called Ghotul, which the tribal people have adapted to solve their accommodation problems. Boys and girls six years of age are entitled to membership. The female workers of the Ghotul are known as "Motiyaris" and they are assigned important administrative duties at the Ghotul. They are responsible for the general cleanliness of the building and premises, the punctual arrival of members, the taking of the attendance, the supervision of sitting arrangements, and the assurance of liberal supply of fire wood, mustard oil, tobacco and landra. Each girl has to attend to a male member of the Ghotul. If he is extremely tired after a day`s work, she massages his body and applies oil. If the boy is pleased, he presents her with a wooden comb and perhaps a plum.

When activities for the night commence, the girls have to intermingle with the boys and distribute themselves around the fire. Together they gossip or make fun of each other. More serious discussions, group singing, playing of musical instruments and dancing follows this. When it is time to retire for the day the girls share beds with boys. These tribals have perfected the art of co-existence from time-immemorial. But one should not misunderstand the intermingling of these tribal people. There are very strict rules and regulations, which needs to be followed for the Ghotul. The mother, it seems, teaches the girl child all the rules so that she can enter the Ghotul. Pre-mature pregnancies are seen very rarely but if anything like this does happen then the girl immediately names the father of the child and a marriage is arranged. A woman has a free hand to select her groom and is never compelled to marry a man against her choice. Child marriage is not permissible and pre-puberty marriages are quite unheard of.

Cool Justice: At times the tribals also run into marital problems. If a husband turns out to be brutal, crude, insane, impotent, unfaithful, criminal or diseased, then the wife has every right to complain about him to the tribal head Manji (or Patel). He in turn assembles his advisory council and gives an opportunity to the couple to plead their cases. If the council is convinced of the husband's guilt, the wife is allowed to get a separation and marry anybody she chooses.

The symbolic Woman: In tribal society women are not treated as inferior or second-class citizens. Although they are on par with the men, they complement rather than compete with each other. This status of the tribal women has existed from ancient times, as can be seen from rock paintings found in the state. These paintings were executed as early as five to fifty centuries before the birth of Christ. Most of these paintings represent hunting scenes, fighting sequences, animal sacrifices, rituals to ward off evil spirits and so on, and hence women do not find much of a place in them. But in the scenes that depict every day life, women are shown to be involved in food gathering, basket weaving, singing and dancing. Pregnant women, women giving birth, and nursing mothers are also depicted. This perhaps indicates that the women represented fertility, motherhood and were the progenitors of the tribe. This special status for women might have given rise to the mother-goddess cult.

The Meghal Women: Besides the usual chores the Meghal women find time for their avidly sought after embroidery work. Their work is distinguished by their primary use of red. This red colour comes from a local pigment produced from crushed insects. The Meghwal women artisans of Thar desert in Sindh and Balochistan, and in Gujarat are considered master of the traditional embroidery and Ralli making. Exotic hand-embroidered items form part of dowry of Meghwal woman.

The Lambani Women: The Lambani, once known as the bee-keeping tribe, the Lambani women, or the great travellers, are found in groups throughout the central and southern parts of India, selling their cloth at markets and on beaches. Their work contributes considerably to the income of their families. The Lambani women embroider bright rainbow-coloured fabrics covered with a mosaic of patchwork mirrors. The Lambani women commonly wear large, silver earrings laden with bells called loila and and a large silver torque around the neck to which two large silver pyramid forms are attached. The Banjara Women: Dedicated to their ancient mode of dressing which is perhaps the most colorful and elaborate of any tribal group in India, this dressing mode sets them apart from the rest of the tribes in India. Their full length skirt, is blazing red with borders embroidered in mustard and green thread. The elaborately embroidered and mirror studded cholis or blouses and the brightly colored odhni (mantle) which covers the head is long enough to drape down their backs almost touching the feet. The women wear pretty silver anklets which clink as they walk barefoot. Long silver earrings, and patterned cowrie shells decorate their hair, and are worn on their wrists and ankles. Silver, brass, some gold, cowries, ivory, animal bone and even plastic are some of the metals used for their ornaments. Mainly labourers, these women still wear all their attire even while doing heavy work road or construction work!

Men and morality: The tribal women were free from sexually transmitted diseases as they have healthy sex. But when the Bhiladela iron ore project commenced a large number of tribal men and women rushed to the construction site in search of a better way of life. Unfortunately, the women became the victims of lust and rape and hence had to take to prostitution to earn their living. Men became the judges of morality of the tribal women. India has observed unequal distribution of resources and this is very apparent by the fact that a tribal mother is over 12 times less likely to be delivered by a medically trained person. A tribal woman is one and a half times more likely to suffer the consequences of chronic malnutrition as compared to women from other social categories.

Migration among tribal women: Thousands of tribal women and girls migrate from their hinterlands in tribal areas to urban city centres mainly in search of employment. They are new to the city life style and environment and find it difficult to make adjustment with the changed situation and environment. They have to face a number of problems in the cities they get migrated. Moreover, the non-tribals in the cities exploit them both financially and sexually. A large majority of migrant tribal women are in the age group of 24 to 47 years and the tribal girls in the age group of 16 to 23 years. They face problems like difficulty of communication in local language, residential accommodation, employment, education of children, local contacts, and adjustment with city life and environment etc.

The Tribal Women of Chattisgarh

For the tribal of India, forests are considered as sacred and an important support system for their lives. Forest resources provide them with food, medicine, fodder and grass, fuel wood and water for irrigation. Women rely on the collection of forest products and also play a part in protecting forests. Between March and May of every year, which is the slow season in agriculture, the tribal households depend almost entirely on forest products for their livelihoods. Early every morning, groups of women set out towards the forest. They collect non-timber products as Tendu Patta, char and sal seeds, Palesh, Sarai, Mahuadori, Harra, Kusum, Sisal, Bamboo, Chhind, Mango, Jamun, Ber. From the products they collect, the women obtain foods such as fruit and oil, and medicines. Forest products also become raw materials for making a number of items for the home, such as Bidi, Brooms, Baskets, Mats, Rope, home-made toothbrushes and leaf plates. Certain tribes collect forest products for their main occupations.

Tribal women collect Tendu leaves, an important forest product, during the "Tendu season". The women rise in the early hours of the morning at around four and spend 6-8 hours collecting the leaves, working without food or water. This is followed by 3-4 hours of counting and stacking the leaves in bundles of 50. If the woman goes out to collect Tendu leaves and her husband stays home, then he cooks and looks after the children. To a limited extent, women also participate in forest protection activities. Ten to fifteen years before the Forest Department came up with the idea of forest protection, several village communities began to organize protection of the forests, as villagers saw outsiders come in and destroy the forests. The forest management committees have had a number of women representatives since then.

Tribal forest economy is primarily a women's economy, and it is women who are most directly affected by the corporate exploitation of their traditional lands. An overview of the local economy, the religious importance of the forests, and traditional sustainable forest management activities are described.

Women's Role in City Agenda Setting

Urban women form half of the population, work two-thirds of work hours, receive one-tenth of the world's income and own only one-hundredth of world's property. Women have limited access to acquire the skills necessary to break the poverty cycle. The problems that face the women in the urban environment are interrelated. The living conditions of the low income women are unhygienic and their children are prone to disease and face a greater threat of dying at a young age. Domestic responsibility and lack of training relegate the women to the lowest paying jobs. Illiteracy and lack of basic education make them unaware of the existing opportunities. Cultural taboos often prevent them exploring income generating areas, which are dominated by the men. They are equally strong, physically and intellectually, but have been suppressed psychologically and culturally. They depend upon men and are excluded from decision making. The total development of the country is not possible unless we harness the potential of silent half of the population. The Social Security, equality for women and economic potential can not be achieved unless the women are brought into the mainstream. It requires establishing an equitous and harmonious society without discrimination.

The Women in Urban India

The urban population of India (270 million in 1991) is roughly split into three equal parts:

i. about one third in the 23 metropolitan cities (more than 1 million)

ii. about one third in the remaining 227 Class cities (100,000-1,000,000); and

iii. about one-third in the remaining 3396.

Women who are nearly half of the urban population account for 73 percent of those below the poverty line. It is observed that gender differences within the incidence of poverty in urban areas are more intense than those in the rural areas. Increased female labour force participation, particularly among the lowest income households, is the single most important coping strategy, making female-headed households and poor women in general a distinct group.

The Draft Country Paper for the 4th World Conference on Women notes that their role in decision making is low, with patriarchal values reinforced through tradition, religion and other socio-political institutions. The family is the primary and apparently a problematic site of gender subordination. Low work force participation, general lack of access to institutional credit mechanisms, low self-esteem, fear of society, men and violence create a vicious inter-generational cycle of poverty and deprivation. Gender discrimination excludes women in India from a right to life (resulting in female infanticide or foeticide), from equal access to food, education and mobility. This means that women have little chance of equal access to jobs, as they are handicapped by their comparative lack of education. Despite the improvements for certain women on many fronts, gender discrimination is apparently increasing.

Constitutional Reforms

During recent years, the Country has witnessed reforms in the context of decentralisation of power from Central/ provincial Governments to local levels, endowing the local bodies with the finances, commensurate with their assigned responsibility. Current scenario in India on 73rd and the 74th amendments to the Constitution (1992) gives a major role to the local bodies and municipalities. There are already more than 60,000 elected representatives, one-third of them being women. Although the reluctance of the power centres is often evident to allow the local bodies to govern, there is a growing demand to restructure the State Governments, enabling the local bodies to discharge their Constitutional obligations.

The framers of Indian Republic's Constitution expected gender equality, implicit within equality of all citizens to be adequate to change the complex systems of social and power relationship. However, recognising the power of institutionalised inequality in certain cases, some special responsibilities of the State were included in the Directive Principles of State Policy (Articles 15 and 16). The provision of one-third women representatives on urban local bodies in 74th Constitutional Amendment Act is a historical step, which should lead to a greater and meaningful role of the women in setting the urban agenda.

Empowerment

The 73rd and 74th Amendments of the Constitution have made the empowerment of women a constitutional mandate. However, we have to go a long way to achieve equality of opportunities for women in both political and administrative system, equal access to resources, basic social services (education, health etc.), equal reward for equal work, elimination of discrimination by gender and prevention of atrocities against women. There is a need to empower and mobilise the women through the legal back-up, administrative reforms and awareness to ensure their active participation in developmental decisions and activities (like sanitation, drinking water supply, education, immunisation, nutrition, etc.). There is a need to strengthen their roles in setting the city-agenda according to the priorities they perceive.

We can not solve our cities' problems until those who suffer most are powerful enough to set the priorities, frame plans and promote solutions. It is necessary to expand gender-balanced dialogue and participation at every level of decision making. The Huairou Commission on women and habitat has among its objectives: to ensure that the Habitat Agenda is implemented with women in central decision-making roles and with sufficient resources to function effectively; and to highlight grassroots women's concerns and perspectives in the development of sustainable human settlements.

From Exclusion to Inclusiveness

Women are often excluded from fully realizing their rights in cities. The legal and regulatory framework, designs of neighbourhoods and transport systems, location of services and facilities, as well as the general security situation, significantly affect women and the extent to which they can have access to the benefits of the city. This is largely due to exclusion of women from the city's agenda-making process. The fact is that urban planning remains gender-biased, both because women are grossly under-represented in the field and because most urban planners do not have data that shows who does what and who benefits most. There is a need for disaggregation of data by gender, so that the policies, programes and projects address to needs in a gender-sensitive manner. There had been tendency to lump women with vulnerable groups such as the elderly, the disabled, and children. It is now recognized that vulnerability is most often caused by exclusion from the socio-economic mainstream, and from the decision-making process. Measures to address vulnerability include programmes, such as safety nets for the vulnerable, but also more fundamentally addressing inequalities from a rights perspective.

Accordingly to Michael Edwards: "Exclusion is the result of three interlocking sets of process; exclusionary economics; social discrimination; and lack of a political voice. These three things come together to keep certain groups of people poor. In addressing this problem, there is increasing interest in the potential of civil society to act as a countervailing force, especially in cities – where NGOs, community organizations and other civic groups are generally more active than in the countryside".

According to Jo Beall: "Seeking ways of accommodating diverse needs and practices is central to creating inclusive cities. This might constitute creating ramps for disabled people, building playgrounds for children or putting in street lighting so that women can feel safe outside their homes at night. However, social relations are underpinned by power and there is an obvious correlation between power and space- what gets built, where, how and for whom. Cities are literally concrete manifestations of ideas on how society was, is and how it should be. Central to understanding the impact of social relations on the city is recognising the specific imprint of gender relations on the city".

Inclusiveness in cities would depend upon local conditions, public policies and on the attitude of citizens. However, there is a need to develop policy instruments and enabling systems, such as legal, procedural, financial, operational supports, in absence of which the inclusiveness of women would remain only in rhetoric terms.

Disaggregation

Human settlement development is generally based upon population and other data in varying national and local contexts. This is often based on segregation of income groups and area-based geographical zoning. This approach usually ignores the targeting to the needs of women. Disaggregation of database is therefore essential to understand and assess the needs of both the sexes and to facilitate their active involvement in the development process and make interventions more effective and efficient. This approach promotes equity between men and women. This disaggregation of data is crucial element of gender-sensitive approach.

Participation

Participation of all the stakeholders is a key ingredient to the success of urban development projects. A World Bank study observes that "the long term sustainability of projects is closely linked to active and informed participation by the poor". Participation is perceived as an instrument for greater effectiveness and a new area for investment. The Government's approach to community participation is implemented through public consultation, elected representatives and by extension staff at the block level and involving community and non-government organisations. Engaging the community in dialogue over provision of services has the potential to increase the sense of ownership. It usually leads to greater sustainability of infrastructure. The thrust of development becomes more community oriented and demand-driven. It also helps in an increased beneficiary contribution to cost recovery and cost sharing. The participation involves developing approaches to project planning, implementation, evaluation of impact, decision-making, training and capacity building, where the role of women is specific and definite.

Decentralisation

According to the 1996 Global Report on Human Settlements,

three factors have contributed to the development of local governance: the decentralisation of policy; the return of democratic principles of government and the growing importance of citizen and community pressure, including social movements. Decentralisation does not simply mean administration, it also implies having the necessary degree of autonomy to govern. It does not mean leaving housing and urban management in the hands of the private sector. To the contrary, it means articulating the participation of different actors, including the women. Decentralisation requires greater degree of professionalism on the part of local bodies and non-governmental organisations. The transfer of power from national entities to local governments has signified new roles and functions for non-governmental organizations, who should activate the engendering the planning and development agenda at all the levels, viz., policy decisions, resource management and implementation.

Engendering Urban Governance

Governments, non-governmental organizations (NGOs), women's groups and international agencies have critical roles in addressing the problem of exclusion of women. They should ensure that women's participation is an integral part of city management and that women's issues are incorporated in community and national development. There is also need for structural and attitudinal changes in the institutions. One of the ways to achieve this is through raising awareness about women's role in city planning and human resource development. It is important not only to desegregate by gender the specific indicators but also to have the capacity to identify crucial indicators to engender the urban development and governance.

According to Jo Beall: "Engendering" the practice of urban governance should begin by addressing issues of gender inequality while at the same time directing attention to broader questions of diversity and democracy in government responsibility and civic engagement".

Localisation

With decentralization the crucial point is the strengthening of local power. It is necessary to strengthen the processes, which optimize the capacity and the participatory planning of local governments. The principle of partnership is no more only a tie-up between the local government and the NGO/CBOs but also a partnership that meets the needs and aspirations of both men and women. It is necessary to have adequate representation of both sexes in non-governmental organizations and organized citizen's groups, who would evolve a 'Localising agenda'.

The "Localizing Agenda" should respond to the particular and contextual challenges of the human settlements and concrete action at the local level. It should aim at lasting change towards equitable mechanism, where both, men and women play an effective role in sustainable development. They can be facilitated to participate in framing up the proposals targeted for grassroot organisations and to open up dialogue with the local authorities.

Social Capital

Women representatives are comparatively at advantage in mobilising low income groups to defend and advance their concerns and a natural role in the formal process of urban governance. They play an important role in fostering the emergence of co-operative values and attitudes, what has come to be known as 'social capital'.

The importance of social capital is recognised in the efficient functioning of financial transactions, in micro-savings and credit, where trust and honesty are essential. This has been successfully demonstrated by SEWA in Ahmedabad and Mahila Milan in Mumbai. Besides this, they have been able in nurturing the capacities required to support negotiated solutions to the problems, relationship of caring, mutual support and successful combating the crime and violence. Social capital is therefore vital in achieving broader social, political and environmental goals such as equity, conservation, non-discrimination, and safety, which in turn is central component of a livable city. As such, they are the foundation for setting the principles of sustainable development.

Another good example is Urban Basic Service Programme (UBSP), which has demonstrated its impact and contribution towards national social sector goals for women and children and poverty reduction. The UBSP scheme aims at empowering urban poor women through information dissemination, community formation and recognises channels for action determined by the women themselves.

Successful cities demonstrate the positive power of government, when harnessed to social capital, mediated through structures which allow all sectors of society a voice and role in decision making. However, new political coalitions are necessary to prioritise the needs of the city and its poorest residents above narrow sectoral interests.

There is a need of deliberate action to strengthen women's role, a commitment to give them more opportunities to represent their concerns and constituents in decision making and respect for their autonomy. The reservation for women in all political and administrative system in the country will give them the equal opportunities and say.

4

Role of Caste in Rural Society of India

Caste stands as a pivot of rural social structure. It acts as the most powerful determinant of individual behaviour and social order in rural unity. Caste is the determinant of individual status and role. It determines the status of the individual as soon as he takes birth. Hutton says that the system provides him from birth a fixed social milieu from which neither wealth nor property, success nor disaster can remove him unless of course he so violates standards of behaviour lay down by the caste. Caste also guides the behaviour of an individual in his conduct, his association and interaction. It has helped maintain the continuity of social order by preserving its pattern of culture and traditions.

It plays a vital role in the process of socialization by teaching individuals the culture and traditions, values and norms of their society. It unifies society in a chain by assigning different places and positions to different groups. It works as the basis of division of labour in society which keeps society away from tensions and conflicts arising out of competition for occupation, power and prestige. Caste also has a deep influence in the religious lives of rural people. The notion of karma and dharma kept social and economic system intact. Performance of rituals, worshipping of different kinds of Gods and Goddesses and celebration of festivals are determined by the caste system. There are some negative aspects according to P. N Bose the caste system has acted essentially to impose that attitude of mind, needed to raise men from savagery but to stop them half way on progress. Caste acts as a barrier to modernization. Modernization essentially needs a change in outlook and mentality along with socio-economic development. It has hindered development as it imposes strict rules regarding occupation of different people. The society characterized by the caste system is a closed one permitting very little or no social mobility. It acts as a perpetuating force of social inequality and untouchability. It is based on inequality of status and opportunities which often creates conflict and tension in the society.

Jajmani System in Rural Society

The notion of the Jajmani system was popularized by colonial ethnography. It tended to conceptualize agrarian social structure in the framework of exchange relations. In its classical construct, different caste groups specialized in specific occupations and exchanged their services through an elabourate system of division of labour. Though asymmetry in position of various caste groups was recognized what it emphasized was not inequality in rights over land but the spirit of community. Wiser argued, each served the other. Each in turn was master. Each in turn was servant. This system of inter relatedness in service within Hindu community was called the Jajmani system. Central to such a construction of exchange is the idea of reciprocity (Gouldner) with the assumption that it was a non-exploitative system where mutual gratification was supposed to be the outcome of the reciprocal exchange.

THE CONCEPT OF JAJMANI SYSTEM

Inter-caste relations at the village level constitute vertical ties. They may be classified into economic, ritual, political and civic ties. The castes living in a village are bound together by economic ties. Generally peasant castes are numerically preponderant in villages and they need the carpenter, blacksmith and leather worker castes to perform agricultural work. Servicing castes such as priest, barber, and washerman and water carrier cater to the needs of everyone except the Harijans. Artisan castes produce goods which are wanted by every one. Most Indian villages do not have more than a few of the essential castes and depend on neighbouring villages for certain services, skills and goods.

In rural India with its largely subsistence and not fully monetized economy the relationship between the different caste groups in a village takes a particular form. The essential artisan and servicing castes are paid annually in grain at harvest time. In some parts of India the artisan and servicing castes are also provided with free food, clothing, fodder and residential site. On such occasions as birth, marriage and death, these castes perform extra duties for which they are paid customary money and some gifts in kind. This type of relationship is found all over India and is called by different names-Jajmani in north, Bara batute in Maharashtra, Mirasi in Tamil Nadu and adade in Karnataka.

Oscar Lewis defined Jajmani system as that under which each caste group within a village is expected to give certain standardized services to the families of other castes. Jajmani is more than a relationship between families than between castes. Jajmani is sort of mutual give and take form of relationship in which one family is hereditarily entitled to supply goods and render services to the other in exchange of the same. The person rendering the services or supplying the goods is known as Kameen or Prajna and the person to whom the services are rendered is called a Jajman. Thus under Jajmani system a permanent informal bond is made between Jajman and Kameen to meet each other's need for good and services.

Main Features of Jajmani System

The Jajmani system is characterized by the following features:

- Unbroken relationship-Under the Jajmani system the Kameen remains obliged to render the services throughout his life to a particular Jajman and the Jajman in turn has the responsibility of hiring services of a Kameen.
- Hereditary relationship-Jajmani rights are enjoyed hereditarily. After the death of a man his son is entitled to work as Kameen for the same Jajman family of families. The son of a Jajman also accepts the son of the Kameen as his Kameen.
- Multidimensional relationship-Due to the permanency of relationship both the Jajman and Kameen families

become mutually dependent on each other. The relationship becomes very deep. They often take part in the personal and family affairs, family rituals and ceremonies.

- Barter exchange-Under Jajmani system the payments are made mainly in terms of goods and commodities. The Kameen gets his necessities from the Jajman in return of his services.

The Jajmani system has gradually decayed in modern society. There are many reasons responsible for it. Modern economic system that measures everything in terms of its monetary value. The decline of belief in caste system and hereditary occupation has given a strong blow to the system. Growth of better employment opportunities outside the village and introduction of new transport options.

Agrarian Changes after Independence in Rural Society

In many ways independence from colonial rule in 1947 marked the beginning of a new phase in the history of Indian agriculture. Having evolved out of a long struggle against colonial rule with the participation of the people from various social categories, the Indian state also took over the task of supervising the transformation of its stagnant and backward economy to make sure that the benefits of economic growth were not monopolized entirely by a particular section of society. It is with this background that development emerged as a strategy of economic change and an ideology of the new regime.

However at the micro-level the structures that evolved during colonial rule still continued to exist. The local interests that had emerged over a long period of time continued to be powerful in the Indian countryside even after the political climate had changed. According to Daniel Thorner the earlier structure of land relations and debt dependencies where a small section consisting of few landlords and money lenders were dominant continued to prevail in the Indian countryside. The nature of property relations, the local values that related social prestige negatively to physical labour and the absence of any surplus with the actual cultivator for investment on land ultimately perpetuated stagnation. This complex of legal, economic and social relations typical of Indian countryside served to produce an effect that Thorner described as a built-in depressor.

Land Reforms in Rural Society

The agrarian question had been an important topic of discussions for Indian freedom struggle leaders as well who wrote extensively and debated on how Indian society and economy should be reorganized. Land reforms became a question of considerable academic interest and debate in the discourse about planning and development. They were viewed as necessary for initiating modernization in agriculture. While there was a general agreement that the prevailing agrarian structures marked by absentee landlordism and semi-feudal relations of production, needed to be reorganized, two extreme positions were taken on the crucial questions-what kind of agrarian reforms were required and which would work the best? Is there an economic logic behind land reforms?

The first view was that of the institutionalists who argued that the way out for Indian agriculture lay in a radical reorganization of land ownership patterns that would not only democratize the village and revive the independent peasant economy but also increase the productivity of land. Thus the slogan came up-land to the tiler. They also argued that smaller-sized holdings gave higher productivity. The second viewpoint argued against the redistribution of land on the grounds that it was both unviable as not enough land was available for everyone and that it worked against the logic of economics. The modernization of agriculture required landlords reorientation. They needed to be motivated to cultivate their own land with wage labour and using modern technology. The land reforms would only divide the land into unviable holdings rendering them unfeasible for the use of modern technology.

However the process of agrarian reforms is inherently a political question. The choices made by the Indian state and the actual implementation of land reforms were determined by the politics of the new regime rather than by the theoretical superiority of a particular position. The Indian state chose to reorganize agrarian relations through redistribution of land but not in a comprehensive and radical manner. Joshi described it as sectorial or sectional reforms. The Government of India directed its states to abolish intermediary tenures, regulate rent and tenancy rights, confer ownership rights on tenants, impose ceilings on holdings, distribute the surplus land among the rural poor and facilitate consolidation of holdings. A large number of legislations were passed by the state government over a short period of time.

However most of the legislations provided loopholes that allowed the dominant landowners to tamper with land records by redistributing land among relatives, evicting their tenants and using other means to escape the legislations. In the absence of concerted political will land reforms could succeed only in regions where the peasantry was politically mobilized and could exert pressure from below.

Despite overall failure, land reforms succeeded in weakening the hold of absentee landlords over rural society and assisted in the emergence of a class of substantial peasants and petty landlords as the dominant political and economic group. For example in Rajasthan though the abolition of Jagirs was far from satisfactory it made considerable difference to the overall land ownership patterns and to the local and regional power structures. The Rajputs possessed much less land after the land reforms than they did before, Most of the village land had moved into the hands of those who could be called small and medium landowners. In qualitative terms most of the land begins to be self-cultivated and the incidence of tenancy declined considerably. The fear of losing land induced many potential losers to sell or rearrange their lands in a manner that escaped legislations.

However in few cases the landless labourers living in the countryside most of whom belonged to the ex-touchable castes received land. The beneficiaries by and large belonged to middle level caste groups who traditionally cultivated land as a part of the calling of their castes. While land reforms were supposed to deal with the problem of landlordism, the hold of moneylenders over the peasantry was to be weakened by providing credit through institutional sources initially by credit societies and later by the nationalized commercial banks. According to the findings of an official survey carried out immediately after Independence from colonial rule up to approximately 91% of the credit needs of cultivators were being met by informal sources of credit. Much of this came from moneylenders. Indian state planned to expand the network of cooperative credit societies. With the imposition of social control and later their nationalization, commercial banks were also asked to lend to the agricultural sector on priority basis. Over the years the dependence of rural households on informal sources has come down significantly. The assessment studies on the cooperative credit societies showed that much of their credit went to the relatively better of sections of rural society and the poor continued to depend on the more expensive informal sources. This was explained as a consequence of the prevailing structure of land tenures. The state response was to bureaucratize the cooperative societies. Though in some regions this helped in releasing credit societies from the hold of big landowners, bureaucratization also led to rampant corruption and increasing apathy among those whom they were supposed to serve.

Yet despite inherent bias of institutional credit against the rural poor, its availability played an important role in making the green revolution a success and definitely helped to marginalize the professional moneylender in the rural power structure.

COMMUNITY DEVELOPMENT PROGRAMME IN RURAL SOCIETY

As a strategy of development, the CDP was different from both land reforms and the idea of making cheap institutional credit available to cultivators. CDP had emanated from the productionist approach to rural development. It was based on a notion of the harmonious village community without any significant internal differences and conflict of interests. There was hardly any mention of the unequal power relations in the village. Its objective was to provide a substantial increase in agricultural production and improvement in basic services which would ultimately lead to a transformation in the social and economic life of the village.

Its basic assumption was that the Indian peasant would of his own free will and because of his felt needs immediately adopt technical improvements the moment he was shown them. The programme was launched on 2 October 1952 in a few selected blocks and it was soon extended to the entire country. However the enthusiasm with which the programme was started could not be sustained. A non-political approach to agrarian transformation resulted in helping only those who were already powerful in the village. Most of the benefits were cornered by a small section of the rural elite.

Green Revolution

Of all the developmental programmes introduced during the post-independence period the green revolution is considered to have been the most successful. The green revolution led to a substantial increase in agricultural output to the extent that it almost solved India's food problem. It also produced significant social and political changes in the Indian village and did bring about an agricultural revolution. In purely economic terms the agricultural sector experienced growth at the rate of 3 to 5 % per annum which was many times more than what the rate of growth had been during the colonial period (less than 1%). The green revolution conceptualized agrarian change in purely technological terms and was based on the trickle down theory of economic growth. The expression green revolution carried the conviction that agriculture was being peacefully transformed through the quiet working of science and technology, reaping the economic gains of modernization while avoiding the social costs of mass upheaval and disorder usually associated with rapid change.

The term green revolution had been first used during the late 1960s to refer to the effects of the introduction of higher yielding variety HYV seeds of wheat and rice in developing countries. The new varieties of seeds required fertility enhancing inputs like chemical fertilizers, controlled irrigation conditions and plant-protecting chemicals. The other components were providing cheap institutional credit, price incentives and marketing facilities. In order to back up the application of new technology on local farms a large number of agricultural universities were also opened in the regions selected for the new programme. It was under the direct supervision of the Ford Foundation that the Intensive Agricultural Development Programme was started in 1961. Initially the IADP operated in 14 districts on an experimental basis it was later extended to 114 districts under the name of the Intensive Agriculture Areas Programme in 1965.

Its advocates argued that the new technology was scale neutral and could be used with as much benefit by small as well as big landowners. However in the actual implementation small holdings were not found to be viable units for technological change. Participating in the green revolution did not mean the same thing to smaller farmers as it did to bigger farmers. While bigger farmers had enough surplus of their own to invest in the new capital-intensive farming for smaller landowners it meant additional dependence on borrowing generally from informal sources. Although theoretically the new technology was scale neutral it was certainly not resource neutral. The new technology also compelled widespread involvement with the market. Cultivators in post-green revolution agriculture had to buy all farm inputs from the market for which they often had to take credit from traders or institutional sources. In order to clear the debts they had no choice but to sell the farm yield in the market even when they needed to keep it for their own consumption. They sold their farm yield immediately after harvesting when prices were relatively low and bought later in the year for consumption when prices were higher. Thus although the small farmers took to the new technologies the fact that their resources were limited meant that these technologies ushered in a new set of dependencies. On the other hand it has strengthened the economic and political position of rich farmers. One of the manifestations of the growing market orientation of agrarian production was the emergence of a totally new kind of mobilization of surplus producing farmers who demanded a better deal for the agricultural sector. These new farmers' movements emerged almost simultaneously in virtually all the green revolution regions. These movements gained momentum during the decade of the 1980s. These movements were led by substantial landowners who had benefited most from the developmental programmes and belonged to the numerically large middle-level caste groups whom Srinivas had called the dominant castes. The members of this new social class not only emerged as a dominant group at village level but they also came to dominate regional/state-level politics in most parts of India. They had an accumulated surplus that they sought to invest in ever more profitable enterprises. Some of them diversified into other economic activities or migrated to urban areas or entered agricultural trade. Culturally also this new class differed significantly from both the classical peasants and old landlords.

The changes produced by the green revolution also generated an interesting debate among Marxist scholars on the question of defining the prevailing mode of production in Indian agriculture. The most contentious revolved around whether capitalism had become dominant in Indian agriculture or was still characterized by the semi-feudal mode of production. Another set of scholars on the basis of their own empirical studies mostly from eastern India asserted that Indian agriculture was still dominated by a semi-feudal mode of production. According to this school landlords cum moneylenders continued to dominate the process of agricultural production. Peasants and labourers were tied to them through the mechanism of debt that led to forced commercialization of labour and agricultural yield. This produced a self-perpetuating stagnant and exploitative agrarian structure that could be described as semi-feudal. The internal logic of this system worked against any possibility of agricultural growth or the development of capitalism in Indian agriculture.

However towards the end of the debate there seems to have emerged a consensus that though it may have its local specificities and considerable regional variations, the capitalist mode of production was on its way to dominating the agrarian economy of India and that regions which had experienced the green revolution.

URBAN SOCIAL ORGANISATION

Some sociologists have used the concept of rural-urban continuum to stress the idea that there are no sharp breaking points to be found in the degree or quantity of rural urban differences. Robert Redfield has given the concept of rural-urban continuum on the basis of his study of Mexican peasants of Tepoztlain. The rapid process of urbanization through the establishment of industries, urban traits and facilities have decreased the differences between villages and cities. There are some sociologists whose treat rural-urban as dichotomous categories have differentiated the two at various levels including occupational differences, environmental differences, differences in the sizes of communities, differences in the density of population, differences in social mobility and direction of migration, differences in social stratification and in the systems of social interaction.

A third view regarding rural and urban communities has been given by Pocock who believe that both village and city are elements of the same civilization and hence neither rural urban dichotomy, nor continuum is meaningful. M. S. A. Rao points out in the Indian context that although both village and town formed part of the same civilization characterized by institution of kinship and caste system in pre-British India, there were certain specific institutional forms and organizational ways distinguishing social and cultural life in towns form that in village. Thus, according to Rao, Rural Urban continuum makes more sense Ghurye believes that urbanization is migration of people from village to city and the impact it has on the migrants and their families. Maclver remarks that though the communities are normally divided into rural and urban the line of demarcation is not always clear between these two types of communities. There is no sharp demarcation to tell where the city ends and country begins. Every village possesses some elements of the city and every city carries some features of the village. R. K Mukherjee prefers the continuum model by talking of the degree of urbanization as a useful conceptual tool for understanding rural-urban relations. P. A Sorokin and Zimmerman in 'Principles of Rural-Urban sociology have stated that the factors distinguishing rural from urban communities include occupation, size and density of population as well as mobility, differentiation and stratification.

Urban Sociological Theories

- The classical theories of urban sociology are divided from the works of European sociologists like Karl Marx, Tonnies, George Simmel, Max Weber and those of American namely Park Burgess, Lowis Wirth and Redfield.
- The reflections of the earlier sociologists throw light on the anti-urban feelings. The great city, metropolis a

paradigm of an inhuman, debasing social environment for Tonnies. Simmel felt that the money economy of the cities destroyed the social life.

- Weber and Wirth explained how mass urbanization nullified opportunities or political participation. Charles Booth and Rowntree wrote the sociography of life in the cities.
- Marx and Engels condemned the consequences of urbanization under capitalism. They viewed the concentration and misery of the mass of workers in the new urban agglomerations as a necessary stage in the creation of a revolutionary force. For them pauperization and material degradation was one aspect of urbanization but equally important was the destruction of the social nexus of the traditional community and its replacement by the utilitarian world of the city. Both for theory and practice communism depended on urbanism.
- Mumford in his book 'The city in history' sees cities as enlarging all dimensions of life as the scattered as the scattered activities of society are brought together so releasing the energies of mankind in a tremendous explosion of creativity. The city has augmented capabilities for participation and widened the basis of personal experience.
- In the writings of Neo-Marxists like Mills, Marcuse, Fromm there is a consensus that conditions of capitalist urbanization are mutilative of the personality, inhibitive of community formation, destructive of social engagement or involvement and conducive to apathy, alienation and anomie. Class consciousness is inhibited and diverted in mass movements, unreason and not reason typifies social response.
- Sociologists from Tonnies to Wirth developed counter-theory to Marxism for the explication of social change led to acceptance of a fundamental cleavage between rural and urban, tradition and modernism which was in sharp opposition to any variant on Marxist theories of development. The urban is accepted as a frame of reference and the urban society as a specific mode of social organization becomes the object of scientific study.

- Tonnies in his book Community and Society explained the impact of the market economy on traditional forms of social association; the implications of urbanization and the development of the state for the conduct of social life and the mechanisms of social solidarity in an individualized society. The distinction he draws between the two forms of human association, gemeniscaft and gesellschaft has become the basis for a succession of typologies of which the best known are the pattern variables formulated by Parsons and folk-urban typology drawn by Redfield and Wirth.
- George Simmel presents social interaction in terms of abstract categories. The study of society could only proceed by means of logical analysis of the forms of association. The forms are cognitive categories. Simmel belonged to the neo-Kantian tradition which frankly denies the possibility of the study of the natural or the social world without selection and ordering by the observer. Simmel was trying to expound on three themes; first the consequences of a money economy for social relationships. Second the significance of numbers for social life and lastly the scope for the maintenance of independence and individuality against the sovereign powers of society.
- Max Weber in his 'The City' has defined the city on the basis of political and administrative conception. To constitute a full urban community a settlement must display a relative predominance of trade-commercial relations with the settlement as a whole displaying the following features:
    - o fortification
    - o market
    - o a court of its own and at least partially autonomous law
    - o a related form of association
    - o partial autonomy and voting rights.

Weber rejects cities governed by religious groups or where the authority is enforced on personal rather than universalistic basis. He recounts a process in which the development of the rational-legal institutions that characterize the modern city enabled the individual to be free from the traditional groups and therefore develop his individuality. He emphasizes the closure, autonomy and separateness of the urban community and stressed that the historical peculiarities of the medieval city were due to the location of the city with in the total medieval political and social organization.

Urban Growth and Urbanization

Urbanization is the movement of population from rural to urban areas and the resulting increasing proportion of a population that resides in urban rather than rural places. It is derived from the Latin 'Urbs' a term used by the Romans to a city. Urban sociology is the sociology of urban living; of people in groups and social relationship in urban social circumstances and situation. Thompson Warren has defined it as the movement of people from communities concerned chiefly or solely with agriculture to other communities generally larger whose activities are primarily centred in government, trade, manufacture or allied interests. Urbanization is a two-way process because it involves not only movement from village to cities and change from agricultural occupation to business, trade, service and profession but it also involves change in the migrants attitudes, beliefs, values and behaviour patterns. The process of urbanization is rapid all over the world. The facilities like education, health-care system, employment avenues, civic facilities and social welfare are reasons attracting people to urban areas. The census of India defines some criteria for urbanization. These are:

- Population is more than 5000
- The density is over 400 persons per sq. km
- 75% of the male population engages in non-agricultural occupations.
- Cities are urban areas with population more than one lakh.
- Metropolises are cities with population of more than one million.

Urbanism

Urbanism is a way of life. It reflects an organization of

society in terms of a complex division of labour, high levels of technology, high mobility, interdependence of its members in fulfilling economic functions and impersonality in social relations. Louis Wirth has given four characteristics of urbanism:

- Transiency: An urban inhabitant's relation with others last only for a short time; he tends to forget his old acquaintances and develop relations with new people. Since he is not much attached to his neighbours members of the social groups, he does not mind leaving them.
- Superficiality: An urban person has the limited number of persons with whom he interacts and his relations with them are impersonal and formal. People meet each other in highly segmental roles. They are dependent on more people for the satisfaction of their life needs.
- Anonymity: Urbanities do not know each other intimately. Personal mutual acquaintance between the inhabitants which ordinarily is found in a neighbourhood is lacking.
- Individualism: People give more importance to their own vested interests.

Town

The town is intermediate between rural and urban communities. It is too large for all inhabitants to be acquainted with one another, yet small enough for informal relationships to predominate. Social behaviour more closely resembles the rural than the metropolitan city pattern. Towns are places with population of 5, 000 and more. Three conditions of a place being classified as a town are:

- The population is more than 5, 000.
- The density is not less than 400 sq. km.
- Not less than 75% of the adult male population is engaged in non-agricultural activities.

City

Cities become possible when an agricultural surplus develops together with improved means of transportation and tend to be located at breaks in transportation. The most significant current developments in city structure are the metropolitan area including the suburb which accounts for current population growth. The city pulls people from various corners towards its nucleus. The rural people faced with various economic problems are attracted by the city and start moving towards the cities. The city provides ample opportunities for personal advancement. It is the centre of brisk economic, commercial, artistic, literary, political, educational, technological, scientific and other activities. Cities are not only the controlling centres of their societies but also the source of innovation and change. They act as the source of new ideas for production, the pace-setters for consumption, guardians of culture and conservers of order in society. Consensus and continuity in a society are maintained from the city centres. Urban culture has become the legitimation for control. Walter Christaller explained the location of urban cities in terms of their functions as service centres. The basic assumption was that a given rural area supports an urban centre which in turn serves the surrounding countryside. There are smaller towns for smaller areas and bigger cities for larger regions. This concept permitted Christaller to build up an integrated system of cities according to their size.

His views conceiving a city as a central place within a rural area was elabourated by Edward L. Ullman with considerable modifications. He admits the vulnerability of the scheme for larger places. In highly industrialized areas the central place schemes is generally distorted by industrial concentration in response to resources and transportation that it may be said to have little significance as an explanation for urban location and distribution. Hyot in his sector theory talked about the growth of cities taking place in sectors and these sectors extend from the centre to periphery.

The concentric zone theory given by Park and Burgess suggested that modern cities consisted of a series of concentric zones. There are five such zones :

- Central business district
- Zone in transition
- Zone of working population
- Residential zone
- Commuter's zone.

Gans and Lewis through compositional theory hold that the composition of a city's population differs from that of a small town in terms of factors such as class, education, ethnicity and marital status. Multiple Nuclie theory given by Harris and Ullman discuss that there is not one centre but several centres for the city. Each of the centres tend to specialize in a particular kind of activity-retailing, wholesaling, finance, recreation, education, government. Several centres may have existed from the beginning of the city or many have developed later in a division from one centre.

According to Castells to understand cities and urbanism one has to understand the process by which spatial forms are created and transformed. The architecture of cities expresses the struggles and conflicts between different groups in society. City is not only a distinct location but also as an integral part of processes of collective consumption.

Features of urban society

i. The urban society is heterogeneous known for its diversity and complexity.

ii. It is dominated by secondary relations.

iii. Formal means of social control such as law, legislation, police, and court are needed in addition to the informal means for regulating the behaviour of the people.

iv. The urban society is mobile and open. It provides more chances for social mobility. The status is achieved than ascribed.

v. Occupations are more specialized. There is widespread division of labour and specialization opportunities for pursuing occupations are numerous.

vi. Family is said to be unstable. More than the family individual is given importance. Joint families are comparatively less in number.

vii. People are more class-conscious and progressive. They welcome changes. They are exposed to the modern developments in the fields of science and technology.

viii. Urban community is a complex multigroup society.

ix. The urban community replaced consensus by dissensus. The social organization is atomistic and illdefined. It is characterized by disorganization, mental illness and anomie.

x. Mass education is widespread in the city increasing democratization of the organizations and institutions demand formal education.

Features of Industrial City

- A large sprawling open city housing a large percent of the population of the society. Relatively low segregation; few outward symbols, segregation based on race. Good transportation and communication.
- A manufacturing, finance and coordinating centre of an industrial society.
- A fluid class structure with an elite of businessmen, professionals and scientists.
- A large middle class with technologically related jobs.
- Wealth by salaries, fees, investment. High status of business activity. Unionization at a national level. Specialization of production and marketing. Large service sector, fixed price.
- Time important and regular work schedule.
- Standardization of process and quality.
- Formal public opinion with a bureaucracy based on technical criteria.
- A weak religious institution separate from other institutions dominated by the middle class. Standardization of religious experience marked by the disappearance of magic.
- Technical and secular education for the masses.

Urban Ecological Processes

It means whereby spatial distribution of people and activities change. They include:

- Centralization clustering of economic and service functions.
- Concentration tendency of people and activities to cluster together.
- Decentralization flight of people and activities from the centre of the city.

- Invasion entrance of new kind of people or activity into an area.
- Segregation concentration of a certain type of people or activities within a particular area.
- Succession completed replacement of one kind of people or activity by another.

Impact of Automation on Society

- It speeds up the developmental processes of the society.
- It increases production.
- Brings further technological changes like information technology.
- Extreme industrialization
- Replacement of human labour with machines.
- Increase in profit margins
- Distance reduction through technological advancements in the field of communication network.
- Makes life dependent on latest gizmos and equipments.

Environment

When physical, chemical and biological projects of the different components of environment: air, water, soil, noise change to the detriment of living of humans it may be said that environment has been affected. Many developing countries are placing more and more reliance on industrialization. It is not only a mechanical but also a social process. Therefore it affects the environment physically as well as socio-culturally. All aspects of pollution are directly or indirectly related to human health and well being. The excessive growth and rush of people from villages to urban areas resulting in over crowding of cities. Rapid urbanization and industrialization have led to an increase in environmental pollutant load that poses serious public health problem. It also affects the socio-cultural environment with the close ties of groups coming under pressure. Traditional ties are replaced with new work based ones. Religion becomes secular. Thus industrialization affects the social fabric making the society more materialistic.

5

Marriage, Family and Kinship

MARRIAGE TYPES AND NORMS

Marriage is one of the universal social institutions established to control and regulate the life of mankind. It is closely associated with the institution of family. Infact both the institutions are complementary to each other. It is an institution with different implications in different cultures. Its purposes, functions and forms may differ from society to society but it is present everywhere as an institution.

Westermarck in 'History of Human marriage' defines marriage as the more or less durable connection between male and female lasting beyond the mere act of propagation till after the birth of offspring. According to Malinowski marriage is a contract for the production and maintenance of children. Robert Lowie describes marriage as a relatively permanent bond between permissible mates. For Horton and Hunt marriage is the approved social pattern whereby two or more persons establish a family.

TYPES OF MARRIAGES

Polygyny: It is a form of marriage in which one man marries more than one woman at a given time. It is of two types— Sororal polygyny and non sororal polygyny

Sororal polygyny: It is a type of marriage in which the wives are invariably the sisters. It is often called sororate.

Non-sororal polygyny: It is a type of marriage in which the wives are not related as sisters.

Polyandry: It is the marriage of one woman with more than one man. It is less common than polygyny. It is of two types—— Fraternal Polyandry and non fraternal polyandry.

Fraternal polyandry: When several brothers share the same wife the practice can be called alelphic or fraternal polyandry. This practice of being mate, actual or potential to one's husband's brothers is called levirate. It is prevalent among Todas.

Non-fraternal polyandry: In this type the husband need not have any close relationship prior to the marriage. The wife goes to spend some time with each husband. So long as a woman lives with one of her husbands; the others have no claim over her.

Monogamy: It is a form of marriage in which one man marries one woman. It is the most common and acceptable form of marriage.

Serial monogamy: In many societies individuals are permitted to marry again often on the death of the first spouse or after divorce but they cannot have more than one spouse at one and the same time.

Straight monogamy: In this remarriage is not allowed.

Group Marriage: It means the marriage of two or more women with two or more men. Here the husbands are common husbands and wives are common wives. Children are regarded as the children of the entire group as a whole.

RULES OF MARRIAGE

No society gives absolute freedom to its members to select their partners. Endogamy and exogamy are the two main rules that condition marital choice.

Endogamy: It is a rule of marriage in which the life-partners are to be selected within the group. It is marriage within the group and the group may be caste, class, tribe, race, village, religious group etc. We have caste endogamy, class endogamy, sub caste endogamy, race endogamy and tribal endogamy etc. In caste endogamy marriage has to take place within the caste. Brahmin has to marry a Brahmin. In sub caste endogamy it is limited to the sub caste groups.

Exogamy: It is a rule of marriage in which an individual has to marry outside his own group. It prohibits marrying within the group. The so-called blood relatives shall neither have marital connections nor sexual contacts among themselves.

Forms of Exogamy

Gotra Exogamy: The Hindu practice of one marrying outside one's own gotra.

Pravara Exogamy: Those who belong to the same pravara cannot marry among themselves.

Village Exogamy: Many Indian tribes like Naga, Garo, Munda etc. have the practice of marrying outside their village.

Pinda Exogamy: Those who belong to the same panda or sapinda (common parentage) cannot marry within themselves.

Isogamy: It is the marriage between two equals (status)

Anisogamy: It is an asymmetric marriage alliance between two individuals belonging to different social statuses. It is of two forms-Hypergamy and Hypogamy.

Hypergamy: It is the marriage of a woman with a man of higher Varna or superior caste or family.

Hypogamy: It is the marriage of high caste man with a low caste woman.

Orthogamy: It is the marriage between selected groups.

Cerogamy: It is two or more men get married to two or more women.

Anuloma marriage: It is a marriage under which a man can marry from his own caste or from those below, but a woman can marry only in her caste or above.

Pratiloma marriage: It is a marriage of a woman to a man from a lower caste which is not permitted.

HINDU MARRIAGE

The Hindu community has been giving great importance for marriage since time immemorial. There are different forms of marriage-

- Brahma Vivaha is where a father marries his daughter to a learned man of good moral character.
- Asura Vivaha is marriage by paying bride price.

- Rakshasa Vivaha is by capture or abduction without obtaining the consent of a girl or her parents.
- Gandharva Vivaha is based on mutual love.
- Prajapatya Vivaha is where no ceremony is performed but the groom is honoured.
- Arsh Vivaha is where the groom gives a pair of cattle or bull to the bride's father before the marriage.
- Daiva Vivaha is where the girl is given in marriage to a priest instead of dakshina or a gift.

In India there is no greater event in a family than a wedding, dramatically evoking every possible social obligation, kinship bond, traditional value, impassioned sentiment, and economic resource. In the arranging and conducting of weddings, the complex permutations of Indian social systems best display themselves.

Marriage is deemed essential for virtually everyone in India. For the individual, marriage is the great watershed in life, marking the transition to adulthood. Generally, this transition, like everything else in India, depends little upon individual volition but instead occurs as a result of the efforts of many people. Even as one is born into a particular family without the exercise of any personal choice, so is one given a spouse without any personal preference involved. Arranging a marriage is a critical responsibility for parents and other relatives of both bride and groom. Marriage alliances entail some redistribution of wealth as well as building and restructuring social realignments, and, of course, result in the biological reproduction of families.

Some parents begin marriage arrangements on the birth of a child, but most wait until later. In the past, the age of marriage was quite young, and in a few small groups, especially in Rajasthan, children under the age of five are still united in marriage. In rural communities, prepuberty marriage for girls traditionally was the rule. In the late twentieth century, the age of marriage is rising in villages, almost to the levels that obtain in cities. Legislation mandating minimum marriage ages has been passed in various forms over the past decades, but such laws have little effect on actual marriage practices. Essentially, India is divided into two large regions with regard to Hindu kinship and marriage practices, the north and the south. Additionally, various ethnic and tribal groups of the central, mountainous north, and eastern regions follow a variety of other practices. These variations have been extensively described and analyzed by anthropologists, especially Irawati Karve, David G. Mandelbaum, and Clarence Maloney.

Broadly, in the Indo-Aryan-speaking north, a family seeks marriage alliances with people to whom it is not already linked by ties of blood. Marriage arrangements often involve looking far afield. In the Dravidian-speaking south, a family seeks to strengthen existing kin ties through marriage, preferably with blood relatives. Kinship terminology reflects this basic pattern. In the north, every kinship term clearly indicates whether the person referred to is a blood relation or an affinal relation; all blood relatives are forbidden as marriage mates to a person or a person's children. In the south, there is no clear-cut distinction between the family of birth and the family of marriage. Because marriage in the south commonly involves a continuing exchange of daughters among a few families, for the married couple all relatives are ultimately blood kin. Dravidian terminology stresses the principle of relative age: all relatives are arranged according to whether they are older or younger than each other without reference to generation.

On the Indo-Gangetic Plain, marriages are contracted outside the village, sometimes even outside of large groups of villages, with members of the same caste beyond any traceable consanguineal ties. In much of the area, daughters should not be given into villages where daughters of the family or even of the natal village have previously been given. In most of the region, brother-sister exchange marriages (marriages linking a brother and sister of one household with the sister and brother of another) are shunned. The entire emphasis is on casting the marriage net ever-wider, creating new alliances. The residents of a single village may have in-laws in hundreds of other villages.

In most of North India, the Hindu bride goes to live with strangers in a home she has never visited. There she is sequestered and veiled, an outsider who must learn to conform to new ways. Her natal family is often geographically distant, and her ties with her consanguineal kin undergo attenuation to varying degrees. In central India, the basic North Indian pattern prevails, with some modifications. For example, in Madhya Pradesh, village exogamy is preferred, but marriages within a village are not uncommon. Marriages between caste-fellows in neighbouring villages are frequent. Brother-sister exchange marriages are sometimes arranged, and daughters are often given in marriage to lineages where other daughters of their lineage or village have previously been wed.

In South India, in sharp contrast, marriages are preferred between cousins (especially cross-cousins, that is, the children of a brother and sister) and even between uncles and nieces (especially a man and his elder sister's daughter). The principle involved is that of return—the family that gives a daughter expects one in return, if not now, then in the next generation. The effect of such marriages is to bind people together in relatively small, tight-knit kin groups. A bride moves to her in-laws' home—the home of her grandmother or aunt—and is often comfortable among these familiar faces. Her husband may well be the cousin she has known all her life that she would marry.

Many South Indian marriages are contracted outside of such close kin groups when no suitable mates exist among close relatives, or when other options appear more advantageous. Some sophisticated South Indians, for example, consider cousin marriage and uncle-niece marriage outmoded.

Rules for the remarriage of widows differ from one group to another. Generally, lower-ranking groups allow widow remarriage, particularly if the woman is relatively young, but the highest-ranking castes discourage or forbid such remarriage. The most strict adherents to the nonremarriage of widows are Brahmans. Almost all groups allow widowers to remarry. Many groups encourage a widower to marry his deceased wife's younger sister (but never her older sister).

Among Muslims of both the north and the south, marriage between cousins is encouraged, both cross-cousins (the children of a brother and sister) and parallel cousins (the children of two same-sex siblings). In the north, such cousins grow up calling each other "brother" and "sister", yet they may marry. Even when cousin marriage does not occur, spouses can often trace between them other kinship linkages.

Some tribal people of central India practice an interesting permutation of the southern pattern. Among the Murias of Bastar in southeastern Madhya Pradesh, as described by anthropologist Verrier Elwin, teenagers live together in a dormitory (*ghotul*), sharing life and love with one another for several blissful years. Ultimately, their parents arrange their marriages, usually with cross-cousins, and the delights of teenage romance are replaced with the serious responsibilities of adulthood. In his survey of some 2, 000 marriages, Elwin found only seventy-seven cases of *ghotul* partners eloping together and very few cases of divorce. Among the Muria and Gond tribal groups, cross-cousin marriage is called "bringing back the milk, " alluding to the gift of a girl in one generation being returned by the gift of a girl in the next.

Finding the perfect partner for one's child can be a challenging task. People use their social networks to locate potential brides and grooms of appropriate social and economic status. Increasingly, urban dwellers use classified matrimonial advertisements in newspapers. The advertisements usually announce religion, caste, and educational qualifications, stress female beauty and male (and in the contemporary era, sometimes female) earning capacity, and may hint at dowry size. In rural areas, matches between strangers are usually arranged without the couple meeting each other. Rather, parents and other relatives come to an agreement on behalf of the couple. In cities, however, especially among the educated classes, photographs are exchanged, and sometimes the couple are allowed to meet under heavily chaperoned circumstances, such as going out for tea with a group of people or meeting in the parlor of the girl's home, with her relatives standing by. Young professional men and their families may receive inquiries and photographs from representatives of several girls' families. They may send their relatives to meet the most promising candidates and then go on tour themselves to meet the young women and make a final choice. In the early 1990s, increasing numbers of marriages arranged in this way link brides and grooms from India with spouses of Indian parentage resident in Europe, North America, and the Middle East.

Almost all Indian children are raised with the expectation that their parents will arrange their marriages, but an increasing number of young people, especially among the college-educated, are finding their own spouses. So-called love marriages are deemed a slightly scandalous alternative to properly arranged marriages. Some young people convince their parents to "arrange" their marriages to people with whom they have fallen in love. This process has long been possible for Indians from the south and for Muslims who want to marry a particular cousin of the appropriate marriageable category. In the upper classes, these semi-arranged love marriages increasingly occur between young people who are from castes of slightly different rank but who are educationally or professionally equal. If there are vast differences to overcome, such as is the case with love marriages between Hindus and Muslims or between Hindus of very different caste status, parents are usually much less agreeable, and serious family disruptions can result.

In much of India, especially in the north, a marriage establishes a structural opposition between the kin groups of the bride and groom—bride-givers and bride-takers. Within this relationship, bride-givers are considered inferior to bride-takers and are forever expected to give gifts to the bride-takers. The one-way flow of gifts begins at engagement and continues for a generation or two. The most dramatic aspect of this asymmetrical relationship is the giving of dowry.

In many communities throughout India, a dowry has traditionally been given by a bride's kin at the time of her marriage. In ancient times, the dowry was considered a woman's wealth—property due a beloved daughter who had no claim on her natal family's real estate—and typically included portable valuables such as jewelry and household goods that a bride could control throughout her life. However, over time, the larger proportion of the dowry has come to consist of goods and cash payments that go straight into the hands of the groom's family. In the late twentieth century, throughout much of India, dowry payments have escalated, and a groom's parents sometimes insist on compensation for their son's higher education and even for his future earnings, to which the bride will presumably have access. Some of the dowries demanded are quite oppressive, amounting to several years' salary in cash as well as items such as motorcycles, air conditioners, and fancy cars. Among some lower-status groups, large dowries are currently replacing traditional bride-price payments. Even among Muslims, previously not given to demanding large dowries, reports of exorbitant dowries are increasing.

The dowry is becoming an increasingly onerous burden for the bride's family. Antidowry laws exist but are largely ignored, and a bride's treatment in her marital home is often affected by the value of her dowry. Increasingly frequent are horrible incidents, particularly in urban areas, where a groom's family makes excessive demands on the bride's family—even after marriage—and when the demands are not met, murder the bride, typically by setting her clothes on fire in a cooking "accident. " The groom is then free to remarry and collect another sumptuous dowry. The male and female in-laws implicated in these murders have seldom been punished.

Such dowry deaths have been the subject of numerous media reports in India and other countries and have mobilized feminist groups to action. In some of the worst areas, such as the National Capital Territory of Delhi, where hundreds of such deaths are reported annually and the numbers are increasing yearly, the law now requires that all suspicious deaths of new brides be investigated. Official government figures report 1, 786 registered dowry deaths nationwide in 1987; there is also an estimate of some 5, 000 dowry deaths in 1991. Women's groups sometimes picket the homes of the in-laws of burned brides. Some analysts have related the growth of this phenomenon to the growth of consumerism in Indian society.

Fears of impoverishing their parents have led some urban middle-class young women, married and unmarried, to commit suicide. However, through the giving of large dowries, the newly wealthy are often able to marry their treasured daughters up the status hierarchy so reified in Indian society.

After marriage arrangements are completed, a rich panoply of wedding rituals begins. Each religious group, region, and caste has a slightly different set of rites. Generally, all weddings involve as many kin and associates of the bride and groom as possible. The bride's family usually hosts most of the ceremonies and pays for all the arrangements for large numbers of guests for several days, including accommodation, feasting, decorations, and gifts for the groom's party. These arrangements are often extremely elabourate and expensive and are intended to enhance the status of the bride's family. The groom's party usually hires a band and brings fine gifts for the bride, such as jewelry and clothing, but these are typically far outweighed in value by the presents received from the bride's side. After the bride and groom are united in sacred rites attended by colorful ceremony, the new bride may be carried away to her in-laws' home, or, if she is very young, she may remain with her parents until they deem her old enough to depart. A prepubescent bride usually stays in her natal home until puberty, after which a separate consummation ceremony is held to mark her departure for her conjugal home and married life. The poignancy of the bride's weeping departure for her new home is prominent in personal memory, folklore, literature, song, and drama throughout India.

DOWERY

Dowry or Dahej is the payment in cash or/and kind by the bride's family to the bridegroom' s family along with the giving away of the bride (called Kanyadaan) in Indian marriage. Kanyadanam is an important part of Hindu marital rites. Kanya means daughter, and dana means gift.

Dowry originated in upper caste families as the wedding gift to the bride from her family. The dowry was later given to help with marriage expenses and became a form of insurance in the case that her in-laws mistreated her. Although the dowry was legally prohibited in 1961, it continues to be highly institutionalized. The groom often demands a dowry consisting of a large sum of money, farm animals, furniture, and electronics.

Dowry System in Indian Marriages can be called the commercial aspect of the marriage. The practice of giving dowry was very common among all people of all nations. A girl gets all the domestic utensils that are necessary to set up a family. Dowry system in India was prevalent since the Vedic period.

In Epic period gifts from parents, brothers and relatives and relatives were recognized as woman‘s property-stridhan. According to Kautilya "Means of subsistence or jewellery constitutes what is called the property of the woman. It is no guilt for a wife to make use of this property in maintaining her son her daughter-in-law or herself if her absent husband has made no provision for her maintenance". Considering the evils of dowry system, the dowry prohibition Act 1961 was passed in India. According to the Act if a person gives or takes dowry then he is liable to be punished for an imprisonment and fine. If a person demands directly or indirectly dowry from the guardians o the wife after the marriage has been solemnized then such a person is liable to be punished for an imprisonment of six months and a fine of Rs. 5000.

Today, in India both divorce and remarriage are completely legal, whereas polygamy and polyandry are both criminal offences for Hindus, punishable by law. The Islamic personal law of Sheriat allows up to four wives for a man, and it is legal for a Muslim to have multiple wives in India.

Marriage, a strong bond, a relationship between a man and a woman. It relies on the pillars of love, complete trust and faith in the spouse. Marriages in India are known with different names like Parinay, Shaadi, Vivah, Kalayanam, and Lagna, etc. The practice of dowry abuse is rising in India. The most severe in "bride burning", the burning of women whose dowries were not considered sufficient by their husband or in-laws. Most of these incidents are reported as accidental burns in the kitchen or are disguised as suicide. It is evident that there exist deep rooted prejudices against women in India. Cultural practices such as the payment of dowry tend to subordinate women in Indian society.

Though prohibited by law in 1961, the extraction of DOWRY from the bride's family prior to marriage still occurs. When the dowry amount is not considered sufficient or is not forthcoming, the bride is often harassed, abused and made miserable. This abuse can escalate to the point where the husband or his family burn the bride, often by pouring kerosene on her and lighting it, usually killing her. The official records of these incidents are low because they are often reported as accidents or suicides by the family. In Delhi, a woman is burned to death almost every twelve hours. The number of dowry murders is increasing. In 1988, 2, 209 women were killed in dowry related incidents and in 1990, 4, 835 were killed. It is important to reiterate that these are official records, which are immensely under reported. The lack of official registration of this crime is apparent in Delhi, where ninety percent of cases of women burnt were recorded as accidents, five percent as suicide and only the remaining five percent were shown as murder.

According to Government figures there were a total of 5, 377 dowry deaths in 1993, an increase of 12% from 1992. Despite the existence of rigorous laws to prevent dowry-deaths under a 1986 amendment to the Indian Penal Code (IPC), convictions are rare, and judges (usually men) are often uninterested and susceptible to bribery. Recent newspaper reports have focused on the alarming rate of deaths of married women in Hamirpur, Mandi and Bilaspur districts in the state of Himachal Pradesh.

BRIDE BURNING

Bride-burning is a form of domestic violence practiced in Bangladesh, India, Pakistan and other countries located on or around the Indian subcontinent. A category of dowry death, bride-burning occurs when a young woman is murdered by her husband or his family for her family's refusal to pay additional dowry. The wife is typically doused with kerosene, gasoline, or other flammable liquid, and set alight, leading to death by fire. Virendra Kumar and Sarita Kanth point out that bride burning has been recognized as an important public health problem in India. They say that it is a historical and cultural issue accounting for around 600-750 deaths per year in India alone. In 1995 Time Magazine reported that dowry deaths in India increased from around 400 a year in the early 1980s to around 5, 800 a year by the middle of the 1990s. A year later CNN ran a story saying that every year police receive more than 2, 500 reports of bride burning.

Ashley K. Jutla MD, and Dr. David Heimbach MD, describe bride burning by saying that "the husband and/or in-laws have determined that the dowry, a gift given from the daughter's parents to the husband, was inadequate and therefore attempt to murder the new bride to make the husband available to remarry or to punish the bride and her family. " In 1961, the Government of India passed the Dowry Prohibition Act, making the dowry demands in wedding arrangements illegal. In 1986, the Indian Parliament added "dowry deaths" as a new domestic violence crime. According to the new section 304-B of the Indian Penal Code, where a bride, "within 7 years of her marriage is killed and it is shown that soon before her death, she was subjected to cruelty or harassment by her husband, or any relative of her husband or in connection with any demand for dowry, such death shall be called 'dowry death' and such husband or relative shall be deemed to have caused her death." The offenders can be sentenced for any period from a minimum of 7 years in prison to a maximum of life. However, many cases of dowry-related domestic violence, suicides and murders have been reported. A 1997 report claimed that at least 5, 000 women die each year because of dowry deaths, and at least a dozen die each day in 'kitchen fires' thought to be intentional.

Suggestions to prevent bride burning are being developed, including: "an increase in the standard of education for women, which will encourage economic and emotional independence; proper implementation of existing laws along with new, stricter legislation to abolish dowry related crimes; and the establishment of voluntary associations to decrease the importance of dowries in general. Community-level programs are essential, and must include doctors, who bear special responsibilities to help change the social milieu in which this phenomenon occurs. "

DOWRY LAW IN INDIA

Payment of a dowry, gift—often financial, has a long history in many parts of the world. In India, the payment of a dowry was prohibited in 1961 under Indian civil law and subsequently by Sections 304B and 498a of the Indian Penal Code were enacted to make it easier for the wife to seek redress from potential harassment by the husband's family. Dowry laws have come under criticism as they have been misused by women and their families.

Dowries

Gifts given by the parents of the bride are considered "stri-dhan", i.e. property of the woman, traditionally representing her share of her parent's wealth.

The 1961 Dowry Prohibition Act

Introduced and taken up by then Indian law minister Ashoka Kumar Sen, this historical act prohibits the request, payment or acceptance of a dowry, "as consideration for the marriage".

Where "dowry" is defined as a gift demanded or given as a precondition for a marriage. Gifts given without a precondition are not considered dowry, and are legal. Asking or giving of dowry can be punished by an imprisonment of up to six months, or a fine of up to Rs. 15000 or the amount of dowry whichever is higher and imprisonment up to 5 years. It replaced several pieces of anti-dowry legislation that had been enacted by various Indian states.

IPC Section 304B

This Section of the Indian Penal Code was inserted by a 1986 amendment. The Dowry deaths law defines a 'dowry death' as the death of a woman caused by any burns or bodily injury or which does not occur under normal circumstances within seven years of her marriage. For a woman's death to be a dowry death, it must also be shown that soon before her death she was subjected to cruelty or harassment by her husband or any relative of her husband for, or in connection with, any demand for dowry. If this is proved, the woman's husband or relative is required to be deemed to have caused her death. Whoever commits dowry death is required to be punished with imprisonment for a term which shall not be less than seven years but which may extend to imprisonment for life.

IPC Section 498A

Section 498A was inserted into the penal code in 1983 it reads: Whoever, being the husband or the relative of the husband of a woman, subjects such woman to cruelty shall be punished with imprisonment for a term which may extend to three years and shall also be liable to fine.

In practice, cruelty is taken to include the demanding of a dowry. This section is non-bailable, non-compoundable (i.e. it cannot be privately resolved between the parties concerned) and cognizable (i.e. the police can arrest the accused without investigation or warrants) on a report from a woman or close relative. Another examples of a cognizable law in India was the Prevention of Terrorist Activities Act.

Police often file charges against the husband, his parents and other relatives (whoever being named on the complaint by the wife or her close relatives) and put them in jail. There is no penalty (even a fine) for filing a false case. Many individuals have claimed this is being abused by the wife or her close relatives. In urban India, the majority of families have inadequate knowledge regarding section 498A of the Indian Penal Code, 1860. The Malimath committee in 2003 proposed making amendments to this section although such amendments have been opposed by women's groups and radical feminists. The Centre for Social Research India has released a research report opposing amendments to section 498A. According to this report, in the studied cases there were no convictions based solely on section 498A. Although the report states that 60. 5 percent of the studied cases were falsified. They also state that many people believe the law has been abused by "educated and independent minded women. " A police official asserted that in his district one-third of dowry murder cases were found totally false by the police..

However, on December 17, 2003, the then Minister of State for Home Affairs, I. D. Swami said: "There is no information available with the Government to come to the conclusion that many families in India are suffering due to exaggerated allegations of harassment and dowry cases made by women against their husbands and other family members involving them in criminal misappropriation and cruelty. "

On 20 July 2005, Justices Arijit Pasayat and H. K. Seema of the Indian Supreme Court declared Section 498A to be constitutional. " The object is to strike at the root of dowry menace. But by misuse of the provision a new legal terrorism can be unleashed. The provision is intended to be used as a shield and not an assassin's weapon. If [the] cry of "wolf" is made too often as a prank, assistance and protection may not be available when the actual wolf appears, " the Bench said.. Several reports of the abuse of Section 498A have involved couples based outside India especially in the US & Canada. The United States Department of State has published the following travel warning: A number of US men who have come to India to marry Indian nationals have been arrested and charged with crimes related to dowry extraction. Many of the charges stem from the US citizen's inability to provide an immigrant visa for his prospective spouse to travel immediately to the United States.

The courts sometimes order the US citizen to pay large sums of money to his spouse in exchange for the dismissal of charges. The courts normally confiscate the American's passport, and he must remain in India until the case has been settled.

It is stated in Travel Advisory by US, since the police may arrest anyone who is accused of committing a crime (even if the allegation is frivolous in nature), the Indian criminal justice system is often used to escalate personal disagreements into criminal charges. This practice has been increasingly exploited by dissatisfied business partners, contractors, estranged spouses, or other persons with whom the US citizen has a disagreement, occasionally resulting in the jailing of US citizens pending resolution of their disputes. At the very least, such circumstances can delay the US citizen's timely departure from India, and may result in an unintended long-term stay in the country. Corruption in India, especially at local levels, is a concern, as evidenced by Transparency International's Corruption Perception Index of 3. 5, ranking India in 72nd place of the world's countries.

In a well publicized case, Dr. Balamurali Ambati, who earned his MD at age 17, and his family were detained in India for over three years in a suit related to alleged dowry demands by the family for his brother's wife Archana, which delayed Dr. Ambati's entry to the ophthalmology program for two years, leaving him to begin his residency in 1998. All charges against him were dismissed in October 1996 and all his family members were acquitted in June 1999. During the course of the trial the Ambatis produced a tape in which the father of Archana demanded US $500, 000 to drop all the charges although the details of this particular case are still debated in India.

FAMILY

The family forms the basic unit of social organization and it is difficult to imagine how human society could function without it. The family has been seen as a universal social institution an inevitable part of human society. According to Burgess and Lock the family is a group of persons united by ties of marriage, blood or adoption constituting a single household interacting with each other in their respective social role of husband and wife, mother and father, brother and sister creating a common culture. P Murdock defines the family as a social group characterized by common residence, economic cooperation and reproduction. It includes adults of both sexes at least two of whom maintain a socially approved sexual relationship and one or more children own or adopted of the sexually co-habiting adults.

Nimkoff says that family is a more or less durable association of husband and wife with or without child or of a man or woman alone with children. According to Maclver family is a group defined by sex relationships sufficiently precise and enduring to provide for the procreation and upbringing of children. Kingsley Davis describes family as a group of persons whose relations to one another are based upon consanguinity and who are therefore kin to one another. Malinowski opined that the family is the institution within which the cultural traditions of a society is handed over to a newer generation. This indispensable function could not be filled unless the relations to parents and children were relations reciprocally of authority and respect. According to Talcott Parsons families are factories which produce human personalities.

Main Characteristics of Family

Universality: There is no human society in which some form of the family does not appear. Malinowski writes the typical family a group consisting of mother, father and their progeny is found in all communities, savage, barbarians and civilized. The irresistible sex need, the urge for reproduction and the common economic needs have contributed to this universality.

Emotional basis: The family is grounded in emotions and sentiments. It is based on our impulses of mating, procreation, maternal devotion, fraternal love and parental care. It is built upon sentiments of love, affection, sympathy, cooperation and friendship.

Limited size: The family is smaller in size. As a primary group its size is necessarily limited. It is a smallest social unit.

Formative influence: The family welds an environment which surrounds trains and educates the child. It shapes the personality and moulds the character of its members. It emotionally conditions the child.

Nuclear position in the social structure: The family is the nucleus of all other social organizations. The whole social structure is built of family units.

Responsibility of the members: The members of the family has certain responsibilities, duties and obligations. Maclver points out that in times of crisis men may work and fight and die for their country but they toil for their families all their lives.

Social regulation: The family is guarded both by social taboos and by legal regulations. The society takes precaution to safeguard this organization from any possible breakdown.

Types and Forms of the Family

On the basis of marriage: Family has been classified into three major types:

- Polygamous or polygynous family
- Polyandrous family
- Monogamous family.

On the basis of the nature of residence family can be classified into three main forms.

- Family of matrilocal residence
- Family of patrilocal residence
- Family of changing residence.

On the basis of ancestry or descent family can be classified into two main types

- Matrilineal family
- Patrilineal family.

On the basis of size or structure and the depth of generations family can be classified into two main types.

- Nuclear or the single unit family
- Joint family.

On the basis of the nature of relations among the family members the family can be classified into two main types.

- The conjugal family which consists of adult members among there exists sex relationship.
- Consanguine family which consists of members among whom there exists blood relationship-brother and sister, father and son etc.

KINSHIP

Kinship is a relationship between any entities that share a genealogical origin, through either biological, cultural, or historical descent. In anthropology the kinship system includes people related both by descent and marriage, while usage in biology includes descent and mating. Human kinship relations through marriage are commonly called "affinity" in contrast to "descent" (also called "consanguinity"), although the two may overlap in marriages among those of common descent. Family relations as sociocultural genealogy lead back to gods, animals that were in the area or natural phenomena (as in origin stories).

Kinship is one of the most basic principles for organizing individuals into social groups, roles, categories, and genealogy. Family relations can be represented concretely (mother, brother, grandfather) or abstractly after degrees of relationship. A relationship may have relative purchase (e.g., father is one regarding a child), or reflect an absolute (e.g., status difference between a mother and a childless woman). Degrees of relationship are not identical to heirship or legal succession. Many codes of ethics consider the bond of kinship as creating obligations between the related persons stronger than those between strangers, as in Confucian filial piety.

Members of a society may use kinship terms without all being biologically related, a fact already evident in Morgan's the use of the term affinity within his concept of the "system of kinship". The most lasting of Morgan's contributions was his discovery of the difference between descriptive and classificatory kinship, which situates broad kinship classes on the basis of imputing abstract social patterns of relationships having little or no overall relation to genetic closeness but do reflect cognition about kinship, social distinctions as they affect linguistic usages in kinship terminology, and strongly relate, if only by approximation, to patterns of marriage.. The major patterns of kinship systems which Lewis Henry Morgan identified through kinship terminology in his 1871 work *Systems of Consanguinity and Affinity of the Human Family* are:

- Iroquois kinship (also known as "bifurcate merging")
- Crow kinship (an expansion of bifurcate merging)

- Omaha kinship (also an expansion of bifurcate merging)
- Dravidian kinship (the classical type of classificatory kinship, with bifurcate merging but totally distinct from Iroquois). Most Australian Aboriginal kinship is also classificatory.
- Eskimo kinship (also referred to as "lineal kinship")
- Hawaiian kinship (also referred to as the "generational system")
- Sudanese kinship (also referred to as the "descriptive system").

The six types (Crow, Eskimo, Hawaiian, Iroquois, Omaha, Sudanese) that are not fully classificatory (Dravidian, Australian) are those identified by Murdock (1949) prior to Lounsbury's (1964) rediscovery of the linguistic principles of classificatory kin terms.

"Kinship System" as Systemic Pattern

The concept of "system of kinship" tended to dominate anthropological studies of kinship in the early 20th century. Kinship systems as defined in anthropological texts and ethnographies were seen as constituted by patterns of behaviour and attitudes in relation to the differences in terminology, listed above, for referring to relationships as well as for addressing others. Many anthropologists went so far as to see, in these patterns of kinship, strong relations between kinship categories and patterns of marriage, including forms of marriage, restrictions on marriage, and cultural concepts of the boundaries of incest. A great deal of inference was necessarily involved in such constructions as to "systems" of kinship, and attempts to construct systemic patterns and reconstruct kinship evolutionary histories on these bases were largely invalidated in later work. However, Dwight Read, a widely published anthropologist, later argued that the way in which kinship categories are defined by individual researchers are substantially inconsistent. This occurs when working within a systemic cultural model that can be elicited in fieldwork, but also allowing considerable individual variability in details, such as when they are recorded through relative products. For example, the English term uncle carries connotations other than "brother of a parent" depending on the writer.

Conflicting Theories of the Mid 20th Century

In trying to resolve the problems of dubious inferences about kinship "systems", George P. Murdock (1949, Social Structure) compiled kinship data to test a theory about universals in human kinship in the way that terminologies were influenced by the behavioural similarities or social differences among pairs of kin, proceeding on the view that the psychological ordering of kinship systems radiates out from ego and the nuclear family to different forms of extended family. Levi-Strauss (1949, Les Structures Elementaires), on the other hand, also looked for global patterns to kinship, but viewed the "elementary" forms of kinship as lying in the ways that families were connected by marriage in different fundamental forms resembling those of modes of exchange: symmetric and direct, reciprocal delay, or generalized exchange.

Kinship Networks and Social Process

A more flexible view of kinship was formulated in British social anthropology. Among the attempts to break out of universalizing assumptions and theories about kinship, Radcliffe-Brown (1922, The Andaman Islands; 1930, The social organization of Australian tribes) was the first to assert that kinship relations are best thought of as concrete networks of relationships among individuals. He then described these relationships, however, as typified by interlocking interpersonal roles.

Malinowski (1922, Argonauts of the Western Pacific) described patterns of events with concrete individuals as participants stressing the relative stability of institutions and communities, but without insisting on abstract systems or models of kinship. Gluckman (1955, The judicial process among the Barotse of Northern Rhodesia) balanced the emphasis on stability of institutions against processes of change and conflict, inferred through detailed analysis of instances of social interaction to infer rules and assumptions. John Barnes, Victor Turner, and others, affiliated with Gluckman's Manchester school of anthropology, described patterns of actual network relations in communities and fluid situations in urban or migratory context, as with the work of J. Clyde Mitchell (1965, Social Networks in Urban Situations). Yet, all these approaches clung to a view of stable functionalism, with kinship as one of the central stable institutions.

Recognition of Fluidity in Kinship Meanings and Relations

Building on Levi-Strauss's (1949) notions of kinship as caught up with the fluid languages of exchange, Edmund Leach (1961, Pul Eliya) argued that kinship was a flexible idiom that had something of the grammar of a language, both in the uses of terms for kin but also in the fluidities of language, meaning, and networks. His field studies devastated the ideas of structural-functional stability of kinship groups as corporations with charters that lasted long beyond the lifetimes of individuals, which had been the orthodoxy of British Social Anthropology. This sparked debates over whether kinship could be resolved into specific organized sets of rules and components of meaning, or whether kinship meanings were more fluid, symbolic, and independent of grounding in supposedly determinate relations among individuals or groups, such as those of descent or prescriptions for marriage. Work on symbolic kinship by David M. Schneider in his (1984, A Critique of The Study of Kinship) reinforced this view. In response to Schneider's 1984 work on Symbolic Kinship, Janet Carsten re-developed the idea of "relatedness" from her initial ideas, looking at what was socialized and biological, from her studies with the Malays (1995, The substance of kinship and the heat of the hearth; feeding, personhood and relatedness among the Malays in Pulau Langkawi, *American Ethnologist*). She uses the idea of relatedness to move away from a pre-constructed analytic opposition which exists in anthropological thought between the biological and the social. Carsten argued that relatedness should be described in terms of indigenous statements and practices, some of which fall outside what anthropologists have conventionally understood as kinship (Cultures of Relatedness, 2000). This kind of approach – recognizing relatedness in its concrete and variable cultural forms – exemplifies the ways that anthropologists have grappled with the fundamental importance of kinship in human society without imprisoning the fluidity in behaviour, beliefs, and meanings in assumptions about fixed patterns and systems.

BIOLOGICAL RELATIONSHIPS

Ideas about kinship do not necessarily assume any biological relationship between individuals, rather just close associations. Malinowski, in his ethnographic study of sexual behaviour on the Trobriand Islands noted that the Trobrianders did not believe pregnancy to be the result of sexual intercourse between the man and the woman, and they denied that there was any physiological relationship between father and child. Nevertheless, while paternity was unknown in the "full biological sense", for a woman to have a child without having a husband was considered socially undesirable. Fatherhood was therefore recognised as a social role; the woman's husband is the "man whose role and duty it is to take the child in his arms and to help her in nursing and bringing it up"; "Thus, though the natives are ignorant of any physiological need for a male in the constitution of the family, they regard him as indispensable socially".

As social and biological concepts of parenthood are not necessarily coterminous, the terms "pater" and "genitor" have been used in anthropology to distinguish between the man who is socially recognised as father (pater) and the man who is believed to be the physiological parent (genitor); similarly the terms "mater" and "genitrix" have been used to distinguish between the woman socially recognised as mother (mater) and the woman believed to be the physiological parent (genitrix). Such a distinction is useful when the individual who is considered the legal parent of the child is not the individual who is believed to be the child's biological parent. For example, in his ethnography of the Nuer, Evans-Pritchard notes that if a widow, following the death of her husband, chooses to live with a lover outside of her deceased husband's kin group, that lover is only considered genitor of any subsequent children the widow has, and her deceased husband continues to be considered the pater. As a result, the lover has no legal control over the children, who may be taken away from him by the kin of the pater when they choose. The terms "pater" and "genitor" have also been used to help describe the relationship between children and their parents in the context of divorce in Britain. Following the divorce and remarriage of their parents, children find themselves using the term "mother" or "father" in relation to more than one individual, and the pater or mater who is legally responsible for the child's care, and whose family name the child uses, may not be the genitor or genitrix of the child, with whom a separate parent-child relationship may be maintained through arrangements such as visitation rights or joint custody.

It is important to note that the terms "genitor" or "genetrix" do not necessarily imply actual biological relationships based on consanguinity, but rather refer to the socially held belief that the individual is physically related to the child, derived from culturally held ideas about how biology works. So, for example, the Ifugao may believe that an illegitimate child might have more than one physical father, and so nominate more than one genitor. J. A. Barnes therefore argued that it was necessary to make a further distinction between genitor and genitrix (the supposed biological mother and father of the child), and the actual genetic father and mother of the child.

Descent and the Family

Descent, like family systems, is one of the major concepts of anthropology. Cultures worldwide possess a wide range of systems of tracing kinship and descent. Anthropologists break these down into simple concepts about what is thought to be common among many different cultures.

Descent Groups

A descent group is a social group whose members claim common ancestry. A unilineal society is one in which the descent of an individual is reckoned either from the mother's or the father's line of descent. With matrilineal descent individuals belong to their mother's descent group. Matrilineal descent includes the mother's brother, who in some societies may pass along inheritance to the sister's children or succession to a sister's son. With patrilineal descent, individuals belong to their father's descent group. Societies with the Iroquois kinship system, are typically uniliineal, while the Iroquois proper are specifically matrilineal. In a society which reckons descent bilaterally (bilineal), descent is reckoned through both father and mother, without unilineal descent groups. Societies with the Eskimo kinship system, like the Eskimo proper, are typically bilateral. The egocentrid kindred group is also typical of bilateral societies.

Some societies reckon descent patrilineally for some purposes, and matrilineally for others. This arrangement is sometimes called double descent. For instance, certain property and titles may be inherited through the male line, and others through the female line. Societies can also consider descent to be ambilineal (such as Hawaiian kinship) where offspring determine their lineage through the matrilineal line or the patrilineal line.

Lineages, Clans, Phratries, Moieties, and Matrimonial Sides

A lineage is a descent group that can demonstrate their common descent from a known apical ancestor. Unilineal lineages can be matrilineal or patrilineal, depending on whether they are traced through mothers or fathers, respectively. Whether matrilineal or patrilineal descent is considered most significant differs from culture to culture. A clan is a descent group that claims common descent from an apical ancestor (but often cannot demonstrate it, or "stipulated descent"). If a clan's apical ancestor is nonhuman, it is called a totem. Examples of clans are found in the Chechen, Chinese, Irish, Japanese, Polish, Scottish, Tlingit, and Somali societies. In the case of the Polish clan, any notion of common ancestry was lost long ago.

A phratry is a descent group containing at least two clans which have a supposed common ancestor. If a society is divided into exactly two descent groups, each is called a moiety, after the French word for *half*. If the two halves are each obliged to marry out, and into the other, these are called matrimonial moieties. Houseman and White (1998b, bibliography) have discovered numerous societies where kinship network analysis shows that two halves marry one another, similar to a matrimonial moieties, except that the two halves—which they call matrimonial *sides* — are neither named nor descent groups, although the egocentric kinship terms may be consistent with the pattern of sidedness, whereas the sidedness is culturally evident but imperfect.

The word *deme* is used to describe an endogamous local population that does not have unilineal descent. Thus, a deme is a local endogamous community without internal segmentation into clans.

Nuclear Family

The Western model of a nuclear family consists of a couple and its children. The nuclear family is ego-centred and impermanent, while descent groups are permanent (lasting beyond the lifespans of individual constituents) and reckoned according to a single ancestor. Kinship calculation is any systemic method for reckoning kin relations. Kinship terminologies are native taxonomies, not developed by anthropologists. *Beanpole family* is a term used to describe expansions of the number of living generations within a family unit, but each generation has relatively few members in it.

Legal Ramifications

Kinship and descent have a number of legal ramifications, which vary widely between legal and social structures. Next of Kin traditionally and in common usage refers to the person closest related to you by blood, such as a parent or your children. In legal terms, for example in intestacy, it has come to mean the person closest to you, which is generally the spouse if married, followed by the natural children of the deceased.

Whilst someone is alive they may nominate any person close to them to be their next of kin. The next of kin is usually asked for as a contact in case of accident, emergency or sudden death. It does not involve completing any forms or registration in the UK, and may be a friend or career unrelated to you by blood or marriage. Most human groups share a taboo against incest; relatives are forbidden from marriage but the rules tend to vary widely when one moves beyond the nuclear family. At common law, the prohibitions are typically phrased in terms of "degrees of consanguinity."

More importantly, kinship and descent enters the legal system by virtue of intestacy, the laws that at common law determine who inherits the estates of the dead in the absence of a will. In civil law countries, the doctrine of legitime plays a similar role, and makes the lineal descendants of the dead person forced heirs. Rules of kinship and descent have important public aspects, especially under monarchies, where they determine the order of succession, the heir apparent and the heir presumptive. One of the great themes pervading Indian life is social interdependence. People are born into groups—

families, clans, subcastes, castes, and religious communities—and live with a constant sense of being part of and inseparable from these groups. A corollary is the notion that everything a person does properly involves interaction with other people. A person's greatest dread, perhaps, is the possibility of being left alone, without social support, to face the necessary challenges of life. This sense of interdependence is extended into the theological realm: the very shape of a person's life is seen as being greatly influenced by divine beings with whom an ongoing relationship must be maintained.

Social interaction is regarded as being of the highest priority, and social bonds are expected to be long lasting. Even economic activities that might in Western culture involve impersonal interactions are in India deeply imbedded in a social nexus. All social interaction involves constant attention to hierarchy, respect, honour, the feelings of others, rights and obligations, hospitality, and gifts of food, clothing, and other desirable items. Finely tuned rules of etiquette help facilitate each individual's many social relationships.

6

Sati and Change of Hindu Social Customs

DOWRY, SATI AND CHILD MARRIAGE

Dahej or Hunda-Dowry and Bride-Price : Dowry is one of those social practices which no educated Indian would own up with pride, although many of us still adhere to this much deplorable practice. Dowry continues to be given and taken. Even among the educated sections of society, dowry continues to form an essential part the negotiations that take place in an arranged marriage. During the marriage ceremony the articles comprising the dowry are proudly displayed in the wedding hall. Dowry is still very much a status symbol. A number of marriage-negotiations break down if there is no consensus between the bride's and groom's families. Dowry deaths of a newly married bride are still regularly in the news. Although the practice of dowry exists in many countries, it has assumed the proportion of a challenge to the forces of modernity and change only in India. Many reasons are put forward for explaining this practice. It is said that a dowry is meant to help the newly-weds to set up their own home.

That dowry is given as compensation to the groom's parents for the amount they have spent in educating and upbringing their son. These explanations may seem logical in the present day context, but they cannot explain how this practice originated. A search for the origins of dowry would have to move backwards into antiquity. Discussion about dowry has to take into account the less prevalent practice of bride price, which is but a reversal or dowry. Although it may not be possible to ascertain when and where these practices originated, it can be supposed that dowry and bride price are posterior to the institution of monogamy. This is the same as saying that dowry and bride price came into being after the practice of monogamous marriage had become prevalent.

But monogamous marriage is itself a culmination of the human adaptation of animal promiscuity. Man's is the only species practicing monogamy, all other species are promiscuous. Thus it is a logical corollary that Man's institution of monogamy came into being at sometime in the long evolution of his species. The practice of monogamy itself evolved in stages as is evident from historical anecdotes as in the Mahabharata where the five Pandava brothers have one wife.

Promiscuity gave way to Polygamy/polyandry, and after various permutations and combinations, monogamy became the established system. As long as promiscuity existed there was no question of dowry or bride price. The origin of these two practices could be linked up with the discarding of promiscuity in favour of Polygamy and Polyandry. These two forms of marriage are themselves mutual opposites. While in polygamy there is pairing between one male and But the existence of the diametrically opposite practices of dowry and bride price, possibly owe their origin to polygamy and polyandry. The formation of polygamous and polyandrous forms of marriage could have been made necessary by changes in the demographic balance between the sexes. A rise in the number of females as compared to that of males is a congenial situation for the emergence of polygamy. Mere the chances of more than one female member of society being in wedlock with one male member are more. In Absence of polygamy, in a society having a larger number of females as compared to males, many female members would have to deprived of marital life. The obligation to get more than one female member into wedlock with one male member could have been the situation which gave birth to dowry as a price exacted by the male and his family from the female's family.

The origin of bride-price could have taken place in opposite circumstances where the sex ratio favoured females and as there was a large number of males for every female, polyandry and bride-price could have been the result. Along with this generalised hypothesis there were many factors specific to different situations which gave birth to dowry and bride-price. These factors can be identified with more certainty. In India's context, these practices can be seen to be a result of the dialectics of our caste system. The conflict of opposing tendencies of the caste hierarchy, as we know have resulted in endogamy, preventing intermarriage between members of different castes. A reason for the origin of dowry and bride-price can also he seen in the same conflict. Hence discussion on these two practices would have to be intertwined.

Dowry (Dahej/Hunda) as we all know is paid in cash or kind by the bride's family to the groom's family alongwith the giving away of the bride (Kanya-dana). The ritual of Kanya-dana is an essential aspect in Hindu marital rites. Kanya = daughter, dana = gift. The word 'Hunda' appears to be derived from 'Handa' which means a pot. This could be due to the now extinct practice of offering dowry in a pot.

Dowry (Dahej/Hunda) as we all know is paid in cash or kind by the bride's family to the groom's family alongwith the giving away of the bride (Kanya-dana). The ritual of Kanya-dana is an essential aspect in Hindu marital rites: Kanya = daughter, dana = gift. A reason for the origin of dowry could perhaps be that the groom and his family had to take up the 'onerous' responsibility of supporting the bride for the rest of her life.

Bride-price on the other hand involves the receipt of presents, in cash or kind, by the bride's family in return for giving away of the bride. Hence bride-price has the character of an exchange. One feature about dowry and bride-price that is conspicuous is that dowry is prevalent among the higher castes while bride-price exists mainly among the lower castes and tribals (Adivasis). We can only conjecture as to why this curious combination could have come into being. In the caste hierarchy it was the lower castes, the Vaishya's and Shudras who did most of the physical labour and menial work. The various occupational divisions into Jatis exist only among these two castes. The two upper castes, the Brahmins and Kshatriyas had only priestly and martial duties allocated to them and hence no occupational subdivision existed among them.

Thus among the lower castes, the coming of a bride into the family meant an increase in the number of members ~ who could work along with other members and become a source of income for the family. While the family from where the bride came suffered the loss of one earning member. Hence a bride-price was paid to the bride's parents to compensate for this loss. Contrarily, among the higher castes to whom no manual labour was assigned in the caste hierarchy, the reverse logic applied.

A marriage meant an additional member who was to be supported and hence was a burden on the groom's family as the bride did not go out to earn and contribute to the family income. Thus a dowry was collected to provide the additional burden resulting from a bride's entry into the groom's family.

SATI (SELF-IMMOLATION BY A WIDOW)

Sati *i.e.* self-immolation by a widow would normally be looked upon as a negative aspect of culture. When confronted with questions as to why such a practice should have existed, a student of history with misplaced national pride would try to explain away such practices. According to Hindu mythology, Sati the wife of Dakhsha was so overcome at the demise of her husband that she immolated herself on his funeral pyre and burnt herself to ashes. Since then her name 'Sati' has come to be symptomatic of self-immolation by a widow.

Today Sati is illegal, it is also generally looked down upon but it continues to exist in the rural corners of our country. One still does hear of stray incidents of woman being forced to or trying to commit Sati. The country owes the abolition of this deplorable practice to the crusading efforts of Raja Ram Mohan Roy the 18th century social reformer. Hand-prints in a temple symbolizing women who have performed Sati. There are many monumets erected in the middle ages which are dedicated to those women who committed Sati (Jauhar) when their honour was in danger of being violated by Saracenic princelings. These temples are called Sati-Mata mandirs.

The reasons why this practice could have come into being are many. But the principal among them could be identified in the same milieu which gave birth to dowry. Closer examination of this practice of immolation supports this inference. Immolation as a widely prevalent practice can be seen only since the mediaeval period but there are reasons which trace its origins in antiquity.

Even a casual observer will notice that immolation is more prevalent among the higher martial caste. Among the lower castes and aboriginal tribes it is nearly absent. The prevalence of Sati among the higher castes is no co-incidence.

As mentioned earlier, among the higher castes, a bride was looked upon as a burden as she represented a drain On the family's income while not contributing anything towards it. If this was her status as a bride, it is not surprising that if she had the misfortune to become a widow, her presence in the family was dreaded. And apart from being considered an object of ill omen, her presence after her husband demise was a dead weight to her in-laws family. A widow's status as an unwanted burden was also a result of the taboos that prevented a widow from participating in the household work as her touch, her voice, her very appearance was considered unholy, impure and something that was to be shunned and abhorred. Thus without her husband a woman's existence was not tolerated and an extreme but logical outcome of this was immolation.

Other auxiliary reasons also went into making immolation a prevalent practice. The near impossibility of widow remarriage arising from the taboos and prejudices that sanctified virginity of a bride was an important reason. Another reason could be the non-recognition of the individuality of a woman who was considered part and parcel of her husband, without whom she was a nullity.

This attitude of looking at women is visible in the legal literature (Dharmashastra) of antiquity. The Manusmriti considered to be one of the most important legal texts guiding ancient Indian polity has injunctions which reflect this attitude. It says "a woman is undeserving for independence" (Ne stree svatantyam arahathi). Beliefs that a widow, especially a young one would fall into immoral practices for sensual pleasures was also used to stoke the fires of Sati. Strangely enough this logic was never applied to the stronger sex. Widowers were never an under-privileged lot. But the most visible factor that perpetrated Sati was the 'halo of honour' given to it. Especially in the medieavel ages Sati was given the status of an act of honour. This was mainly so among the Rajput martial caste of northern India among whom Sati took the form of a collective suicide after a battle in which male members had suffered death at the enemy's hands.

Sati was even committed by women before their husbands were actually death when their city or town was beseiged by the enemy and faced certain defeat. This form of Sati was more popularly known as Jouhar. The Jouhar committed by Rant Padmini of Chittor when faced by the prospect of dishonour at the hands of a Sultan from Delhi has been immortalised in Indian history.

In those days North India was under foreign subjugation. The most powerful kingdomset up by the invaders was the Sultanate of Delhi. But in Rajputana, the Rajputs had defiantly preserved their writ by resisting the Delhi Sultans. One such Rajput kingdom was at Chittor. In those days of the aribitrary feudal power structure, any feudal lord who took a fancy for any lady would claim her for himself even at the cost of killing her husband if she happened to be married or even by waging a war if she was queen or princess. One such lady of unsurpassable beauty was the Rana of Chittor named Padmini.

Chittor was under the Rule of King Ratnasen, a brave and noble warrior-king. Apart, from being a loving husband and a just ruler, Ratansen was also a patron of the arts. In his court were many talented People one of whom was a musician named Raghav Chetan. But unknown to anybody, Raghav Chetan was also a sorcerer. He used his evil talents to run down his rivals and unfortunately for him was caught red-handed in his dirty act of arousing evil spirits. On hearing this King Ratansen was furious and he banished Raghav Chetan from his kingdom after blackening his face with face and making him ride a donkey. This harsh Punishment earned king Ratansen an uncompromising enemy. Sulking after his humiliation, Raghav Chetan made his way towards Delhi with-the aim of trying to incite the Sultan of Delhi Allah-ud-din Khilji to attack Chittor.

On approaching Delhi, Raghav Chetan settled down in one of the forests nearby Delhi which the Sultan used to frequent for hunting deer. One day on hearing the Sultan's hunt party entering the forest, Raghav-Chetan started playing a melodious tone on his flute. When the alluring notes of Raghav-Chetan flute reached the Sultan's party they were surprised as to who could be playing a flute in such a masterly way in a forlorn forest.

The Sultan despatched his soldiers to fetch the person and when Raghav-Chetan was brought before him, the Sultan Allah-ud-din Khilji asked him to come to his court at Delhi. The cunning Raghav-Chetan asked the king as to why he wants to have a ordinary musician like himself when there were many other beautiful objects to be had. Wondering what Raghav-Chetan meant, Allah-ud-din asked him to clarify. Upon being told of Rani Padmini's beauty, Allah-ud-din's lust was aroused and immediately on returning to his capital he gave orders to his army to march on Chittor.

But to his dismay, on reaching Chittor, Allah-ud-din found the fort to be heavily defended. Desperate to have a look at the legendary beauty of Padmini, he sent word to King Ratansen that he looked upon Padmini as his sister and wanted to meet her. On hearing this, the unsuspecting Ratansen asked Padmini to see the 'brother'. But Padmini was more wordily-wise and she refused to meet the lustful Sultan personally.

But on being persuaded she consented to allow Allah-ud-din to see her only in a mirror. On the word being sent to Allah-ud-din that Padmini would see him he came to the fort with his selected his best warriors who secretly made a careful examination of the fort's defences on their way to the Palace.

On seeing Padmini, in the mirror, the lustful 'brother', Allah-ud-din Khilji decided that he should secure Padmini for himself. While returning to his camp, Allah-ud-din was accompanied for some way by King Ratansen. Taking this opportunity, the wily Sultan treacherously kidnapped Ratansen and took him as a prisoner into his camp and demanded that Padmini come and surrender herself before Allah-ud-din Khilji, if she wanted her husband King Ratansen alive again. On seeing Padmini, the lustful 'brother' decided that he should secure Padmini for himself. While returning to his camp, Allah-ud-din was accompanied for some way by King Ratansen. Taking this opportunity, the wily Sultan treacherously kidnapped

Ratansen and took him as a prisoner into his camp. Allah-ud-din showed his true colours and demanded, that Padmini be given to him and in return Ratnasen was to get his liberty. Word was sent into the palace about the Sultan's demand.

The Rajput generals decided to beast the Sultan at his own game and sent back a word that Padmini would be given to Ala-ud-din the next morning. On the following day at the crack of dawn, one hundred and fifty palaquins (covered cases in which royal ladies were carried in medieval times) left the fort and made their way towards Ala-ud-din's camps The palanquins stopped before the tent where king Ratansen was being held prisoner.. Seeing that the palanquins had come from Chittor; and thinking that they had brought along with them his queen, king Ratansen was mortified. But to his surprise from the palanquins came out, not his queen and her women servants but fully armed soldiers, who quickly freed; Ratansen and galloped away towards Chittor on horses grabbed from Ala-ud-din's stables.

On hearing that his designs had been frustrated, the lustful Sultan was furious and ordered his army to storm Chittor. But hard as they tried the Sultans army could not break into the fort. Then Ala-ud-din decided to lay siege to the fort. The siege was a long drawn one and gradually supplied within the fort were depleted. Finally King Ratnasen gave orders that the Rajputs would open the gates and fight to finish with the besieging troops. On hearing of this decision, Padmini decided that with their menfolk going into the unequal struggle with the Sultan's army in which they were sure to perish, the women of Chittor had either to commit suicides or face dishonour at the hands of the victorious enemy.

The choice was in favour of suicide through Jauhar. A huge pyre was lit and followed by their queen, all the women of Chittor jumped into the flames and deceived the lustful enemy waiting outside. With their womenfolk dead, the men of Chittor had nothing to live for. Their charged out of the fort and fought on furiously with the vastly Powerful array of the Sultan, till all of them perished. After this phyrrhic victory the Sultan's troops entered the fort only to be confronted with ashes and burnt bones of the women whose honour they were going to violate to satisfy their lust.

These women who committed Jawahar had to perish but their memory has been kept alive till today by bards and songs which glorify their act which was right in those days and circumstances. Thus a halo of h our is given to their supreme sacrifice.

But this halo of honour has to be seen in the light of the above compulsions of alien rule in India during the medieval ages. From the 13th century onwards up to the coming of the British, the position of women was insecure due to the arbitrary power structure associated with the feudal society and the rule of the Sultans of Delhi. Although during the reign of the later Mughals the situation had improved relatively, women in the medieaval ages were often exposed to the lust of feudal overlords. Their insecurity increased after the demise of their husbands. This compulsion which was resultant of a particular age was by far the most important reason for the prevalence of Sati during the middle ages.

Although the Mughal emperor Akbar tried to curb this practice, he could not eradicate it completely. As long as circumstances made necessary the existence of such an anomalous and inhuman practice, all efforts to stamp it out were bound to fail. But with the passing of the feudal power structure and entry of the industrial age under the British, the compulsions of the medieaval age which helped the existence of Sati were no longer there. Hence the efforts of Raja Ram Mohan Roy succeeded while those of emperor Akbar could not.

One last reason that needs to be mentioned in this context is that of grief and remorse experienced by a widowed lady. Women as such are more sensitive and emotional than menu This explains in part the readiness of some woman to commit Sati. But it should be borne in mind that the proportion of voluntary Sati was far less and the reasons behind voluntary Sati Though facts were blown out of proportion to justify this practice. However, in conclusion it can be observed that a complexity of factors contributed over different periods to make Sati a prevalent custom.

CHILD-MARRIAGE (BAL VIVAHA)

Child-marriage is another 'blessing' of the medieaval age and it was born from the same compulsions that; perpetuated

Sati. Child-marriage was not prevalent in ancient India. The most popular form of marriage was Swayamvara where grooms assembled at the bride's house and the bride selected her spouse. Svayam-vara can be translated as self selection of one's husband, Svayam = self, Vara = husband. Instances of Swayamvara ceremony are found in our national epics, the Ramayana and Mahabharata. Various types of marriages were prevalent in ancient India Gandharva Vivaha (love marriage), Asura Viviha (marriage by abduction) etc., But among these Bal-Viviha is conspicuous its absence.

There are many reasons to believe that this custom originated in the medieval ages. As mentioned earlier in the turbulent atmosphere of the medieavel ages, law and order was not yet a universal phenomenon and arbitrary powers were concentrated in the hands of a hierarchy led by a despotic monarch. In India the Sultans of Delhi who held the place of the despotic monarch, came from a different type of culture. They were orthodox in their beliefs with a fanatical commitment to their religion and a ruthless method in its propagation. Intolerant as they were to all forms of worship other than their own, they also exercised contempt for members of other faiths.

Women as it is are at the receiving and during any war, arson, plunder, etc. During the reign of the Delhi Sultans these were the order of the day and the worst sufferers were Hindu women. During these dark days were spawned customs like child-marriage and selection of women from the rest of the society, wearing of the Ghungat (veil). This age also perpetuated customs like Sati and looking upon the birth of a female baby as an ill omen, even killing newly born baby girls by drowning them in a tub of milk. Amidst the feeling of insecurity, the presence of young unmarried girls was a potential invitation for disaster.

The predatory Sarasenic feudal lords and princelings of Sarasenic origins who stalked all over India in the middle ages were a source of constant threat. Hence parents would seek to get over with the responsibilities of their daughters by getting them married off before they reached the marriage age. The custom of child marriages with the 'bride' and 'groom' still in their cradles was a culmination of this tendency. This way the danger to a growing girl's virginity was somewhat reduced.

Many marriages during the middle ages were performed in the cradle itself. The predatory Sarasenic feudal lords and princelings of Sarasenic origins who stalked all over India in the middle ages were a source of constant threat. Hence parents would seek to get over with the responsibilities of their daughters by getting them married off before they reached the marriage age. The custom of child marriages with the 'bride' and 'groom' still in their cradles was a culmination of this tendency. This way the danger to a growing girl's virginity was somewhat reduced.

Alongwith this principal reason, there were a few other reasons arising from the nature of the feudal society which were conducive for the prevalence of this practice. In a feudal society, qualities like rivalry, personal honour, hereditary friendship or enmity are rated very highly. Because of this, military alliances play a very important role in preserving or destroying the balance of power between the various kingdoms and fiefdoms. To ensure that the military alliances entered into were observed by both parties, practices like exchanging Juvenile members of the respective families who were educated and brought up at each other's palaces were followed.

They were a sort of captives who were held to ensure that the military alliances between the two kingdoms or clans were honoured. But a more lasting bond that could back up military alliances were-matrimonial alliances between members of the two families. But such matrimonial alliances could be worked out smoothly only if the bride and groom were ready to accept each others Young men and women of marriageable age are bound to be choosy. This difficulty could be avoided when the marriage was between two children or babies where there was no question of their having any sense of choice as to who their partners in life should be.

The caste hierarchy also perhaps had its role to play in perpetuating such a system. Caste which is based on birth and heredity does not allow marriages between members of different castes. But as youngsters whose emotions and passions could be ruled by other considerations might violate this injunction. Out of the necessity to preserve itself, the hereditary caste system could have helped in nourishing the practice of child-marriage.

Among other subsidiary considerations which could have helped to preserve this custom might be the belief that adults (or adolescent) boys and girls would indulge in loose moral practices. This consideration would have-been more relevant in the context of the puritanical and orthodox environment of the bygone ages. The practice could also have been perpetuated, especially among-the economically weaker sections, by the consideration of keeping marriage expenses to a minimum. A child-marriage need not have been as grand an affair as adult marriages.

Note on Sati and Child-marriage

Sati, Child-marriage, Ghunghat, etc. were largely caused by the arbitrary tryannical rule of the Sultans of Delhi. The temperament of these Sultans was a result of socio-cultural reasons. They had imbibed these their tryannical traits alongwith their religion from the Arabs who display traits like fanaticism and short-temperateness in their extreme. The reasons why these traits should exist among those Arabs who originate from the Saudi Arabian Peninsula are to be found in their harsh natural environment.

Saudi Arabia, the birthplace of Islam is devoid of fertile plains and river valleys which are congenial to the development of a settled civilized life. This was responsible for the atrophy of residents of the Arabian peninsula into barbarism, and their exclusion from civilization. The same cannot be said of the people of Mesopotamia, Assyria and Egypt who today consider themselves to be Arabs but were the founders of great riparian civilizations of the ancient world. The absence of a civilized way of life among the Arabs (from the Arabian peninsula) nourished the fanatical attitude which later became a characteristic of Islamic thought and way of life.

This attitude was transmitted to other people who were converted to Islam. Added to this was Islam's monotheistic character because of which Mohammedans regarded all other religions in exclusion from their own. This singularistic and exclusive character of monotheistic Islam precluded any possibility of assimilation into itself of other deities or forms of worship. And whenever it had the support or the force of arms, its fanatical and intolerant nature found brutal expression in the annihilative repression it unleashed whenever it came in contact with another religion or culture.

Such was the cultural lineage of the Sultans of Delhi. It made itself evident in the forcible conversion of peoples of other faiths to Islam at the point of the sword, destruction of places of worship belonging to other faiths, the imposition of Jazia tax on non-muslims and other policies whose objective was to stamp out all other religions and to Islamize the country.

SATI PRACTICE

Sati (practice)

The practice of sati (or suttee) was a funeral custom in which the widow immolated herself alive on her husband's funeral pyre. The term is derived from the original name of a goddess, who immolated herself, unable to bear the humiliation of her (living) husband. The term may also be used to refer to the widow herself. The term sati is now sometimes interpreted as 'chaste woman'.

Origin

Few reliable records exist of the practice before the time of the Gupta empire, approximately 400 AD. While sati is described in the Mahabharata and other works that may be considered at least partly historical accounts, it is known that large parts of these works are relatively late interpolations into an original story. There is an early Greek account of the practice however. This describes an account of an Indian soldier in Persia, whose two wives vied to die on his funeral pyre, in 316 BC.

Voluntary death at funerals has been described in northern India before the Gupta empire. The original practices were called anumarana, and were not common. They were not necessarily practices that would be understood as sati at present, since it was not necessarily a widow who died. Those who died could be anyone, male or female with a personal loyalty to the dead person. They included other relatives of the dead person, servants, followers or friends. Sometimes these deaths were because of vows of loyalty taken in life. Compare with later Japanese seppuku. Widow burning, the practice as understood today, started to become more extensive after about 1200 AD, and the end of the hindu empire. This is sometimes ascribed to the decline of Hinduism in India, the rise of Islam societies. Some accounts claim that this rise in the incidences of sati was in response to the Islamic conquest of South Asia. The women didn't want to be enslaved by the conquerors and chose death over dishonor. At about this time, instances of sati began to be marked by inscribed memorial stones. The earliest of these is in Sagar, Madhya Pradesh, though the largest collections are some centuries later, in Rajasthan. These stones, called devli, or sati-stones, became shrines where the dead woman became an object of reverence and worship. They are most common in western India.

By about the 10th century sati, as understood today, was known across much of the subcontinent. It continued to occur, usually at a low frequency and with regional variations, until the early 19th century. It has continued to occur occasionally to the present day.

Self-immolation

The Practice: The act of sati was always supposed to take place voluntarily, and from the existing accounts, many of them were indeed voluntary. The act may have been expected of widows in some communities. The extent to which any social pressures or expectations should be considered as compulsion has been the matter of much debate in modern times. It is frequently stated that a widow could expect little of life after her husband's death, especially if she was childless. However, there were also instances where the wish of the widow to commit sati was not welcomed by others, and where efforts were made to prevent the death. Traditionally, the funeral of any dead person would usually have taken place within a day of the death. Thus a decision by a widow to die at her husband's funeral would often have to be made quickly. In some cases, such as when the husband died elsewhere, then it was still possible for the widow to die by immolation, but at a later date.

The connection with the original marriage between the widow and the deceased was emphasised. Unlike other mourners, the sati at the funeral was often dressed in marriage robes, or in other finery. Her death may have been seen as a culmination of the marriage. In the preliminaries of the related act of Jauhar, both the husbands and wives have been known to dress in their marriage clothes and re-enact their wedding ritual, before going to their separate deaths.

There are accounts of many different approaches of the widow to her death. The majority have the widow seated or lying down on the funeral pyre beside her dead husband. There are also many descriptions of widows who walked or jumped into the flames after the fire had been lit, and there are descriptions of widows who lit their own funeral pyres after seating themselves on it.

Compulsion: As stated previously, sati is supposed to be a voluntary act. Leaving aside the matter of social pressures, it is likely that some widows were physically forced to their deaths. Sometimes the woman was seated on the unlit pyre and tied or otherwise restrained to keep her from fleeing after the fire was lit. Some accounts say that the woman was drugged. There is one description of men with long poles preventing a widow from fleeing the flames.

Royal Funerals: Royal funerals sometimes have included the deaths of many wives and concubines. A number of examples of these occur in the history of Rajasthan.

Symbolic Sati: There have been accounts of symbolic sati in some Hindu communities. A widow lies down next to her dead husband, and certain parts of both the marriage ceremony and the funeral ceremonies are enacted, but without her death.

Jauhar: The practice of jauhar, only known from Rajasthan, was the collective suicide of a community. It consisted of the mass immolation of women, and sometimes also of the children, the elderly and the sick, at the same time that their fighting men died in battle with muslim kings who were after hindu women. It is detailed in a separate article.

Burials: In some Hindu communities, it is conventional to bury the dead. It has been known for similar widow deaths to occur in these communities, but with the widow being buried alive with the husband, in ceremonies that are otherwise largely as in the immolation.

Prevalence: Records exist of sati across most of the subcontinent. However, there seem to have been major differences historically, in different regions, and among different communities.

Numbers: There are no reliable figures for the numbers who died by sati across the country. A local indication of the numbers is given in the records kept by the Bengal Presidency of the British East India Company. The total figure of known occurrences for the period 1813 to 1828 is 8,135, thus giving an average of about 600 per year. Bentinck, in his 1829 report, states that 420 occurrences took place in one (unspecified) year in the 'Lower Provinces' of Bengal, Bihar and Orissa, and 44 in the 'Upper Provinces' (the upper Gangetic plain). Given a population of over 50 million at the time for the Presidency, this suggests a maximum frequency of immolation among widows of well under 1%.

Communities: It is said by some authorities that the practice was much more common among the higher castes, and among those who considered themselves to be rising in social status. It was little known or unknown in the lowest castes and the tribal groups. According to at least one source, it was very rare for anyone in the later Mughal empire except royal wives to be burnt. However, it has been said elsewhere that it was unusual in higher caste women in the south (quoted from Kamat).

Regional Variations

It was known in Rajasthan from the earliest (6th century) to the present. About half the known sati stones (about 150 in total) in India are in Rajasthan. However, the extent to which individual instances of deaths resulted in veneration (glorification) implies that was not very common. It is known to have occurred in the south from the 9th century through the period of the Vijayanagara empire, up to the 17th century. Madhavacharya, who is probably the best known of those historical figures who justified the practice, was originally a minister of the court of this empire. The practice continued to occur after the collapse of the empire, though apparently at a fairly low frequency. A record exists of a minister of the kingdom of Mysore giving permission for a widow to commit sati in 1805.

In the Upper Gangetic plain, while it occurred, there is no indication that it was especially widespread. The earliest known attempt by a government to stop the practice took place here, that of Muhammad Tughlaq, in the Sultanate of Delhi in the 14th century.

In the Lower Gangetic plain, the practice may have reached a high level fairly late in history. It appears possible, based on available evidence and the existing reports of the occurrences of it, that the greatest incidence of sati in any region and period, in terms of total numbers, occurred in Bengal and Bihar in the late 18th and early 19th centuries. This was during the earlier period of British rule, and before the abolition. The Bengal Presidency kept records from 1813 to 1829. The frequency increased in periods of hardship and famine. Ram Mohan Roy suggested that it was more prevalent in Bengal than in the rest of the subcontinent. An unusually large number of the surviving reports for this period are from Bengal, also suggesting that it was most common there.

In modern times, it has been largely confined to Rajasthan, mostly in or near Shekhawati, with a few instances in the Gangetic plain. The custom of the immolation of a widow (or other close relatives and slaves) was also practiced by the ancient peoples of Scythia, Egypt, Scandinavia and China.

Recent Incidence

Sati still occurs occasionally, mostly in rural areas. About 40 cases have occurred in India since independence in 1947, the majority in the Shekhawati region of Rajasthan. The last clearly documented case was that of Roop Kanwar. However there are claims that other more recent deaths have also been cases of Sati. Roop Kanwar, a childless 19-year old widow, committed Sati in 1988, some allege forcibly, dressed in her red wedding dress, in Rajasthan's Deorala village. Several thousand people were said to have been at the event.

The event quickly turned into a national case of outrage, pitting a modern Indian ideology against a traditional one. A much-publicised investigation led to the arrest of a large number of people from Deorala, said to have been present in the ceremony, or participants in it. Eventually, 11 people were charged. On January 31, 2004, a special court in Jaipur acquitted all of the 11 accused in the case, observing that the prosecution had failed to prove charges that they glorified Sati.

Justifications and Criticisms

Brahmin scholars of the second millennium justified the practice, and gave reasonings as to how the scriptures could be said to justify them. Among them were Vijnanesvara, of the Chalukya court, and later Madhavacharya, theologian and minister of the court of the Vijayanagara empire, according to Shastri, who quotes their reasoning. It was lauded by them as exemplary conduct in pious women, and it was explained that this was considered not to be suicide (suicide was otherwise variously banned or discouraged in the scriptures). It was deemed an act of peerless piety, and was said to purge the couple of all accumulated sin, guarantee their salvation and ensure their reunion in the afterlife.

Law Books

These are relatively late works. Justifications for the practice are given in the Vishnu Smriti. Now the duties of a woman (are)... After the death of her husband, to preserve her chastity, or to ascend the pile after him. (Vishnu Smriti, 25-14). There is justification also in the later work of the Brihaspati Smriti (25-11). Both this and the Vishnu Smriti date from the first millennium AD. The Manu Smriti is often regarded as the culmination of classical Hindu law, and hence its position is important. It does not mention or sanction sati though it does prescribe life-long asceticism for most widows.

Scriptures

Although the legend of the goddess Sati is that of a wife who dies by her own volition on a fire, this is not a case of the practice of sati. The goddess was not widowed, and the legend is quite unconnected with the justifications for the practice. The Puranas have examples of women who commit sati and there are suggestions in them that this was considered desirable or praiseworthy: A wife who dies in the company of her husband shall remain in heaven as many years as there are hairs on his person. (Garuda Purana 1.107.29) According to 2.4.93 she stays with her husband in heaven during the rule of 14 Indras, *i.e.* a kalpa.

It is notable that in the Ramayana, Tara, in her grief at the death of husband Vali, wish to commit sati. Hanuman,

Rama, and the dying Vali dissuade her and she finally does not immolate herself. Examples of the act in the puranas include the following. In the Mahabharata, Madri, the second wife of Pandu, commits sati. She holds herself responsible for the death of her husband, who had been cursed with death if he ever had intercourse. He died while performing the forbidden act with Madri, who blamed herself for not having rejected his advances, although she was well aware of the curse.

The Tantras strictly condemn the practice. It is often claimed that this most ancient text sanctions or prescribes sati. This is based on verse 10.18.7, part of the verses to be used at funerals. Whether they even describe sati or something else entirely, is disputed, The hymn is about funeral by burial, and not by cremation. There are differing translations of the passage. The translation below is one of those said to prescribe it.

Let these women, whose husbands are worthy and are living, enter the house with ghee (applied) as collyrium (to their eyes). Let these wives first step into the pyre, tearless without any affliction and well adorned. The text does not mention widowhood, and other translations differ in their translation of the word here rendered as 'pyre'; for instance as 'house'. In addition, the following verse, which is unambiguously about widows, then contradicts any suggestion of the woman's death; it explicitly states that the widow should return to her house. Rise, come unto the world of life, O woman-come, he is lifeless by whose side thou liest. Wifehood with this thy husband was thy portion, who took thy hand and wooed thee as a lover.

A reason given for the discrepancy in translation and interpretation of verse 10.18.7, is that one consonant in a word that meant house, yomiagre, was deliberately changed by those who wished claim scriptural justification, to a word that meant fire, yomiagne.

Counter-Arguments within Hinduism

No early criticisms of the practice within Hinduism, (or in the other native religions of Buddhism or Jainism), are known before the Gupta period. This is possibly because the practice was little known at that time. Explicit criticisms in the first millennium AD, included that of Medhatithi, a commentator on various theological works. He considered it suicide, which was forbidden by the Vedas. One shall not die before the span of one's life is run out, Another critic was Bana, who wrote during the reign of Harsha. Bana condemned it both as suicide, and as a pointless and futile act. There does not seem to be any thought or suggestion among any of these critics that the act would not be voluntary. Reform and bhakti movements within Hinduism tended to be anti-caste, favoured egalitarian societies, and in line with the tenor of these beliefs, they generally condemned the practice, sometimes explicitly. The Alvars condemned sati, in the 8th century. The Virashaiva movement in the 12th and 13th centuries, also condemned it. In the early 19th century, Ram Mohan Roy wrote and disseminated arguments that the practice was not part of Hinduism, as part of his campaign to ban the practice.

Non-Hindu Views and Criticisms

The Sikh religion explicitly proscribed the practice, by about 1500 AD. The principal foreign early visitors to the subcontinent whose have left records of the practice, are from Western Asia, mostly Muslim, and later on, Europeans. Both groups were fascinated by the practice, and sometimes described it as horrific, but often also as an incomparable act of devotion. Ibn Battuta described an instance, but said that he collapsed or fainted and had to be carried away from the scene. European artists in the eighteenth century produced many images for their own native markets, showing the widows as heroic women, and moral exemplars.

Europeans also showed a change in their attitude to local customs as they became dominant local powers. The earliest Europeans to establish themselves were the Portuguese in Goa. They tried early on to override local customs and practices, including sati, as they attempted to Christianise territories in their control. The British entered India as a trading body, and in the earlier periods of their rule, they were largely indifferent to local practices. A campaign against sati was however set up by the evangelical movement in Britain, particularly by William Wilberforce, as part of a campaign to increase missionary activity in India. The practice of sati, and its later legal abolition by the British (along with the suppression of thuggee) went on to become one of the standard justifications for British rule. British attitudes in their later history in India are usually given in the following much repeated quote, usually ascribed to General Napier. You say that it is your custom to burn widows. Very well. We also have a custom: when men burn a woman alive, we tie a rope around their necks and we hang them. Build your funeral pyre; beside it, my carpenters will build a gallows. You may follow your custom. And then we will follow ours.

Suppression

The first known instance of official attempts to stop the practice were those of the Sultanate of Delhi, under Muhammad Tughlaq. They required formal permits to be issued before the act could take place, from about 1325.

Mughal Period

Humayun issued a royal fiat against sati, which he later withdrew. Akbar required that permission be granted by his officials, and these officials were instructed to delay the woman's decision for as long as possible. The reasoning was that she was less likely to chose to die once the emotions of the moment had passed. In the reign of Shah Jahan, widows with children were not allowed in any circumstances to burn. In other cases governors did not readily give permission, but could be bribed to do so. Later on in the Mughal period, pensions, gifts and rehabilitative help were offered to the potential sati to wean her away from committing the act. Children were strictly forbidden from the practice. The later Moghuls continued to put obstacles in the way but the practice carried on in the areas outside their capitals.

The strongest attempts to control it were made by Aurangzeb. In 1663, he "issued an order that in all lands under Mughal control, never again should the officials allow a woman to be burnt". In spite of such attempts however, the practice continued, especially in conditions of war and upheaval.

British and other European Territories

By the end of the 18th century, the practice had been banned in territories held by some European powers. The Portuguese banned the practice in Goa by about 1515, though it is not believed to have been especially prevalent there. The Dutch and the French had also banned it in Chinsurah and

Pondicherry. The British who by then ruled much of the subcontinent, and the Danes, who held the small territory of Shrirampur, permitted it into the 19th century.

Attempts to limit or ban the practice had been made by individual British officers in the 18th century, but without the backing of the British East India Company. The first formal British ban was in 1798, in the city of Calcutta only. The practice continued in surrounding regions. Toward the end of the 18th century, the evangelical church in Britain, and its members in India, started campaigns against sati. Leaders of these included William Carey and William Wilberforce, and both appeared to be motivated partly by a desire to convert Indians to Christianity. These movements put pressure on the company to ban the act, and the Bengal Presidency started collecting figures on the practice in 1813.

From about 1812, the Bengali reformer Ram Mohan Roy started his own campaign against the practice. He was motivated by the experience of seeing his own sister-in-law commit sati. Among his actions, he visited Calcutta cremation grounds to persuade widows not to so die, formed watch groups to do the same, and wrote and disseminated articles to show that it was not required by scripture.

On 4 December 1829, the practice was formally banned in the Bengal Presidency lands, by the then governor, Lord William Bentinck. It was mainly due to the efforts of Raja Ram Mohan Roy. The ban was challenged in the courts, and the matter went to the Privy Council in London, but was upheld in 1832. Other company territories also banned it shortly after. Although the original ban in Bengal was fairly uncompromising, later in the century British laws include provisions that provided mitigation for murder when "the person whose death is caused, being above the age of 18 years, suffers death or takes the risk of death with his own consent".

Sati remained legal in some princely states for a time after it had been abolished in lands under British control. The last such state to permit it, Jaipur, banned the practice in 1846.

Modern Times

In modern India, following outcries after each instance, there have been various fresh measures passed against the practice, which now effectively make it illegal to be a bystander at an event of sati. The law now makes no distinction between passive observers to the act, and active promoters of the event; all are supposed to be held equally culpable. Other measures include efforts to stop the 'glorification' of the dead women. Glorification includes the erection of shrines to the dead, the encouragement of pilgrimages to the site of the pyre, and the derivation of any income from such sites and pilgrims. Enforcement of these measures is not always consistent however. The enforcement of some measures, such as the possible stopping of worship at ancient shrines, is a matter of modern controversy.

Influences on Art and Culture

A famous fictional depiction of sati is found in Around the World in Eighty Days (1872). The English gentleman Phileas Fogg and his servant Passepartout are travelling India when they find a sati. They risk their lives battling the Indians and rescue the drugged princess Aouda from death.

CENTRAL SATI ACT-AN ANALYSIS

Four months after the Roop Kanwar incident at Deorala, the focus of attention shifted to the need for central legislation to stamp out the oppressive practice of Sati. Two rallies in Delhi, Rajasthan women activists, MP's in the State and at the Centre all called for stringent legislation against Sati. By 1 October, the Rajasthan Legislature had already promulgated an ordinance against Sati which is now a State Act passed by assembly and upheld by the Rajasthan High Court. By the new year, the Commission of Sati (Prevention), Act had passed through both houses with a minimum of debate or amendment.

The particular barbarism of consigning a vibrant life to the flames of a funeral pyre has always provoked the rulers of India to prevent this horror, despite the spurious sanctity that has come to be attached to the practice. Historically, efforts to prevent Sati by formal means were extent even before the Moghul rulers came to power. Under the Delhi Sultanates (circa 1325) permission had to be sought prior to any Sati. In time this check against compulsion became a mere formality. In any case Hindu women from royal families continued to burn unchecked. Humayun tried, but withdrew a royal fiat against Sati. Akbar insisted that no woman could commit Sati without the specific permission of his Kotwals. They were instructed to delay the woman's decision for as long as possible. Pensions, gifts and rehabilitative help was offered to the potential Sati to wean her away from committing the Act. Children were strictly forbidden from the practice. The later Moghuls continued to put obstacles in the way but the practice carried on in the areas outside Agra. In their own sphere of influence the Portuguese, Dutch and French banned Sati but efforts to stamp out Sati were formalised only under Lord William Bentinck after 1829.

British Regulation

The British were by no means certain of their approach to the custom no matter how abhorrent they found it. Following Mughal example, for a while they tried to regulate it by requiring that it be carried out in the presence of their officials and strictly according to custom. Perhaps Bentinck was spurred on to Legislation by the unacceptable rise in Satis in his province, Bengal. In the 10 years between 1815 and 1825, the figure had doubled to 639 deaths by burning. He was certainly egged on by the constant entreaties of the missionaries and encouraged to action by the sea change being wrought amongst an influential section of Hindus led by Raja Ram Mohan Roy's Brahmo Samaj.

Despite this, Bentinck approached the question with caution. He sent circulars to 58 of his administrators to discover whether the army would revolt, whether legislation was advisable and whether Hindu resistance could be contained. The consensus of opinion was that the army would pose no problem. Finally, within 18 months of having assumed the governorship of Bengal, Lord William Bentinck passed the Sati Regulation, XVII of 1827 on 4 December. The regulation was clear, concise and unequivocal in its condemnation of Sati, declaring it illegal and punishable by the criminal courts. It made zamindars, petty land owners, local agents and officers in charge of revenue collection especially accountable for immediate communication to the officers of their nearest police station of any intended sacrifice of the nature described. In case of wilful neglect the responsible officer was liable to a fine of Rs.200 or 6 months in jail for default.

Immediately on receiving intelligence that a sacrifice was to take place, the police daroga accompanied by others was to go to the spot and declare the gathering illegal, prevail upon the crowd to disperse, explain that any persistence was likely to make them all liable to a crime and if necessary prevent the Sati from taking place or go and inform the nearest magistrate of the names and addresses of all those present. If the sacrifice was over, a full and immediate inquiry had to be undertaken in the same way as for any unnatural death.

Most significantly the regulation eschewed any debate about voluntariness which has so much in the forefront of the Sati debate in 1987. Aiding and abetting a sacrifice whether voluntary or not was to deemed culpable homicide. Punishment was at the discretion of the court according to the nature and circumstances of the case. No justification was to be made that the victim desired to sacrificed. The death penalty was specially spelled out for any violence or compulsion or helping or assisting in burning of a widow while she laboured under a state of intoxication or stupefaction or because any other cause impeded her free will. In such cases the court was instructed to show no mercy.

Fundamental Opposition

Even before the regulation was out, some three hundred orthodox Hindus petitioned Lord Bentinck to stop the abolition. They pleaded that the practise of "self immolation", was not merely a sacred duty but a "privilege" of believers. Bentinck however would not relent. The sequence of events that followed are and eerie precursor to the events after Roop Kanwars Sati in 1987. Orthodox Bengali Brahmins formed themselves into the Dharma Sabha, just as today we have the Dharam Raksha Samiti in Rajasthan. In all they collected more than Rs.30,000/-a huge sum in those days, to fight the Regulation all the way upto the highest court. By contrast Raja Ram Mohan Roy was given Rs.5000/-to assist the Government in their representations before the Privy Council in England. Both sides gathered petitions and pamphleteered extensively. In 1832 the appeal was heard by the Privy Council. The petitioners argued that it went against the basic assurance given in George III Statute 37 whereby the Hindus were assured complete noninterference with their religion. The abolitionists argued that there was really no freedom of religion that could go beyond what was "compatible with the paramount claims of humanity and justice." Of 7 privy councillors, three finally voted against Bentinck's regulation but finally it was it was upheld.

With the last hurdle cleared, Madras and then Bombay followed suit with their own legislation banning Sati. Slowly local rulers who came under the yoke of the British also conceded legislation against Sati in conformity with the British regulations. The rulers of Jaipur banned it in 1846.

Indian Penal Code

The 1833 Charter to the East India Company empowered the government to make laws for British India with due respect for native custom and usage. T.B. Macaulay, brilliant academician and lawyer was given the brief of formulating a comprehensive criminal code of universal application through the entire subcontinent. He had no doubt in his mind that Sati was a barbarous practice which could brook no justification. But the administration of 1860 and the Law Commissioners who revised the first draft, were unnecessarily alive to the sensitivities of high caste brahmanical feeling and watered down the murder provisions in their relation to Sati by enacting exception 5 of section 300. Under this, a mitigation was provided for murder when "the person whose death is caused, being above the age of 18 years, suffers death or takes the risk of death with his own consent." Despite this concession under the IPC, taking of life is absolutely prohibited to everyone in every circumstance. But Punishment varies depending on the nature and circumstances of the offense.

If on the facts, the ritualistic public burning or burying alive of a woman is shown to be involuntary, it is murder plain and simple (Section 300 IPC 1860). In the unlikely even that the woman was a willing participant, her death still amounts to culpable homicide (Section 299 or via exception 5 of Section 300) or at the very least to abetment to suicide (Section 306). Even where a Sati is deemed to be a suicide *i.e.* voluntary self-killing, the presence of any intoxicant or anything which in fact inhibits free will makes the abettor as culpable as if he had helped murder the victim (section 305 IPC). The punishment for this is exactly the same as for murder. Where the Sati is incomplete, a person helping to achieve it is caught by the attempt sections of the IPC. Depending again on the circumstances, the crime may be attempt to murder (section 307); attempt to culpable homicide not amounting to murder (Section 308); or abetment to suicide punishable with one year's imprisonment and attempt to commit suicide which is an offence for the woman as well. Under the present IPC no one who abets a Sati should escape the consequences of his acts. Abetment can take the form of instigation, conspiracy to do an act or make an illegal omission, intentional aiding, or wilful misrepresentation or wilful concealment (Section 107). Again depending on the facts, the aider could be abeting murder, culpable homicide. Form all the above it is clear that there are enough and more laws on the statute books to punish those guilty of making any human sacrifice including widow burning.

Fresh Sati Legislation

Despite this, the Central government has passed the Commission of Sati Prevention Act of 1987. Womens groups had been asked for suggestions. Had the Central government taken time to consider and passed judicious amendments to the present laws which are compatible and in consonance with the general jurisprudence of the country, the anomalies that have now arisen would not have come about.

While an entirely new act has the advantage of bringing under one, enactment scattered offenses so as to form a ready code, it also fuels the belief that there was no law against Sati in the first place. A special law again Sati related offenders also has the disadvantage of elevating a run of the mill criminal to the status of a conscientious offender. Specific legislation also provides a rallying point for pro-Sati lobbyists and a ready made cause in the name of religion and identity. Though the High Court at Rajasthan has already upheld the constitutionality of the State legislation which the Central law copies, both acts undoubtedly suffer from all the ills of hastily drafted and ill-considered legislation.

Burden of Proof

The least attractive feature of the new law is Section 16, which reverses the burden of proof on to the accused. Under the philosophy or criminal law adopted in India and used uniformly throughout the Penal Code, each accused is innocent until proven guilty. In every case the prosecution must prove its case positively beyond reasonable doubt. The only argument for shifting the burden of proof sometimes put forward is that the prosecution is so extremely disadvantaged in some circumstances that there would be absolutely minimal chance of catching the culprit. In statutory minimal chance of catching the culprit. In statutory cases where burden of proof is shifted, the offenses are relatively minor and the accused has a generally easy time proving his innocence. In the public, even tamasha atmosphere of a sati, witnesses are available; independent, corroborative evidence is there for the authorities to gather and there is no justification for reversing the burden of proof for a mere abettor to sati when a brutal sadistic or psychotic murderer in any other circumstances has the full protection of the law requiring the prosecution to prove its case in each and every particular.

If the new law had been in the form of an amendment in the homicide sections of the IPC, declaring that henceforth all Satis (or any ritual killings) shall be presumed to be as murder unless otherwise established by the defense, the problem of women killers getting off lightly for merely abetting to suicide would have been solved. The woman herself in this case would have always been the victim. But under the new act a woman who attempts Sati is herself liable to punishment for 6 months jail.

Abetting Sati

Without the principal there can be no abettor so the new act in its muddled way has to treat the woman as an offender in order to catch all those who take part in the commission of a Sati. Justice requires that the punishment fit the crime. The Penal Code while absolutely forbidding all killing carefully differentiates between degrees of moral opprobrium society attaches to a crime. This is reflected in the punishments handed out for different types of killing.

The new Sati Act throws these fine and necessary distinctions to the winds. Section 4 first of all obfuscates the difference between abetment to a crime and the principle offender. It lumps together all sorts into a single section entitled 'Abatement of Sati'. It punishes both the person who actually prevents or obstructs a widow from saving herself from being burnt or buried alive in the same measure as a person who participates "in any procession in connection with the commission of Sati". Yet the degree of guilt is totally varied. In fact the man who intoxicates a woman or prevents her getting out of the fire is not an abettor at all but a murderer and should be treated as such. The bystander may be deemed an abettor and should be punished accordingly.

The does not mean that an abettor to the attempt would go free. Abetment to Sati can cover a wide variety of activities, such as standing around shouting 'sati mata ki jai' and attending a ceremonial killing. The degree of culpability should matter but under the new law the latter person is as liable to the death sentence as the person who actually holds down the widow and prevents her from escaping from the pyre. The bystander at a Sati ceremony is now certainly more disadvantaged than the gruesome murderer or his aide is under the ordinary law. In their case at least the prosecution must prove the case beyond reasonable doubt.

Under the Indian Penal Code what is worrisome is the willingness of the authorities to treat cases of widow burning as suicide rather than murder or culpable homicide, because by its very definition a classic Sati is self immolation. The result is that abettors are let off comparatively lightly and escape the ignominy and moral opprobrium that attaches to these. Of course a great deal depends on the willingness of the police to pursue inquiries and lodge an appropriate FIR. Even in the Roop Kanwar case, one cannot help but feel that but for the hue and cry raised, the matter would not have been taken up and under the murder sections of the IPC.

HINDU SOCIAL ORDER AND THE HUMAN RIGHTS OF DALITS

Combat Law, Issue 4-Social scientists have inquired into whether the religious and societal notions (or ideologies) of behaviour in different societies confirm or come in conflict with the secular and universalistic approach to human rights. They have tried to identify the (religious and social) codes of behaviour that conflicted with or supported the universal rights. Some have considered the UN human rights framework to be the particular expression of secular humanists against which other religious and social traditions are examined and compared.

We will discuss how the Hindu social order (particularly its main pillar, the caste system and untouchability) in its classical form comes in direct conflict with the universal human rights framework. And how the continuation of the practice of caste system and untouchability in modified forms leads to the ubiquitous violations of human rights, particularly of the dalits. Despite the legal provisions, since the caste system and the institution of untouchability continue to govern the social behaviour of high caste Hindus it makes the enforcement of human rights difficult, if not impossible.

The drafting of the Indian Constitution in late 1947-48 coincided with the UN Declaration on Human Rights in 1948. The section of the Constitution on "Fundamental Rights" and the "Directive Principles" emulates the UN Declaration. The provision in the Constitution reads: [It is solemnly resolved] to secure to all citizens Justice: Social, Economic and Political, Liberty of thought, expression, belief, faith and worship. And equality of status and of opportunity, and to promote among them all fraternity, assuring the dignity of individual and unity.

Though the situation has changed gradually, dalit residential settlements are still 'outside the pale'. The Constitution also states that: The state shall not discriminate against any citizen on grounds of religion, race, caste, place and birth or any form. In the Directive Principles it is added that The State shall promote with special care the educational and economic interest of the scheduled castes/tribes and shall protect them from social injustice and all forms of exploitation.

In accordance with these Constitutional provisions a number of measures have been initiated by the government for providing protection to untouchables (Scheduled Castes or SCs). These measures are both protective and developmental. In the 'protective' sphere untouchability was legally abolished and its practice in any form forebidden by the Protection of Civil Rights (Anti-Untouchability) Act of 1955.

Nearly two decades later, protections for SCs were reviewed to make them more stringent and effective in the Bonded Labour (Abolition) Act 1976. In 1989, the Government enacted yet another Act, namely the Scheduled Castes and Tribes (Prevention of Atrocities) Act in order to prevent atrocities against SC/STs. The need for this additional Act was felt because under the circumstances, PCR 1955 and normal provisions of the Indian Penal Code had been found to be inadequate to provide safeguards to SC/ST against several crimes. In the economic, educational and political spheres provisions have been made through the reservation and representation to improve their access and participation. The provision of political reservation in various bodies, reservation in government services, admission to educational institutions and in several other areas are some of the promotional measures under this category. It must be mentioned that discrimination in private sphere-social or economic-is not covered by this legislation.

HUMAN RIGHTS UNDER HINDU SOCIAL ORDER

The Hindu social order, particularly its main pillars: the caste system and untouchability, presents a unique case. As a system of social, economic and religious governance it is founded not on the principle of liberty (or freedom), equality and fraternity-the values which formed the basis of universal human rights-but on the principle of inequality in every sphere of life. In Ambedkar's view, the doctrine of inequality is the core and heart of the Hindu social order. It leaves no difference between legal philosophy (and law) and moral philosophy (morality). (Ambedkar 1987 first published, Deepak Lal, 1988). The three unique features of the caste system need to be understood.

In the social sphere the caste system involves (a) division of people in social groups (castes). The social, religious, cultural and economic rights of members of the castes are predetermined in advance by birth into that caste and are hereditary (b) an unequal distribution of these rights across caste groups (c) provision of a mechanism of social and economic ostracism calculated to ensure rigid adherence to the system and justification of the social system by the philosophy of Hinduism. In the sphere of economic rights, the Hindu social order also lays down a scheme of distribution, namely (a) it fixes the occupations for each caste by birth and its hereditary continuation; (b) unequal distribution of these economic rights related to property, trade, employment, wages, education etc., among the caste groups; and (c) hierarchy of occupation based on social stigma.

These features imply that the Hindu social order is based on three interrelated elements, namely predetermination of social, religious and economic rights of each caste based on birth; the unequal and hierarchical (graded) division of these rights among the castes; and provision of strong social, religious and economic ostracism supported by social and religious ideology to maintain the Hindu social order.

In this framework the concept of "human rights" under the Hindu social system takes on a specific meaning. Unlike other human societies, the Hindu social order in its classical form does not recognize the individual and his distinctiveness as the centre of the social purpose. The unit of the Hindu society is not the individual. Even the family is not regarded as a unit of society except for the purposes of marriages and inheritance (Ambedkar 1987, first published). The primary unit of society is caste. There is no room for individual merit and the consideration of individual justice. Rights that an individual has are not due to him personally; it is due to him because he belongs to a particular caste. Similarly, if an individual suffers from a lack of rights, it is not because he deserves it by his conduct. The disability is imposed upon the caste and as a member of the caste that is his lot.

The other implication is that, the caste system also involves the principle of rank and gradation, in so far as the rights increase in ascending order from untouchable to Brahmin. It is a hierarchically interlinked system. In this framework castes are artfully interlinked with each other in a manner such that the right and privileges of higher castes become the disabilities of the lower castes, particularly the untouchables. In this sense, in Ambedakar's view the caste in a single number cannot exist. Caste can exist only in plural number. There cannot be such a thing as caste as a singular phenomenon. So one has to look at the castes as a system, where each is interlinked with other in unequal measures of social, religious, economic relations and rights. This hierarchically interlinked character of the caste system implies a concept of "human rights" and "humanhood" which is different and unique. In this particular order of hierarchy the Brahmins are not only placed at the top but are considered to be "superior social beings" worthy of special rights and privileges. At the bottom, the untouchables are treated as "sub-human beings or lesser human beings" considered unworthy of many rights. Untouchables are considered as inferior social beings and therefore not entitled to any individual rights i.e., civic, religious, political and economic. In fact, the disabilities are so severe that they are physically and socially isolated and excluded from the rest of the Hindu society. Isolation and exclusion of untouchables is a unique feature of the Hindu social order. Classes or social groups are common to all societies, but as long as the classes or social groups do not practice isolation and exclusiveness they are only non-social in their relations towards one another. "Isolation and exclusiveness" makes them anti-social and inimical to one another. (Ambedkar, first published 1987).

The Evidence: The annual reports of the Commission for Scheduled Caste and Schedule Tribe provide the data on the registered cases of untouchability and atrocities against the Scheduled Castes. That average number of cases registered under Anti Untouchability Act (or Human Right Act) were 480 during the 1950s, 1903 during the 1960s, 3240 during the 1970s, 3875 during the 1980s and 1672 during the first half of the 1990s. During the nine year period between 1981-86 and 1995-97 a total of two lakhs cases of atrocities on the SC were registered, which means on an average three thousand cases of atrocities were committed on them annually.

The break-up of the atrocities for the year 1997 shows 504 cases of murder, 3452 of grievous hurt, 384 of arson, 1002 of rape and 12149 cases of other offences. The data for the period between 1981 and 1997 showed that on an average annually about 508 SC persons were murdered, about 2343 hurt, 847 subjected to arson, 754 became victims of physical violence and about 12,000 were subjected to other offences.

7

Changes of Social Systems in Indian Society

India is justly famous for its complex social systems. Indian society is multifaceted to an extent perhaps unknown in any other of the world's great civilizations. Virtually no generalization made about Indian society is valid for all of the nation's multifarious groups. Comprehending the complexities of Indian social structure has challenged scholars and other observers over many decades.

The ethnic and linguistic diversity of Indian civilization is more like the diversity of an area as variable as Europe than like that of any other single nation-state. Living within the embrace of the Indian nation are vast numbers of different regional, social, and economic groups, each with different cultural practices. Particularly noteworthy are differences between social structures in the north and the south, especially in the realm of kinship systems. Throughout the country, religious differences can be significant, especially between the Hindu majority and the large Muslim minority; and other Indian groups—Buddhists, Christians, Jains, Jews, Parsis, Sikhs, and practitioners of tribal religions—all pride themselves on being unlike members of other faiths.

Access to wealth and power varies considerably, and vast differences in socioeconomic status are evident everywhere. The poor and the wealthy live side by side in urban and rural areas. It is common in city life to see a prosperous, well-fed man or woman chauffeured in a fine car pass gaunt street dwellers huddled beneath burlap shelters along the roadway. In many villages, solid cement houses of landowners rise not far from the flimsy thatched shacks of landless laborers. Even when not so obvious, distinctions of class are found in almost every settlement in India.

Urban-rural differences can be immense. Nearly 74 percent of India's population dwells in villages, with agriculture providing support for most of these rural residents. In villages, mud-plastered walls ornamented with traditional designs, dusty lanes, herds of grazing cattle, and the songs of birds at sunset provide typical settings for the social lives of most Indians. In India's great cities, however, millions of people live amidst cacophony—roaring vehicles, surging crowds, jammed apartment buildings, busy commercial establishments, loudspeakers blaring movie tunes—while breathing the poisons of industrial and automotive pollution.

Gender distinctions are pronounced. The behaviour expected of men and women can be quite different, especially in villages, but also in urban centres. Prescribed ideal gender roles help shape the actions of both sexes as they move between family and the world outside the home.

Crosscutting and pervading all of these differences of region, language, wealth, status, religion, urbanity, and gender is the special feature of Indian society that has received most attention from observers: caste. The people of India belong to thousands of castes and castelike groups—hierarchically ordered, named groups into which members are born. Caste members are expected to marry within the group and follow caste rules pertaining to diet, avoidance of ritual pollution, and many other aspects of life. Given the vast diversity of Indian society, any observation must be tempered with the understanding that it cannot apply to all Indians. Still, certain themes or underlying principles of life are widely accepted in India.

THEMES IN INDIAN SOCIETY

India is a hierarchical society. Within Indian culture, whether in the north or the south, Hindu or Muslim, urban or village, virtually all things, people, and groups of people are ranked according to various essential qualities. If one is attuned to the theme of hierarchy in India, one can discern it everywhere. Although India is a political democracy, in daily life there is little advocacy of or adherence to notions of equality. Castes and castelike groups—those quintessential groups with which almost all Indians are associated—are ranked. Within most villages or towns, everyone knows the relative rankings of each locally represented caste, and people's behaviour toward one another is constantly shaped by this knowledge. Between the extremes of the very high and very low castes, however, there is sometimes disagreement on the exact relative ranking of castes clustered in the middle.

Castes are primarily associated with Hinduism but also exist among other Indian religious groups. Muslims sometimes expressly deny that they have castes—they state that all Muslims are brothers under God—but observation of Muslim life in various parts of India reveals the existence of castelike groups and clear concern with social hierarchy. Among Indian Christians, too, differences in caste are acknowledged and maintained.

Throughout India, individuals are also ranked according to their wealth and power. For example, there are "big men" (*bare admi*, in Hindi) and "little men" (*chhote admi*) everywhere. "Big men" sit confidently on chairs, while "little men" come before them to make requests, either standing or crouching down on their haunches, certainly not presuming to sit beside a man of high status as an equal. Even men of nearly equal status who might share a string cot to sit on take their places carefully—the higher-ranking man at the head of the cot, the lower-ranking man at the foot.

Within families and kinship groupings, there are many distinctions of hierarchy. Men outrank women of the same or similar age, and senior relatives outrank junior relatives. Several other kinship relations involve formal respect. For example, in northern India, a daughter-in-law of a household shows deference to a daughter of a household. Even among young siblings in a household, there is constant acknowledgment of age differences: younger siblings never address an older sibling by name, but rather by respectful terms for elder brother or elder sister. However, an older sibling may address the younger by name. Even in a business or academic setting, where colleagues may not openly espouse traditional observance of caste or class ranking behaviour, they may set up fictive kinship relations, addressing one another by kinship terms reflecting family or village-style hierarchy. For example, a younger colleague might respectfully address an older colleague as *chachaji* (respected father's younger brother), gracefully acknowledging the superior position of the older colleague.

Purity and Pollution

Many status differences in Indian society are expressed in terms of ritual purity and pollution. Notions of purity and pollution are extremely complex and vary greatly among different castes, religious groups, and regions. However, broadly speaking, high status is associated with purity and low status with pollution. Some kinds of purity are inherent, or inborn; for example, gold is purer than copper by its very nature, and, similarly, a member of a high-ranking Brahman, or priestly, caste is born with more inherent purity than a member of a low-ranking Sweeper (Mehtar, in Hindi) caste. Unless the Brahman defiles himself in some extraordinary way, throughout his life he will always be purer than a Sweeper. Other kinds of purity are more transitory—a Brahman who has just taken a bath is more ritually pure than a Brahman who has not bathed for a day. This situation could easily reverse itself temporarily, depending on bath schedules, participation in polluting activities, or contact with temporarily polluting substances.

Purity is associated with ritual cleanliness—daily bathing in flowing water, dressing in properly laundered clothes of approved materials, eating only the foods appropriate for one's caste, refraining from physical contact with people of lower rank, and avoiding involvement with ritually impure substances. The latter include body wastes and excretions, most especially those of another adult person. Contact with the products of death or violence are typically polluting and threatening to ritual purity.

During her menstrual period, a woman is considered polluted and refrains from cooking, worshiping, or touching anyone older than an infant. In much of the south, a woman spends this time "sitting outside," resting in an isolated room or shed. During her period, a Muslim woman does not touch the Quran. At the end of the period, purity is restored with a complete bath. Pollution also attaches to birth, both for the mother and the infant's close kin, and to death, for close relatives of the deceased. Members of the highest priestly castes, the Brahmans, are generally vegetarians (although some Bengali and Maharashtrian Brahmans eat fish) and avoid eating meat, the product of violence and death. High-ranking Warrior castes (Kshatriyas), however, typically consume nonvegetarian diets, considered appropriate for their traditions of valour and physical strength.

A Brahman born of proper Brahman parents retains his inherent purity if he bathes and dresses himself properly, adheres to a vegetarian diet, eats meals prepared only by persons of appropriate rank, and keeps his person away from the bodily exuviae of others (except for necessary contact with the secretions of family infants and small children).

If a Brahman happens to come into bodily contact with a polluting substance, he can remove this pollution by bathing and changing his clothing. However, if he were to eat meat or commit other transgressions of the rigid dietary codes of his particular caste, he would be considered more deeply polluted and would have to undergo various purifying rites and payment of fines imposed by his caste council in order to restore his inherent purity.

In sharp contrast to the purity of a Brahman, a Sweeper born of Sweeper parents is considered to be born inherently polluted. The touch of his body is polluting to those higher on the caste hierarchy than he, and they will shrink from his touch, whether or not he has bathed recently. Sweepers are associated with the traditional occupation of cleaning human feces from latrines and sweeping public lanes of all kinds of dirt. Traditionally, Sweepers remove these polluting materials in baskets carried atop the head and dumped out in a garbage pile at the edge of the village or neighbourhood. The involvement of Sweepers with such filth accords with their low-status position at the bottom of the Hindu caste hierarchy, even as their services allow high-status people, such as Brahmans, to maintain their ritual purity.

Members of the Leatherworker (Chamar) caste are ascribed a very low status consonant with their association with the caste occupation of skinning dead animals and tanning the leather. Butchers (Khatiks, in Hindi), who kill and cut up the bodies of animals, also rank low on the caste hierarchy because of their association with violence and death. However, castes associated with ruling and warfare—and the killing and deaths of human beings—are typically accorded high rank on the caste hierarchy. In these instances, political power and wealth outrank association with violence as the key determinant of caste rank.

Maintenance of purity is associated with the intake of food and drink, not only in terms of the nature of the food itself, but also in terms of who has prepared it or touched it. This requirement is especially true for Hindus, but other religious groups hold to these principles to varying degrees. Generally, a person risks pollution—and lowering his own status—if he accepts beverages or cooked foods from the hands of people of lower caste status than his own. His status will remain intact if he accepts food or beverages from people of higher caste rank. Usually, for an observant Hindu of any but the very lowest castes to accept cooked food from a Muslim or Christian is regarded as highly polluting.

In a clear example of pollution associated with dining, a Brahman who consumed a drink of water and a meal of wheat bread with boiled vegetables from the hands of a Sweeper would immediately become polluted and could expect social rejection by his caste fellows. From that moment, fellow Brahmans following traditional pollution rules would refuse food touched by him and would abstain from the usual social interaction with him. He would not be welcome inside Brahman homes—most especially in the ritually pure kitchens—nor would he or his close relatives be considered eligible marriage partners for other Brahmans. Generally, the acceptance of water and ordinary foods cooked in water from members of lower-ranking castes incurs the greatest pollution. In North India, such foods are known as *kaccha khana*, as contrasted with fine foods cooked in butter or oils, which are known as *pakka khana*. Fine foods can be accepted from members of a few castes slightly lower than one's own. Local hierarchies differ on the specific details of these rules.

Completely raw foods, such as uncooked grains, fresh unpeeled bananas, mangoes, and uncooked vegetables can be accepted by anyone from anyone else, regardless of relative status. Toasted or parched foods, such as roasted peanuts, can also be accepted from anyone without ritual or social repercussions. (Thus, a Brahman may accept gifts of grain from lower-caste patrons for eventual preparation by members of his own caste, or he may purchase and consume roasted peanuts or tangerines from street vendors of unknown caste without worry.)

Water served from an earthen pot may be accepted only from the hands of someone of higher or equal caste ranking, but water served from a brass pot may be accepted even from someone slightly lower on the caste scale. Exceptions to this rule are members of the Waterbearer (Bhoi, in Hindi) caste, who are employed to carry water from wells to the homes of the prosperous and from whose hands members of all castes may drink water without becoming polluted, even though Waterbearers are not ranked high on the caste scale.

These and a great many other traditional rules pertaining to purity and pollution constantly impinge upon interaction between people of different castes and ranks in India. Although to the non-Indian these rules may seem irrational and bizarre, to most of the people of India they are a ubiquitous and accepted part of life. Thinking about and following purity and pollution rules make it necessary for people to be constantly aware of differences in status. With every drink of water, with every meal, and with every contact with another person, people must ratify the social hierarchy of which they are a part and within which their every act is carried out. The fact that expressions of social status are intricately bound up with events that happen to everyone every day—eating, drinking, bathing, touching, talking—and that transgressions of these rules, whether deliberate or accidental, are seen as having immediately polluting effects on the person of the transgressor, means that every ordinary act of human life serves as a constant reminder of the importance of hierarchy in Indian society.

There are many Indians, particularly among the educated urban elite, who do not follow traditional purity and pollution practices. Dining in each others' homes and in restaurants is common among well-educated people of diverse backgrounds, particularly when they belong to the same economic class. For these people, guarding the family's earthen water pot from inadvertent touch by a low-ranking servant is not the concern it is for a more traditional villager. However, even among those people whose words and actions denigrate traditional purity rules, there is often a reluctance to completely abolish consciousness of purity and pollution from their thinking. It is surely rare for a Sweeper, however well-educated, to invite a Brahman to dinner in his home and have his invitation unself-consciously accepted. It is less rare, however, for educated urban colleagues of vastly different caste and religious heritage to enjoy a cup of tea together. Some high-caste liberals pride themselves on being free of "casteism" and seek to accept food from the hands of very low-caste people, or even deliberately set out to marry someone from a significantly lower caste or a different religion. Thus, even as they deny it, these progressives affirm the continuing significance of traditional rules of purity, pollution, and hierarchy in Indian society.

Social Interdependence

One of the great themes pervading Indian life is social interdependence. People are born into groups—families, clans, subcastes, castes, and religious communities—and live with a constant sense of being part of and inseparable from these groups. A corollary is the notion that everything a person does properly involves interaction with other people. A person's greatest dread, perhaps, is the possibility of being left alone, without social support, to face the necessary challenges of life. This sense of interdependence is extended into the theological realm: the very shape of a person's life is seen as being greatly influenced by divine beings with whom an ongoing relationship must be maintained.

Social interaction is regarded as being of the highest priority, and social bonds are expected to be long lasting. Even economic activities that might in Western culture involve impersonal interactions are in India deeply imbedded in a social nexus. All social interaction involves constant attention to hierarchy, respect, honour, the feelings of others, rights and obligations, hospitality, and gifts of food, clothing, and other desirable items. Finely tuned rules of etiquette help facilitate each individual's many social relationships.

Western visitors to India are sometimes startled to find that important government and business officials have left their posts—often for many days at a time—to attend a cousin's wedding or participate in religious activities in a distant part of the country. "He is out of station and will be back in a week or two," the absent official's officemates blandly explain to the frustrated visitor. What is going on is not laziness or hedonistic recreation, but is the official's proper recognition of his need to continually maintain his social ties with relatives, caste fellows, other associates, and God. Without being enmeshed in such ties throughout life, a person cannot hope to maintain long-term efficacy in either economic or social endeavours. Social bonds with relatives must be reinforced at family events or at rites crucial to the religious community. If this is not done, people who could offer vital support in many phases of life would be alienated.

In every activity, there is an assumption that social ties can help a person and that their absence can bring failure. Seldom do people carry out even the simplest task on their own. From birth onward, a child learns that his "fate" has been "written" by divine forces and that his life will be shaped by a plan decided by more powerful beings. When a small child eats, his mother puts the mouthfuls of food into his mouth with her own hand. When a boy climbs a tree to pluck mangoes, another stands below with a basket to receive them. When a girl fetches water from the well in pots on her head, someone at her home helps her unload the pots. When a farmer stacks sheaves of grain onto his bullock cart, he stands atop the cart, catching the sheaves tossed up to him by his son.

A student applying to a college hopes that he has an influential relative or family friend who can put in a good word for him with the director of admissions. At the age of marriage, a young person expects that parents will take care of finding the appropriate bride or groom and arranging all the formalities. At the birth of a child, the new mother is assured that the child's kin will help her attend to the infant's needs. A businessman seeking to arrange a contract relies not only on his own abilities but also on the assistance of well-connected friends and relatives to help finalize the deal. And finally, when facing death, a person is confident that offspring and other relatives will carry out the appropriate funeral rites, including a commemorative feast when, through gifts of clothing and food, continuing social ties are reaffirmed by all in attendance.

FAMILY

Family Ideals

In India, people learn the essential themes of cultural life within the bosom of a family. In most of the country, the basic units of society are the patrilineal family unit and wider kinship groupings. The most widely desired residential unit is the joint family, ideally consisting of three or four patrilineally related generations, all living under one roof, working, eating, worshiping, and cooperating together in mutually beneficial social and economic activities. Patrilineal joint families include men related through the male line, along with their wives and children. Most young women expect to live with their husband's relatives after marriage, but they retain important bonds with their natal families.

Despite the continuous and growing impact of urbanization, secularization, and Westernization, the traditional joint household, both in ideal and in practice, remains the primary social force in the lives of most Indians. Loyalty to family is a deeply held ideal for almost everyone.

Large families tend to be flexible and well-suited to modern Indian life, especially for the 67 percent of Indians who are farmers or agricultural workers or work in related activities. As in most primarily agricultural societies, few individuals can hope to achieve economic security without being part of a cooperating group of kinsmen. The joint family is also common in cities, where kinship ties can be crucial to obtaining scarce jobs or financial assistance. Numerous prominent Indian families, such as the Tatas, Birlas, and Sarabhais, retain joint family arrangements even as they work together to control some of the country's largest financial empires.

The joint family is an ancient Indian institution, but it has undergone some change in the late twentieth century. Although several generations living together is the ideal, actual living arrangements vary widely depending on region, social status, and economic circumstance. Many Indians live in joint families that deviate in various ways from the ideal, and many live in nuclear families—a couple with their unmarried children—as is the most common pattern in the West. However, even where the ideal joint family is seldom found (as, for example, in certain regions and among impoverished agricultural laborers and urban squatters), there are often strong networks of kinship ties through which economic assistance and other benefits are obtained. Not infrequently, clusters of relatives live very near each other, easily available to respond to the give and take of kinship obligations. Even when relatives cannot actually live in close proximity, they typically maintain strong bonds of kinship and attempt to provide each other with economic help, emotional support, and other benefits.

As joint families grow ever larger, they inevitably divide into smaller units, passing through a predictable cycle over time. The breakup of a joint family into smaller units does not necessarily represent the rejection of the joint family ideal. Rather, it is usually a response to a variety of conditions, including the need for some members to move from village to city, or from one city to another to take advantage of employment opportunities. Splitting of the family is often blamed on quarrelling women—typically, the wives of coresident brothers. Although women's disputes may, in fact, lead to family division, men's disagreements do so as well. Despite cultural ideals of brotherly harmony, adult brothers frequently quarrel over land and other matters, leading them to decide to live under separate roofs and divide their property. Frequently, a large joint family divides after the demise of elderly parents, when there is no longer a single authority figure to hold the family factions together. After division, each new residential unit, in its turn, usually becomes joint when sons of the family marry and bring their wives to live in the family home.

Variations in Family Structure

Some family types bear special mention because of their unique qualities. In the sub-Himalayan region of Uttar Pradesh, polygyny is commonly practiced. There, among Hindus, a simple polygynous family is composed of a man, his two wives, and their unmarried children. Various other family types occur there, including the supplemented subpolygynous household—a woman whose husband lives elsewhere (perhaps with his other wife), her children, plus other adult relatives. Polygyny is also practiced in other parts of India by a tiny minority of the population, especially in families in which the first wife has not been able to bear children. Among the Buddhist people of the mountainous Laddakh District of Jammu and Kashmir, who have cultural ties to Tibet, fraternal polyandry is practiced, and a household may include a set of brothers with their common wife or wives. This family type, in which brothers also share land, is almost certainly linked to the extreme scarcity of cultivable land in the Himalayan region, because it discourages fragmentation of holdings.

The peoples of the northeastern hill areas are known for their matriliny, tracing descent and inheritance in the female line rather than the male line. One of the largest of these groups, the Khasis—an ethnic or tribal people in the state of Meghalaya—are divided into matrilineal clans; the youngest daughter receives almost all of the inheritance including the house. A Khasi husband goes to live in his wife's house. Khasis, many of whom have become Christian, have the highest literacy rate in India, and Khasi women maintain notable authority in the family and community.

Perhaps the best known of India's unusual family types is the traditional Nayar *taravad*, or great house. The Nayars are a cluster of castes in Kerala. High-ranking and prosperous, the Nayars maintained matrilineal households in which sisters and brothers and their children were the permanent residents. After an official prepuberty marriage, each woman received a series of visiting husbands in her room in the *taravad* at night. Her children were all legitimate members of the *taravad*. Property, matrilineally inherited, was managed by the eldest brother of the senior woman. This system, the focus of much anthropological interest, has been disintegrating in the twentieth century, and in the 1990s probably fewer than 5 percent of the Nayars live in matrilineal *taravads*. Like the Khasis, Nayar women are known for being well-educated and powerful within the family.

Malabar rite Christians, an ancient community in Kerala, adopted many practices of their powerful Nayar neighbours, including naming their sons for matrilineal forebears. Their kinship system, however, is patrilineal. Kerala Christians have a very high literacy rate, as do most Indian Christian groups.

Large Kinship Groups

In most of Hindu India, people belong not only to coresident family groups but to larger aggregates of kin as well. Subsuming the family is the patrilineage (known in northern and central India as the *khandan*, *kutumb*, or *kul*), a locally based set of males who trace their ancestry to a common progenitor a few generations back, plus their wives and unmarried daughters. Larger than the patrilineage is the clan, commonly known as the *gotra* or *got*, a much larger group of patrilineally related males and their wives and daughters, who often trace common ancestry to a mythological figure. In some regions, particularly among the high-ranking Rajputs of western India, clans are hierarchically ordered. Some people also claim membership in larger, more amorphous groupings known as *vansh* and *sakha*.

Hindu lineages and clans are strictly exogamous—that is, a person may not marry or have a sexual alliance with a member of his own lineage or clan; such an arrangement would be considered incestuous. In North India, rules further prohibit marriage between a person and his mother's lineage members as well. Among some high-ranking castes of the north, exogamy is also extended to the mother's, father's mother's, and mother's mother's clans. In contrast, in South India, marriage to a member of the mother's kin group is often encouraged. Muslims also recognize kinship groupings larger than the family. These include the *khandan*, or patrilineage, and the *azizdar*, or kindred. The *azizdar* group differs slightly for each individual and includes all relatives linked to a person by blood or marriage. Muslims throughout India encourage marriage within the lineage and kindred, and marriages between the children of siblings are common.

Within a village or urban neighbourhood, members of a lineage recognize their kinship in a variety of ways. Mutual assistance in daily work, in emergencies, and in factional struggles is expected. For Hindus, cooperation in specific annual rituals helps define the kin group. For example, in many areas, at the worship of the goddess deemed responsible for the welfare of the lineage, patrilineally related males and their wives join in the rites and consume specially consecrated fried breads or other foods. Unmarried daughters of the lineage are only spectators at the rites and do not share in the special foods.

Upon marriage, a woman becomes a member of her husband's lineage and then participates regularly in the worship of her husband's lineage goddess. Lineage bonds are also evident at life-cycle observances, when kin join together in celebrating births, marriages, and religious initiations. Upon the death of a lineage member, other lineage members observe ritual death pollution rules for a prescribed number of days and carry out appropriate funeral rites and feasts.

For some castes, especially in the north, careful records of lineage ties are kept by a professional genealogist, a member of a caste whose traditional task is maintaining genealogical tomes. These itinerant bards make their rounds from village to village over the course of a year or more, recording births, deaths, and glorious accomplishments of the patrilineal descent group. These genealogical services have been especially crucial among Rajputs, Jats, and similar groups whose lineages own land and where power can depend on fine calculations of pedigree and inheritance rights.

Some important kinship linkages are not traced through men but through women. These linkages involve those related to an individual by blood and marriage through a mother, married sisters, or married daughters, and for a man, through his wife. Anthropologist David Mandelbaum has termed these "feminal kin." Key relationships are those between a brother and sister, parents and daughters, and a person and his or her mother's brother. Through bonds with these close kin, a person has links with several households and lineages in many settlements. Throughout most of India, there are continuous visits—some of which may last for months and include the exchange of gifts at visits, life-cycle rites, and holidays, and many other key interactions between such relatives. These relationships are often characterized by deep affection and willingly offered support.

These ties cut across the countryside, linking each person with kin in villages and towns near and far. Almost everywhere a villager goes—especially in the north, where marriage networks cover wide distances—he can find some kind of relative. Moral support, a place to stay, economic assistance, and political backing are all available through these kinship networks. The multitude of kinship ties is further extended through the device of fictive kinship. Residents of a single village usually use kinship terms for one another, and especially strong ties of fictive kinship can be ceremonially created with fellow religious initiates or fellow pilgrims of one's village or neighbourhood. In the villages and cities of the north, on the festival of Raksha Bandhan (the Tying of the Protective Thread, during which sisters tie sacred threads on their brothers' wrists to symbolize the continuing bond between them), a female may tie a thread on the wrist of an otherwise unrelated male and "make him her brother." Fictive kinship bonds cut across caste and class lines and involve obligations of hospitality, gift-giving, and variable levels of cooperation and assistance.

Neighbours and friends may also create fictive kinship ties by informal agreement. Actually, any strong friendship between otherwise unrelated people is typically imbued with kinship-like qualities. In such friendships, kinship terms are adopted for address, and the give and take of kinship may develop. Such bonds commonly evolve between neighbours in urban apartment buildings, between special friends at school, and between close associates at work. The use of kinship terms enhances affection in the relationship. In Gujarat, personal names usually include the word for "sister" and "brother," so that the use of someone's personal name automatically sounds affectionate and caring.

Family Authority and Harmony

In the Indian household, lines of hierarchy and authority are clearly drawn, shaping structurally and psychologically complex family relationships. Ideals of conduct are aimed at creating and maintaining family harmony. All family members are socialized to accept the authority of those ranked above them in the hierarchy. In general, elders rank above juniors, and among people of similar age, males outrank females. Daughters of a family command the formal respect of their brothers' wives, and the mother of a household is in charge of her daughters-in-law. Among adults in a joint family, a newly arrived daughter-in-law has the least authority. Males learn to command others within the household but expect to accept the direction of senior males. Ideally, even a mature adult man living in his father's household acknowledges his father's authority on both minor and major matters.

Women are especially strongly socialized to accept a position subservient to males, to control their sexual impulses, and to subordinate their personal preferences to the needs of the family and kin group. Reciprocally, those in authority accept responsibility for meeting the needs of others in the family group.

There is tremendous emphasis on the unity of the family grouping, especially as differentiated from persons outside the kinship circle. Internally, efforts are made to deemphasize ties between spouses and between parents and their own children in order to enhance a wider sense of harmony within the entire household. Husbands and wives are discouraged from openly displaying affection for one another, and in strictly traditional households, they may not even properly speak to one another in the presence of anyone else, even their own children. Young parents are inhibited by "shame" from ostentatiously dandling their own young children but are encouraged to play with the children of siblings.

Psychologically, family members feel an intense emotional interdependence with each other and the family as an almost organic unit. Ego boundaries are permeable to others in the family, and any notion of a separate self is often dominated by a sense of what psychoanalyst Alan Roland has termed a more inclusive "familial self." Interpersonal empathy, closeness, loyalty, and interdependency are all crucial to life within the family.

Family resources, particularly land or businesses, have traditionally been controlled by family males, especially in high-status groups. Customarily, according to traditional schools of Hindu law, women did not inherit land or buildings and were thus beholden to their male kin who controlled these vital resources. Under Muslim customary law, women are entitled to inherit real estate and often do so, but their shares have typically been smaller than those of similarly situated males. Under modern law, all Indian women can inherit land.

VEILING AND THE SECLUSION OF WOMEN

A particularly interesting aspect of Indian family life is purdah (from the Hindi *parda*, literally, curtain), or the veiling and seclusion of women. In much of northern and central India, particularly in rural areas, Hindu and Muslim women follow complex rules of veiling the body and avoidance of public appearance, especially in the presence of relatives linked by marriage and before strange men. Purdah practices are inextricably linked to patterns of authority and harmony within the family. Rules of Hindu and Muslim purdah differ in certain key ways, but female modesty and decorum as well as concepts of family honour are essential to the various forms of purdah. In most areas, purdah restrictions are stronger for women of high-status families.

The importance of purdah is not limited to family life; rather, these practices all involve restrictions on female activity and access to power and the control of vital resources in a male-dominated society. Restriction and restraint for women in virtually every aspect of life are the basic essentials of purdah. In India, both males and females are circumscribed in their actions by economic disabilities, hierarchical rules of deference in kinship groups, castes, and the larger society. But for women who observe purdah, there are additional constraints.

For almost all women, modest dress and behaviour are important. Clothing covering most of the body is common; only in tribal groups and among a few castes do women publicly bare their legs or upper bodies. In most of the northern half of India, traditionally dressed women cover the tops of their heads with the end of the sari or scarf (*dupatta*). Generally, females are expected to associate only with kin or companions approved by their families and to remain sexually chaste. Women are not encouraged to roam about on pleasure junkets, but rather travel only for explicit family-sanctioned purposes. In North India, women do relatively little shopping; most shopping is done by men. In contrast to females, males have much more freedom of movement and observe much less body modesty.

For both males and females, free association with the opposite sex is limited, and dating in the Western sense is essentially limited to members of the educated urban elite. In all areas, illicit liaisons do occur. Although the male may escape social repudiation if such liaisons become known, the female may suffer lasting damage to her own reputation and bring dishonor to her family. Further, if a woman is sexually linked with a man of lower caste status, the woman is regarded as being irremediably polluted, "like an earthen pot." A male so sullied can be cleansed of his temporary pollution, "like a brass pot," with a ritual bath.

Such rules of feminine modesty are not considered purdah but merely proper female behaviour. For traditional Hindus of northern and central India, purdah observances begin at marriage, when a woman acquires a husband and in-laws. Although she almost never observes purdah in her natal home or before her natal relatives, a woman does observe purdah in her husband's home and before his relatives. As a young woman, she remains inside her husband's house much of the time (rather than going out into lanes or fields), absents herself or covers her face with her sari in the presence of senior males and females related by marriage, and, when she does leave the house in her marital village, covers her face with her sari.

Through use of the end of the sari as a face veil and deference of manner, a married woman shows respect to her affinal kin who are older than or equal to her husband in age, as well as certain other relatives. She may speak to the women before whom she veils, but she usually does not converse with the men. Exceptions to this are her husband's younger brothers, before whom she may veil her face, but with whom she has a warm joking relationship involving verbal banter.

Initially almost faceless and voiceless in her marital home, a married woman matures and gradually relaxes some of these practices, especially as elder in-laws become senescent or die and she herself assumes senior status. In fact, after some years, a wife may neglect to veil her face in front of her husband when others are present and may even speak to her husband in public.

Such practices help shield women from unwanted male advances and control women's sexuality but also express relations within and between groups of kin. Familial prestige, household harmony, social distance, affinal respect, property ownership, and local political power are all linked to purdah. Restricting women to household endeavours rather than involving them in tasks in fields and markets is associated with prestige and high rank in northern India. There the wealthiest families employ servants to carry water from the well and to work in the fields alongside family males. Mature women of these families may make rare appearances in the fields to bring lunch to the family males working there and sometimes to supervise laborers. Thus elitism is expressed in women's exclusive domesticity, with men providing economic necessities for the family. Only women of poor and low-ranking groups engage in heavy manual labour outside the home, especially for pay. Such women work long hours in the fields, on construction gangs, and at many other tasks, often veiling their faces as they work.

For Muslim women, purdah practices involve less emphasis on veiling from in-laws and more emphasis on protecting women from contact with strangers outside the sphere of kinship. Because Muslims often marry cousins, a woman's in-laws may also be her natal relatives, so veiling her face within the marital home is often inappropriate. Unlike Hindus, Muslim women do not veil from other women as do Hindus. Traditional Muslim women and even unmarried girls, however, often refrain from appearing in public, or if they do go out, they wear an all-covering garment known as a *burka*, with a full face covering. A *burka* protects a woman—and her family—from undue familiarity with unknown outsiders, thus emphasizing the unity of the family vis-à-vis the outside world. Because Muslim women are entitled to a share in the family real estate, controlling their relationships with males outside the family can be crucial to the maintenance of family property and prestige.

In rural communities and in older sections of cities, purdah observances remain vital, although they are gradually diminishing in intensity. Among the educated urban and rural elite, purdah practices are rapidly vanishing and for many have all but disappeared. Chastity and female modesty are still highly valued, but, for the elite, face-veiling and the *burka* are considered unsophisticated. As girls and women become more widely and more highly educated, female employment outside the home is commonplace, even for women of elite families.

LIFE PASSAGES

In India, the ideal stages of life have been most clearly articulated by Hindus. The ancient Hindu ideal rests on childhood, followed by four stages: undergoing religious initiation and becoming a celibate student of religious texts, getting married and becoming a householder, leaving home to become a forest hermit after becoming a grandparent, and becoming a homeless wanderer free of desire for all material things. Although few actually follow this scheme, it serves as a guide for those attempting to live according to valued standards. For Hindus, dharma (a divinely ordained code of proper conduct), karma (the sum of one's deeds in this life and in past lives), and *kismat* (fate) are considered relevant to the course of life. Crucial transitions from one phase of life to another are marked by sometimes elaborate rites of passage.

Children and Childhood

Throughout much of India, a baby's birth is celebrated with rites of welcome and blessing—songs, drums, happy distribution of sweets, auspicious unguents, gifts for infant and mother, preparation of horoscopes, and inscriptions in the genealogist's record books. In general, children are deeply desired and welcomed, their presence regarded as a blessing on the household. Babies are often treated like small deities, pampered and coddled, adorned with makeup and trinkets, and carried about and fed with the finest foods available to the family. Young girls are worshiped as personifications of Hindu goddesses, and little boys are adulated as scions of the clan.

In their children, parents see the future of the lineage and wider kin group, helpers in daily tasks, and providers of security in the parents' old age. These delightful ideals are articulated and enacted over and over again; yet, a coexisting harsher reality emerges from a close examination of events and statistics. Many children lead lives of striking hardship, and many die premature deaths. In general, conditions are significantly worse for girls than for boys.

Birth celebrations for baby daughters are more muted than for sons and are sometimes absent altogether. Although India was once led by a woman prime minister, Indira Gandhi, and Indian women currently hold a wide range of powerful positions in every walk of life, there is a strong cultural bias toward males. Girls are frequently victims of underfeeding, medical neglect, sex-selective abortion, and outright infanticide. According to the 1991 census final population totals, there were

927 females per 1,000 males in India—a figure that has gradually declined from 972 females per 1,000 males in 1901 and from 934 just since 1981. Much of this imbalance is attained through neglecting the nutritional and health needs of female children, and much is also the result of inadequate health care for women of childbearing years. The sex ratio is even more imbalanced in urban areas (894 per 1,000 in 1991) than in rural areas (938 per 1,000 in 1991), partially because a large number of village men go to work in cities, leaving their wives and children behind in their rural homes.

That girls are victims of fatal neglect and murder has been thoroughly discussed in the Indian press and in scholarly investigations. It has been noted that infant girls are killed with potions of opium in Rajasthan and pastes of poisonous oleander in Tamil Nadu—most especially girls preceded by the birth of several sisters. Clinics offering ultrasound and amniocentesis in order to detect and abort female fetuses have become popular in various parts of the country, and many thousands of female fetuses have been so destroyed. In Maharashtra, Rajasthan, and Punjab such selective abortions have been outlawed because of pressure from feminist groups. More usually, girls are simply fed and cared for less well than their brothers.

The sex ratio is particularly unfavorable to females in the central northern section of the country. For example, in Uttar Pradesh there are only eighty-eight females per 100 males; in Haryana, eighty-seven per 100; and in Rajasthan ninety-one per 100. By contrast, in Kerala, on the southwest coast, a region traditionally noted for matriliny, the sex ratio is reversed, with females outnumbering males 104 to 100. In Andhra Pradesh and Tamil Nadu, two large southern states, there are ninety-seven females per 100 males.

Parents favor boys for various reasons. In the north, a boy's value in agricultural endeavours is higher than a girl's, and after marriage a boy continues to live with his parents, ideally supporting them in their old age. Political scientist Philip Oldenburg notes that in some violence-prone regions of the north, having sons may enhance families' capacity to defend themselves and to exercise power. A girl, however, moves away to live with her husband's relatives, and with her goes a dowry.

In the late twentieth century, the values of dowries have been increasing, and, furthermore, groups that never gave dowries in the past are being pressured to do so. Thus, a girl child can represent a significant economic liability to her parents. In rice-growing areas, especially in the south, girls receive better treatment, and there is some evidence that the better treatment is related to the value of women as field workers in wet-rice cultivation. Throughout most of India, for Hindus it is important to have a son conduct funeral rites for his parents; a daughter, as a member of her husband's lineage, has not traditionally been able to do so.

For both boys and girls, infant mortality rates tend to be high, and in the absence of confidence that their infants will live, parents tend to produce numerous offspring in the hope that at least two sons will survive to adulthood. Family planning measures are used to a modest degree in India; perhaps 37.5 percent of couples use contraceptives at least occasionally. Abortion is legal, condoms are advertised on colorful billboards, and government health services offer small bounties for patients undergoing vasectomies and tubal ligations. In some regions, most notably Kerala, better health care and higher infant survival rates are associated with lowered fertility rates.

Most children survive infancy and do not fall victim to the cultural and economic pressures alluded to above. The majority of children grow up as valued members of a family, treasured by their parents and encouraged to participate in appropriate activities. Although relative ages of children are always known and reflected in linguistic and deference behaviour, there is little age-grading in daily life. Children of all ages associate with each other and with adults, unlike the situation in the West, where age-grading is common.

Studies of Indian psychology by Sudhir Kakar, Alan Roland, and others stress that the young Indian child grows up in intimate emotional contact with the mother and other mothering persons. Because conjugal marital relationships are deemphasized in the joint household, a woman looks to her children to satisfy some of her intimacy needs. Her bond to her children, especially her sons but also her daughters, becomes enormously strong and lasting. A child is suckled on demand, sometimes for years, sleeps with a parent or grandparent, is bathed by doting relatives, and is rarely left alone. Massaged with oil, carried about, gently toilet-trained, and gratified with treats, the young child develops an inner core of well-being and a profound sense of expectation of protection from others. Such indulgent and close relationships produce a symbiotic mode of relating to others and effect the development of a person with a deeply held sense of involvement with relatives, so vital to the Indian family situation.

The young child learns early about hierarchy within the family, as he watches affectionate and respectful relationships between seniors and juniors, males and females. A young child is often carried about by an older sibling, and strong and close sibling bonds usually develop. Bickering among siblings is not as common as it is in the West; rather, most siblings learn to think of themselves as part of a family unit that must work together as it meets the challenges of the outside world. Young children are encouraged to participate in the numerous rituals that emphasize family ties. The power of sibling relationships is recognized, for example, when a brother touches his sister's feet, honoring in her the principle of feminine divinity, which, if treated appropriately, can bring him prosperity. In calendrical and life-cycle rituals in both the north and the south, sisters bless their brothers and also symbolically request their protection throughout life.

After about four or five years of indulgence, children typically experience greater demands from family members. In villages, children learn the rudiments of agricultural labour, and young children often help with weeding, harvesting, threshing, and the like. Girls learn domestic chores, and boys are encouraged to take cattle for grazing, learn plowing, and begin to drive bullock carts and ride bicycles. City children also learn household duties, and children of poor families often work as servants in the homes of the prosperous. Some even pick through garbage piles to find shreds of food and fuel.

In some areas, children work as exploited laborers in factories, where they weave carpets for the export market and make matches, glass bangles, and other products. At Sivakasi, in Tamil Nadu, some 45,000 children work in the match, fireworks, and printing industries, comprising perhaps the largest single concentration of child labour in the world. Children reportedly as young as four years old work long hours each day. Education in a school setting is available for most of India's children, and many young people attend school. Officials state that education is "compulsory," but the reality is that a significant percentage of children—especially girls—fail to become literate and instead carry out many other tasks in order to contribute to family income. More than half of India's children between the ages of six and fourteen—82.2 million—are not in school. Instead they participate in the labour force, even as more privileged children study at government and private schools and prepare for more prestigious jobs. Thus children learn early the realities of socioeconomic and urban-rural differentiation and grow up to perpetuate India's hierarchical society.

For many children, especially boys, an important event of young adolescence is religious initiation. Initiation rituals vary among different regions, religious communities, and castes. In the north, girls reach puberty without public notice and in an atmosphere of shyness, whereas in much of the south, puberty celebrations joyously announce to the family and community that a young girl has grown to maturity.

MARRIAGE

In India there is no greater event in a family than a wedding, dramatically evoking every possible social obligation, kinship bond, traditional value, impassioned sentiment, and economic resource. In the arranging and conducting of weddings, the complex permutations of Indian social systems best display themselves.

Marriage is deemed essential for virtually everyone in India. For the individual, marriage is the great watershed in life, marking the transition to adulthood. Generally, this transition, like everything else in India, depends little upon individual volition but instead occurs as a result of the efforts of many people. Even as one is born into a particular family without the exercise of any personal choice, so is one given a spouse without any personal preference involved. Arranging a marriage is a critical responsibility for parents and other relatives of both bride and groom. Marriage alliances entail some redistribution of wealth as well as building and restructuring social realignments, and, of course, result in the biological reproduction of families.

Some parents begin marriage arrangements on the birth of a child, but most wait until later. In the past, the age of marriage was quite young, and in a few small groups, especially in Rajasthan, children under the age of five are still united in marriage. In rural communities, prepuberty marriage for girls traditionally was the rule. In the late twentieth century, the age of marriage is rising in villages, almost to the levels that obtain in cities. Legislation mandating minimum marriage ages has been passed in various forms over the past decades, but such laws have little effect on actual marriage practices.

Essentially, India is divided into two large regions with regard to Hindu kinship and marriage practices, the north and the south. Additionally, various ethnic and tribal groups of the central, mountainous north, and eastern regions follow a variety of other practices. These variations have been extensively described and analyzed by anthropologists, especially Irawati Karve, David G. Mandelbaum, and Clarence Maloney.

Broadly, in the Indo-Aryan-speaking north, a family seeks marriage alliances with people to whom it is not already linked by ties of blood. Marriage arrangements often involve looking far afield. In the Dravidian-speaking south, a family seeks to strengthen existing kin ties through marriage, preferably with blood relatives. Kinship terminology reflects this basic pattern. In the north, every kinship term clearly indicates whether the person referred to is a blood relation or an affinal relation; all blood relatives are forbidden as marriage mates to a person or a person's children. In the south, there is no clear-cut distinction between the family of birth and the family of marriage. Because marriage in the south commonly involves a continuing exchange of daughters among a few families, for the married couple all relatives are ultimately blood kin. Dravidian terminology stresses the principle of relative age: all relatives are arranged according to whether they are older or younger than each other without reference to generation.

On the Indo-Gangetic Plain, marriages are contracted outside the village, sometimes even outside of large groups of villages, with members of the same caste beyond any traceable consanguineal ties. In much of the area, daughters should not be given into villages where daughters of the family or even of the natal village have previously been given. In most of the region, brother-sister exchange marriages (marriages linking a brother and sister of one household with the sister and brother of another) are shunned. The entire emphasis is on casting the marriage net ever-wider, creating new alliances. The residents of a single village may have in-laws in hundreds of other villages. In most of North India, the Hindu bride goes to live with strangers in a home she has never visited. There she is sequestered and veiled, an outsider who must learn to conform to new ways. Her natal family is often geographically distant, and her ties with her consanguineal kin undergo attenuation to varying degrees.

In central India, the basic North Indian pattern prevails, with some modifications. For example, in Madhya Pradesh, village exogamy is preferred, but marriages within a village are not uncommon. Marriages between caste-fellows in neighboring villages are frequent. Brother-sister exchange marriages are sometimes arranged, and daughters are often given in marriage to lineages where other daughters of their lineage or village have previously been wed.

In South India, in sharp contrast, marriages are preferred between cousins (especially cross-cousins, that is, the children of a brother and sister) and even between uncles and nieces (especially a man and his elder sister's daughter). The principle involved is that of return—the family that gives a daughter expects one in return, if not now, then in the next generation. The effect of such marriages is to bind people together in relatively small, tight-knit kin groups. A bride moves to her in-laws' home—the home of her grandmother or aunt—and is often comfortable among these familiar faces. Her husband may well be the cousin she has known all her life that she would marry. Many South Indian marriages are contracted outside of such close kin groups when no suitable mates exist among close relatives, or when other options appear more advantageous. Some sophisticated South Indians, for example, consider cousin marriage and uncle-niece marriage outmoded.

Rules for the remarriage of widows differ from one group to another. Generally, lower-ranking groups allow widow remarriage, particularly if the woman is relatively young, but the highest-ranking castes discourage or forbid such remarriage. The most strict adherents to the nonremarriage of widows are Brahmans. Almost all groups allow widowers to remarry. Many groups encourage a widower to marry his deceased wife's younger sister (but never her older sister).

Among Muslims of both the north and the south, marriage between cousins is encouraged, both cross-cousins (the children of a brother and sister) and parallel cousins (the children of two same-sex siblings). In the north, such cousins grow up calling each other "brother" and "sister", yet they may marry. Even when cousin marriage does not occur, spouses can often trace between them other kinship linkages.

Some tribal people of central India practice an interesting permutation of the southern pattern. Among the Murias of Bastar in southeastern Madhya Pradesh, as described by anthropologist Verrier Elwin, teenagers live together in a dormitory (*ghotul*), sharing life and love with one another for several blissful years. Ultimately, their parents arrange their marriages, usually with cross-cousins, and the delights of teenage romance are replaced with the serious responsibilities of adulthood. In his survey of some 2,000 marriages, Elwin found only seventy-seven cases of *ghotul* partners eloping together and very few cases of divorce. Among the Muria and Gond tribal groups, cross-cousin marriage is called "bringing back the milk," alluding to the gift of a girl in one generation being returned by the gift of a girl in the next.

Finding the perfect partner for one's child can be a challenging task. People use their social networks to locate potential brides and grooms of appropriate social and economic status. Increasingly, urban dwellers use classified matrimonial advertisements in newspapers. The advertisements usually announce religion, caste, and educational qualifications, stress female beauty and male (and in the contemporary era, sometimes female) earning capacity, and may hint at dowry size.

In rural areas, matches between strangers are usually arranged without the couple meeting each other. Rather, parents and other relatives come to an agreement on behalf of the couple. In cities, however, especially among the educated classes, photographs are exchanged, and sometimes the couple are allowed to meet under heavily chaperoned circumstances, such as going out for tea with a group of people or meeting in the parlor of the girl's home, with her relatives standing by. Young professional men and their families may receive inquiries and photographs from representatives of several girls' families.

They may send their relatives to meet the most promising candidates and then go on tour themselves to meet the young women and make a final choice. In the early 1990s, increasing numbers of marriages arranged in this way link brides and grooms from India with spouses of Indian parentage resident in Europe, North America, and the Middle East.

Almost all Indian children are raised with the expectation that their parents will arrange their marriages, but an increasing number of young people, especially among the college-educated, are finding their own spouses. So-called love marriages are deemed a slightly scandalous alternative to properly arranged marriages. Some young people convince their parents to "arrange" their marriages to people with whom they have fallen in love. This process has long been possible for Indians from the south and for Muslims who want to marry a particular cousin of the appropriate marriageable category.

In the upper classes, these semi-arranged love marriages increasingly occur between young people who are from castes of slightly different rank but who are educationally or professionally equal. If there are vast differences to overcome, such as is the case with love marriages between Hindus and Muslims or between Hindus of very different caste status, parents are usually much less agreeable, and serious family disruptions can result.

In much of India, especially in the north, a marriage establishes a structural opposition between the kin groups of the bride and groom—bride-givers and bride-takers. Within this relationship, bride-givers are considered inferior to bride-takers and are forever expected to give gifts to the bride-takers. The one-way flow of gifts begins at engagement and continues for a generation or two. The most dramatic aspect of this asymmetrical relationship is the giving of dowry. In many communities throughout India, a dowry has traditionally been given by a bride's kin at the time of her marriage. In ancient times, the dowry was considered a woman's wealth—property due a beloved daughter who had no claim on her natal family's real estate—and typically included portable valuables such as jewelry and household goods that a bride could control throughout her life. However, over time, the larger proportion of the dowry has come to consist of goods and cash payments that go straight into the hands of the groom's family. In the late twentieth century, throughout much of India, dowry payments have escalated, and a groom's parents sometimes insist on compensation for their son's higher education and even for his future earnings, to which the bride will presumably have access. Some of the dowries demanded are quite oppressive, amounting to several years' salary in cash as well as items such as motorcycles, air conditioners, and fancy cars. Among some lower-status groups, large dowries are currently replacing traditional bride-price payments. Even among Muslims, previously not given to demanding large dowries, reports of exorbitant dowries are increasing.

The dowry is becoming an increasingly onerous burden for the bride's family. Antidowry laws exist but are largely ignored, and a bride's treatment in her marital home is often affected by the value of her dowry. Increasingly frequent are horrible incidents, particularly in urban areas, where a groom's family makes excessive demands on the bride's family—even after marriage—and when the demands are not met, murder the bride, typically by setting her clothes on fire in a cooking "accident." The groom is then free to remarry and collect another sumptuous dowry. The male and female in-laws implicated in these murders have seldom been punished. Such dowry deaths have been the subject of numerous media reports in India and other countries and have mobilized feminist groups to action. In some of the worst areas, such as the National Capital Territory of Delhi, where hundreds of such deaths are reported annually and the numbers are increasing yearly, the law now requires that all suspicious deaths of new brides be investigated. Official government figures report 1,786 registered dowry deaths nationwide in 1987; there is also an estimate of some 5,000 dowry deaths in 1991. Women's groups sometimes picket the homes of the in-laws of burned brides. Some analysts have related the growth of this phenomenon to the growth of consumerism in Indian society.

Fears of impoverishing their parents have led some urban middle-class young women, married and unmarried, to commit suicide. However, through the giving of large dowries, the newly wealthy are often able to marry their treasured daughters up the status hierarchy so reified in Indian society.

After marriage arrangements are completed, a rich panoply of wedding rituals begins. Each religious group, region, and caste has a slightly different set of rites. Generally, all weddings involve as many kin and associates of the bride and groom as possible. The bride's family usually hosts most of the ceremonies and pays for all the arrangements for large numbers of guests for several days, including accommodation, feasting, decorations, and gifts for the groom's party. These arrangements are often extremely elaborate and expensive and are intended to enhance the status of the bride's family. The groom's party usually hires a band and brings fine gifts for the bride, such as jewelry and clothing, but these are typically far outweighed in value by the presents received from the bride's side.

After the bride and groom are united in sacred rites attended by colorful ceremony, the new bride may be carried away to her in-laws' home, or, if she is very young, she may remain with her parents until they deem her old enough to depart. A prepubescent bride usually stays in her natal home until puberty, after which a separate consummation ceremony is held to mark her departure for her conjugal home and married life. The poignancy of the bride's weeping departure for her new home is prominent in personal memory, folklore, literature, song, and drama throughout India.

ADULTHOOD

In their new status, a young married couple begin to accept adult responsibilities. These include work inside and outside of the home, childbearing and child-rearing, developing and maintaining social relationships, fulfilling religious obligations, and enhancing family prosperity and prestige as much as possible. The young husband usually remains resident with his natal family, surrounded by well-known relatives and neighbours. The young bride, however, is typically thrust into a strange household, where she is expected to follow ideal patterns of chaste and cheerfully obedient behaviour.

Ideally, the Hindu wife should honour her husband as if he were her personal god. Through her marriage, a woman becomes an auspicious wife (*suhagan*), adorned with bangles and amulets designed to protect her husband's life and imbued with ritual powers to influence prosperity and procreation. At her wedding, the Hindu bride is likened to Lakshmi, the Goddess of Wealth, in symbolic recognition of the fact that the groom's patrilineage can increase and prosper only through her fertility and labours. Despite this simile, elegantly stated in the nuptial ritual, the young wife is pressed into service as the most subordinate member of her husband's family. If any misfortunes happen to befall her affinal family after her arrival, she may be blamed as the bearer of bad luck. Not surprisingly, some young women find adjusting to these new circumstances extremely upsetting. A small percentage experience psychological distress so severe that they seem to be possessed by outspoken ghosts and spirits.

In these difficult early days of a marriage, and later on throughout her life, a woman looks to her natal kin for moral and often economic support. Although she has become part of another household and lineage, she depends on her natal relatives—especially her brothers—to back her up in a variety of circumstances. A wide range of long visits home, ritual obligations, gifts, folklore, and songs reflect the significance of a woman's lifelong ties to her blood relatives.

By producing children, especially highly valued sons, and, ultimately, becoming a mother-in-law herself, a woman gradually improves her position within the conjugal household. In motherhood the married woman finds social approval, economic security, and emotional satisfaction.

A man and his wife owe respect and obedience to his parents and other senior relatives. Ideally, all cooperate in the joint family enterprise. Gradually, as the years pass, members of the younger generation take the place of the older generation and become figures of authority and respect. As this transition occurs, it is generally assumed that younger family members will physically care for and support elders until their demise.

In their adult years, men and women engage in a wide variety of tasks and occupations strongly linked to socioeconomic status, including caste membership, wealth, place of residence, and many other factors. In general, the higher the status of a family, the less likely its members are to engage in manual labour and the more likely its members are to be served by employees of lower status. Although educated women are increasingly working outside the home, even in urbane circles some negative stigma is still attached to women's employment. In addition, students from high-status families do not work at temporary menial jobs as they do in many Western countries.

People of low status work at the many menial tasks that high-status people disdain. Poor women cannot afford to abstain from paid labour, and they work alongside their menfolk in the fields and at construction projects. In low-status families, women are less likely than high-status women to unquestioningly accept the authority of men and even of elders because they are directly responsible for providing income for the family. Among Sweepers, very low-status latrine cleaners, women carry out more of the traditional tasks than do men and hold a relatively less subordinate position in their families than do women of traditional high-status families. Such women are, nonetheless, less powerful in the society at large than are women of economically prosperous high-status families, who control and influence the control of more assets than do poor women. Along with economically supporting themselves, their elders, and their children, adults must maintain and add to the elaborate social networks upon which life depends. Offering gracious hospitality to guests is a key ingredient of proper adult behaviour. Adults must also attend to religious matters, carrying out rites intended to protect their families and communities. In these efforts, men and women constantly work for the benefit of their kin groups, castes, and other social units.

DEATH AND BEYOND

The death of an infant or young child—a common event in India—causes sorrow but usually not major social disruption. The death of a married adult has wider repercussions. Among Hindus, the demise of a lineage member immediately ritually pollutes the entire lineage for a period of several days. As part of the mourning process, closely related male mourners have their heads and facial hair shaved, thus publicly declaring their close links to the deceased. Various funeral rites, feasts, and mourning practices affirm kinship ties with the deceased and among survivors. Crucial social bonds become visible to all concerned. Although a man may grieve for his deceased wife, a widow may face not only a personal loss but a major restructuring of her life. Becoming a widow in India is not a benign or neutral event. A man's death, particularly if it occurs when he is young, may be attributed to ill fortune brought upon him by his wife, possibly because of her sins in a past life.

With the death of her husband, a woman's auspicious wifehood ends, and she is plunged into dreaded widowhood. The very word *widow* is used as an epithet. As a widow, a woman is devoid of reason to adorn herself. If she follows tradition, she may shave her head, shed her jewelry, and wear only plain white or dark clothing. Widows of low-ranking groups have always been allowed to remarry, but widows of high rank have been expected to remain unmarried and chaste until death. In earlier times, for child brides married to older men and widowed young, these strictures caused great hardship and inspired reform movements in some parts of the country.

In past centuries, the ultimate rejection of widowhood occurred in the burning of the Hindu widow on her husband's funeral pyre, a practice known as sati (meaning, literally, true or virtuous one). Women who so perished in the funeral flames were posthumously adulated, and even in the late twentieth century are worshiped at memorial tablets and temples erected in their honour. In western India, Rajput lineages proudly point to satis in their history. Sati was never widespread, and it has been illegal since 1829, but a few cases of sati still occur in India every year. In choosing to die with her husband, a woman evinces great merit and power and is considered able to bring boons to her husband's patrilineage and to others who honour her. Thus, through her meritorious death, a widow avoids disdain and achieves glory, not only for herself, but for all of her kin as well.

By restricting widow remarriage, high-status groups limit restructuring of the lineage on the death of a male member. An unmarried widow remains a member of her husband's lineage, with no competing ties to other groups of in-laws. Her rights to her husband's property, traditionally limited though they are to management rather than outright inheritance, remain uncomplicated by remarriage to a man from another lineage. It is among lower-ranking groups with lesser amounts of property and prestige that widow remarriage is most frequent.

Most Indians see their present lifetimes as but a prelude to an afterlife, the quality of which depends on their behaviour in this life. Muslims envision heaven and hell, but Hindus conceptualize a series of rebirths ideally culminating in union with the divine. Some Hindus believe they are destined to marry the same person in each of their lifetimes. Thus people feel connected with different permutations of themselves and others over cosmic cycles of time.

8

Changes of Vedas System in Indian Religion

The final *Veda*, the *Atharva-Veda*, is attributed to a sage, or *rishi*, named Atharvan, and consists of a number of hymns and magical incantations. Some scholars believe that this scripture may have originated with the original pre-Aryan culture of indigenous peoples, and because it deviated form the other *Vedas*, it was not at first readily accepted. Eventually it too was adopted as a ritual handbook by the Brahmans, the higest class of priests. Although the *Rig-Veda* is still considered the most important of these ancient texts, it was still never very popular. Much of this comes from the fact of its composition by and for a religious aristocracy.

In contrast, the *Atharva-Veda*, compiled perhaps as late as 500 BC, frequently refers to many lesser functional gods considered useful in the daily lives and simple rituals of the ordinary Aryan that did not need the mediation of priests. What little we know of the Vedic Age comes from the *Rig-Veda*. By the time the oral tradition of the Aryan religion was comitted to Sanskrit, however, some of the gods mentioned had already begun to lose their importance. Nevertheless, The *Rig-Veda* represented a blend of beliefs held by several Aryan tribes. Each of the gods, of the Vedic Period, had a primary function, or *Vrata*. Usually these functions were closely connected to the forces of nature such as light, fire, and heaven which in turn followed the cosmic order (*rta*) of the universe. The demons of darkness and chaos, headquartered under the earth, arrayed their power against the righteousness of the gods. In this dualistic approach, the demons sought to disrupt the system of nature, therefore practicing *anrta*. During a later period, *rta* gave way to the concept of *dharma*, which could be translated as "virtue."

Although the deities of the *Rig-Veda* are not organized hierarchically, each could, in its own right, be looked upon as the supreme god. Nevertheless, Indra, the god of war and weather, receives the most attention in the ancient Vedic text, and is frequently referred to as the *eka deva*, or "one god." According to the *Rig-Veda* (6.7), creation began once Indra slew Vritra, the serpent demon, who had locked up the waters necessary for human existence in mountain caves. With the waters now released, he then placed the sun in the sky thus establishing the cosmic order (*rta*) under the god Varuna. Varuna, then, sits in the palace of heaven and oversees the world below. As the guardian of the moral order, both earthly and cosmic, Varuna punishes the sinner with disease, or for all time by condemning them to the House of Clay following death. Aryans who practiced right deeds, or performed the proper ritual would forever celebrate happiness after death. Varuna is aided in his efforts by many spies who fly through the cosmos at his command.

Less important than Indra, but still held in high regard among the numerous deities of the Aryan religion, was Agni, the fire god. Agni descends from the darkened clouds as lightning, shines on the world as the sun, and manifests in the flame of the sacrifice. Through the sacrificial offering, Agni served as the intermediary between the gods and man, and the correct performance of this important ritual could beneficially reward the devotee. Rituals based on the fire sacrifice could be as personal as dumping clarified butter in the family hearth, to the production of soma juice. As part of the sacrificial ritual, parts of the soma plant were pressed between stones, mixed with milk, and filtered through a sheepskin. An hallucinogen, soma consumed during sacrifices supposedly produced a sense of superhuman strength and visions of the gods. Soma would later become the moon god.

The cosmic order of the Aryan universe remained fairly simple. The heavens served as the residence of the major gods and the souls of the righteous. The region between heaven and earth was called the *antariksa*. This region, where the birds flew and the clouds crossed the sky, was also home to the demigods. Below the earth, in the darkness of the House of Clay, dwelled the spirits of the unrighteousness and the demons that sought to disrupt *rta*. The concept of birth and rebirth had not yet become part of the Indian cosmology that would later be indicative of all Indian religion.

Religion during the Vedic Age revolved around the sacrifice. Within the home, the patriarch of the family daily sacrificed at the domestic hearth while the brahmans performed great rituals slaughtering numerous animals to the gods. In each case, the idea was to communicate with the gods who would descend from the heavens granting the devotees health, happiness, and success. Over time, these rituals became so complex that the brahmans, who knew the correct ritual, became indispensable. Between 800 and 400 BC, significant changes began to occur in the lives of religious peoples in all of the civilized parts of the world. Independent thinkers, discontented with the traditional explanations of the cosmic order, and specifically man's place within that cosmos, began to develop new, more simple and rational, doctrines. Scholars frequently refer to this period as the Axial Age. There is, however, no solid explanation why such dramatic religious changes would occur throughout the world during the same period.

Prominent among the rising sages were the Greek philosophers led by Socrates. In Persia, Zarathustra extracted the elements of the supernatural from religion and created a new faith, Zoroastrianism. In China, Confucius devoted himself to teaching moral persuasion and good government, which would become the mainstay of Chinese thought. The Hebrew prophets formulated a monotheistic religious tradition notably different from the polytheistic religions of Greece, China, Mesopotamia, and India. While all of this was happening in the rest of the world, *kshatriya* ascetics, throughout India, began to challenge the proliferation of brahmin ritual that personified the Aryan religion of the Vedic Age.

During this time, the Vedas were still held in high regard, but this new generation of seekers sought a more enlightened meaning to life. This period is commonly referred to as the Vedantic Age. The collection of teachings generated by the ascetics who meditated on the mysteries of human existence became known as the *Upanishads*, and the seekers who produced the writings were called Upanishads, which literally means "sitting near" the gurus. Over a hundred *Upanishads* have survived, but only a dozen, or so, are considered authentic. To lend credibility to the teachings, they were invariably compiled as appendages to the Vedas. Vedanta, then, means the "end of the Vedas." In this respect, the Vedas are considered the foundation of the faith while the *Upanishads* are considered the vehicle whereby the devotee may attain enlightenment as to the nature of god and man's role in the cosmos.

Scholars continue to debate over the beginning of Hinduism. Some insists that this tradition began with the Indus civilization and its proto-Shiva personified by the horned god. Others point to the development of the Aryan religion of the Vedic Age as the genesis of the Hindu tradition. Still others point to the Vedantic Age, with the development of *karma* (deed), and the doctrine of *samsara* or the transmigration of birth and rebirth, as the fundamental beginning. Unfortunately, unlike many other religions, Hinduism can not be attributed to the teachings of any single individual. This sort of ambiguity naturally lends itself to debate and speculation. Although we are unable to accurately date the beginning of Hinduism, we can point to the Vedantic Age as the period in Indian history where the Hindu religious tradition began to solidify. The principles of *karma* and *samsara* directly appealed to a populace caught in the stranglehold of the rigidity of the caste system. In this respect, one's deeds in the present life would directly effect their future as the soul passes form life to life.

Interestingly, the *Upanishads*, nor the thinkers reponsible for the new orthodoxy of the Hindu religion, ever directly challenged the Vedic beliefs, the existing gods, or the practice of sacrifice. Instead, a quiet transformation gradually occurred that formulated a new system of thought that became the cornerstone of Hinduism. Increasingly, the common people directed their faith toward lesser deities that filled their specific needs. Rising to the top of the nonexistent hierarchy of the gods, the religious practices, although still based in the Vedic scripture, decidedly shifted from Indra and Varuna to the two current sects of Hinduism which worship Vishnu and Shiva.

During the Axial Age, enlightened thinkers, throughout the known world, were developing new explanations of existence, and man's place within the order of the universe. In India, the Upanishads redefined the Aryan religious tradition. Led by ksatriya ascetics, this new development rebelled against the ritual superiority of the brahman class proliferated during the Vedic period. This movement gradually led to an integral transformation of Hindu thought. But, while these new thinkers quietly transmuted the Aryan belief system, two other luminaries, not only challenged the ritualism of the former tradition, but openly rejected the rigidity of class distinction, forming new religions.

Similar to the seekers, who reformed Hinduistic thought, the individuals responsible for the growth of these new religions came from the *ksatryia* caste that sought a release from the brahman's domination of ritual. Also significant, in this quest for change, were the members of the *vaishya* caste. With the collapse of tribalism, India experienced great material and economic growth from which this class, which included an increasing number of merchants, craftsmen, and professional, benefited. Many of the *vaishya*, therefore, resented the privileges afforded the upper two castes, which invariably prepared them for religious ferment.

Most prominent of the two individuals seeking answers to the orthodox Vedism, and the injustice of the caste system was Siddhartha Gautama(c. 563 BC-483 BC) who founded the religion known as Buddhism. Although this tradition significantly diminished in the land of its birth, it remained a powerful force in the rest of the world. Central to Buddhist thought are the Four Noble Truths: that all life is suffering (*dukkha*); the cause of suffering is desire; escape from *dukkha* can be attained by ending desire; the path to the cessation of desire can be achieved through the Noble Eight-Fold Path comprised by right views, motives, speech, conduct, livelihood, effort, thought and meditation. Although Buddhism became more important because of its spread outside of India, Jainism, at least within the confines of the subcontinent, gathered equal support. Western scholars frequently list Vardhamana Mahavira (c. 540 BC- 468 BC), as the founder of Jainism. According to Jain legend, however, Mahavira was the last in line of twenty-four *Tirthankaras*, or those who had successfully crossed the river of suffering and attained enlightenment.

Like Siddhartha Gautama, Mahavira came from the *ksatriya* caste, and eventually abandoned his family and earthly possessions to become a wandering ascetic in search of spiritual enlightenment. After an extended period of meditation, Mahavira attained full enlightenment and became a *kevalin* (completed soul), and a jina (conqueror). Mahavira continued his teachings for a number of years accompanied by a band of naked monks. Purportedly he died at the age of seventy-two as a result of starvation.

The codification of Jain religious doctrines did not occur until nearly two hundred years after Mahavira's death, but contained many of his teachings. According to Mahavira, all living things are divided into five categories and are delineated by the number of senses they posses. The highest class, which have five senses include men, gods, and animals with higher intelligence. The second class, with four senses (touch, smell, taste, and sight), include most larger insects. The third classification, supposedly devoid of sight, contains smaller insects such as fleas and ants. Included in the second group, with only touch and taste, are worms, some shellfish, and leeches. The final class of one sensed creatures, not only includes plants, but such inanimate objects such as minerals, fire, and water. In this respect, then, everything in nature contains *karmic* matter, and *karma* is the cause of bondage. Thusly, all Jains are instructed to respect all things unconditionally, and to practice *ahimsa*, or nonviolence, towards all things. Salvation, or enlightenment, according to Jain principles, can only be attained by freeing one's soul from karmic matter to reach a level of purity.

VEDAS AND UPANISHADS

Although they did use some writing with pictographic symbols at Mohenjo-daro, they were not extensive nor alphabetic nor have they been deciphered yet, and the Indo-European Sanskrit which did develop in India is probably quite different. Nevertheless the Harappan civilization of the Indus Valley in what is now Pakistan did borrow many ideas from Mesopotamia and is considered the third civilization to develop. Two seals of the Mohenjo-daro type were discovered at Elam and Mesopotamia, and a cuneiform inscription was unearthed at Mohenjo-daro.

The pastoral villages that spread out east of Elam through Iran and Baluchistan prepared the way for the cities that were to develop around the Indus River, particularly at Harappa and Mohenjo-daro. By about 3000 BC they were building mud-brick houses; burials in the houses included funereal objects; and pottery had fine designs and the potters' marks. After 2500 BC farmers moved out into the alluvial plain of the Indus River valley and achieved full-sized villages using copper and bronze pins, knives, and axes; figurines of women and cattle indicate probable religious attitudes.

The urban phase began about 2300 BC and lasted for about six hundred years with elaborate cities like Mohenjo-daro (called locally Mound of the Dead), which was excavated in the 1920s. This city and others not yet excavated had about 40,000 inhabitants congregated in well built houses with private showers and toilets that drained into municipal sewer lines. Suffering from occasional flooding by the Indus, Mohenjo-daro was rebuilt seven times. The largest structures were the elevated granary and the great bath or swimming pool which was 12 by 7 meters. Around the pool were dressing rooms and private baths.

The people of the Harappan culture did not seem to be very warlike, although they hunted wild game and domesticated cattle, sheep, and goats. Wheat and barley were the main food supplemented by peas, sesame, and other vegetables and fruits, beef, mutton, pork, eggs, fish, and milk. Compared to other ancient civilizations, the houses were of nearly equal size, indicating a more egalitarian social structure. The potter's wheel and carts were used; children played with miniature toy carts. Cotton, perhaps first used here, and wool were made into clothing. A bronze figurine was found of an expressive dancing girl with her hand on her hip, naked except for jewellery. The numerous figurines of the Mother Goddess indicate a likely source for what later became the Shakti worship of the feminine power in India. A male god in a yoga posture, depicted with three faces and two horns, has been identified with Shiva, another important figure in later Indian religion. Phallic lingams, also associated with Shiva, have been found. A civilization that endured dangerous flooding for six hundred years very likely had a strong religion to help hold people together. With no written histories the decline of this civilization is subject to much speculation. The traditional theory is that the Aryans invaded from the northwest. Although this is likely, the decline of Harappan culture was quite gradual and indicates problems beyond foreign conquest. One theory is deforestation, because of all the wood needed for the kilns to make the bricks used to keep out the flood waters that gradually brought about salinization of the soil, as it had to Sumer over centuries, so that the Harappan culture had greatly declined by 1900 BC.

However, a more comprehensive explanation comes from an analysis of the consequences of the extensive herds of cattle that indicate overgrazing and a general degradation of the ecosystem, including salinization of water supplies. This led farmers to move on to greener pastures, leaving behind abandoned villages and depopulated cities. Even though fodder was probably grown to feed the cattle, this would not have been enough; and the overgrazing by the bullocks and milk cows could have caused the surrounding land to deteriorate. By 1500 BC the Harappan civilization had faded away into a culture that was spreading throughout India with new ideas from the west.

The traditional theory, well documented by the ancient hymns of the *Vedas,* is that a people calling themselves Aryans conquered the native peoples of India and destroyed their forts. Because of language similarities these Aryans are associated particularly with the Iranians and even further back with the origins of the Indo-European language group. The general consensus seems to be that this culture must have begun somewhere in the Russian steppes and Central Asia about 2000 BC, though some have put their origin in Lithuania because of similarity to that language. The branch of these speakers, who came to India under the name Aryans, which means "noble ones," is the Indo-Iranian group. In fact "Iran" derives from the Persian cognate of the word for Aryan. Other branches spread into Greece and western Asia as Hittites, Kassites, and Mitanni. A rock inscription found at Boghaz Koi dated about 1400 BC, commemorating a treaty between the

Mitanni and Hittites, invokes the Aryan gods Indra, Varuna, Mitra, and the twins Nasatya (Asvins).

The ancient writings of the Persian *Avesta* and the Hindu *Vedas* share many gods and beliefs. Eventually they must have split, causing later authors to demonize the divinities of their adversaries. In early Hindu writings the *asuras* were respected gods, but later they became the demons most hated, while Ahura Mazda became the chief god of the Zoroastrians. (Persian often uses an h where Sanskrit uses an s, such as *haoma* for *soma*.) On the other hand the Hindu term for divinities, devas, was used by Zoroastrians to describe the devils from which even our English word is derived. Some scholars have concluded that the ancient Hindus did not want to admit that they came from Iran, and therefore the origin of the Aryans is never mentioned in the ancient texts, although they frankly boast of their conquest over the indigenous Dasas or Dasyus in India.

The word *Veda* means knowledge, and the *Vedas* are considered the most sacred scripture of Hinduism referred to as *sruti*, meaning what was heard by or revealed to the *rishis* or seers. The most holy hymns and mantras put together into four collections called the *Rig*, *Sama*, *Yajur*, and *Atharva Vedas* are difficult to date, because they were passed on orally for about a thousand years before they were written down. More recent categories of *Vedas* include the *Brahmanas* or manuals for ritual and prayer, the *Aranyakas* or forest texts for religious hermits, and the *Upanishads* or mystical discourses.

RIG VEDA

The hymns of the *Rig Veda* are considered the oldest and most important of the *Vedas*, having been composed between 1500 BC and the time of the great Bharata war about 900 BC. More than a thousand hymns are organized into ten mandalas or circles of which the second through the seventh are the oldest and the tenth is the most recent. The Hindu tradition is that even the *Vedas* were gradually reduced from much more extensive and ancient divine revelations but were perverted in the recent dark age of *Kaliyuga*. As the only writings from this ancient period of India, they are considered the best source of knowledge we have; but the ethical doctrines seem to have improved from the ancient hymns to the mystical *Upanishads*.

Essentially the *Rig Veda* is dominated by hymns praising the Aryan gods for giving them victories and wealth plundered from the local Dasas through warfare.

The Aryans apparently used their advances in weaponry and skill in fighting to conquer the agricultural and tribal peoples of the fading Harappan culture. Numerous hymns refer to the use of horses and chariots with spokes which must have given their warriors a tremendous advantage. Spears, bows, arrows, and iron weapons are also mentioned. As a nomadic and pastoral culture glorifying war, they established a new social structure of patriarchal families dominated by warriors and, eventually with the power of the *Vedas* themselves, by priests also.

The *Rig Veda* does mention assemblies, but these were probably of the warrior elite, which may have had some controlling influence on the kings and the tribal priest called a *purohita*. The gods worshiped resemble the Indo-European gods and were headed by the powerful Indra, who is often credited with destroying ninety forts. Also popular was Agni, the fire-god considered a messenger of the gods.

Varuna and Mitra, the gods of the night and day sky, have been identified with the Greek Uranos and the Persian Mithras respectively. Dyaus, who is not mentioned nearly as often, has been correlated with the Greek Zeus. Surya the sun-god is referred to as the eye of Varuna and the son of Dyaus and rides through the sky on his chariot led by his twin sons, the Asvins who represent his rays; Ushas the dawn is his wife or daughter. Maruts are storm-gods shaped by Rudra, who may have been one of the few indigenous deities adopted by the Aryans. Like the Iranian *Avesta*, the *Rig Veda* refers to the thirty-three gods.

Generally the hymns of the *Rig Veda* praise the gods and ask them for worldly benefits such as wealth, health, long life, protection, and victory over the Dasa peoples.

> *He, self-reliant, mighty and triumphant, brought low the dear head of the wicked Dasas.*
>
> *Indra the Vritra-slayer, Fort-destroyer, scattered the Dasa hosts who dwelt in darkness.*
>
> *For men hath he created earth and waters, and ever helped the prayer of him who worships.*

To him in might the Gods have ever yielded, to Indra in the tumult of battle.

When in his arms they laid the bolt, he slaughtered the Dasyus and cast down their forts of iron.

They call upon Brihaspati or Brahmanaspati, who has been related to a Hittite thunder-god, to avenge the sinner and protect them from the deceitful and wicked man. The Aryans did have a concept of eternal law called *rita*, which the immortal Agni in serving the gods is said to never break (*Rig Veda* III:3:1).

In *Rig Veda* III:34:9 Indra killed the Dasyus and "gave protection to the Aryan colour." Not only did the Aryans shamelessly pray for booty in war, but they based their militarily won supremacy on the lightness of their skin colour compared to the dark colors of the native Dasyus. They arrogantly proclaimed, "Let those who have no weapons suffer sorrow." (*Rig Veda* IV:5:14.)

Renowned is he when conquering and when slaying:

'tis he who wins cattle in the combat.

When Indra hardens his indignation all that is fixed and all that moves fear him.

Indra has won all kine, all gold, all horses, -

Maghavan, he who breaks forts in pieces;

Indra is praised for killing thousands of the abject tribes of Dasas with his arrow and taking great vengeance with "murdering weapons." (*Rig Veda* IV:28:3-4) One hymn mentions sending thirty thousand Dasas "to slumber" and another hymn sixty thousand slain. A hymn dedicated to the weapons of war (*Rig Veda* VI:75) refers to a warrior "armed with mail," using a bow to win cattle and subdue all regions, "upstanding in the car the skillful charioteer guides his strong horses on whithersoe'er he will." The arrows had iron mouths and shafts "with venom smeared" that "not one be left alive." Hymn VII:83 begins, "Looking to you and your alliance, O ye men, armed with broad axes they went forward, fain for spoil. Ye smote and slew his Dasa and his Aryan enemies."

Only occasionally did the authors of these hymns look to their own sins.

Free us from sins committed by our fathers, from those wherein we have ourselves offended.

O king, loose, like a thief who feeds the cattle, as from the cord a calf, set free Vasishtha.

Not our own will betrayed us, but seduction, thoughtlessness, Varuna! wine, dice or anger.

The old is near to lead astray the younger: even sleep removes not all evil-doing.

A hymn to the frogs compares the repetitions of the priests around the soma bowl to the croaking of the frogs around a pond after the rains come. (*Rig Veda* VII:103)

The basic belief of the prayers and sacrifices is that they will help them to gain their desires and overcome their enemies, as in *Rig Veda* VIII:31:15: "The man who, sacrificing, strives to win the heart of deities will conquer those who worship not." Some awareness of a higher law seems to be dawning in the eighth book in hymn 75: "The holy law hath quelled even mighty men of war. Break ye not off our friendship, come and set me free." However, the enemies are now identified with the Asuras and still are intimidated by greater weapons: "Weaponless are the Asuras, the godless: scatter them with thy wheel, impetuous hero." (*Rig Veda* VIII:85:9)

Many of the hymns refer to the intoxicating soma juice, which is squeezed from the mysterious soma plant and drank. All of the hymns of the ninth book of the *Rig Veda* are dedicated to the purifying soma, which is even credited with making them feel immortal, probably because of its psychedelic influence. The first hymn in this book refers to the "iron-fashioned home" of the Aryans.

In the first book of the *Rig Veda* the worshipers recognize Agni as the guard of eternal law (I:1:8) and Mitra and Varuna as lovers and cherishers of law who gained their mighty power through law (I:2:8). In the 24th hymn they pray to Varuna, the wise Asura, to loosen the bonds of their sins. However, the prayers for riches continue, and Indra is thanked for winning wealth in horses, cattle, and gold by his chariot. Agni helps to slay the many in war by the hands of the few, "preserving our wealthy patrons with thy succors, and ourselves." (*Rig Veda* I:31:6, 42) Indra helped win the Aryan victory:

He, much invoked, hath slain Dasyus and Simyus, after his wont, and laid them low with arrows.

The mighty thunderer with his fair-complexioned friends won the land, the sunlight, and the waters.

Control of the waters was essential for agricultural wealth. Indra is praised for crushing the godless races and breaking down their forts. (*Rig Veda* I:174)

In the tenth and last book of the *Rig Veda* some new themes are explored, but the Dasyus are still condemned for being "riteless, void of sense, inhuman, keeping alien laws," and Indra still urges the heroes to slay the enemies; his "hand is prompt to rend and burn, O hero thunder-armed: as thou with thy companions didst destroy the whole of Sushna's brood." (*Rig Veda* X:22)

One unusual hymn is on the subject of gambling with dice. The speaker regrets alienating his wife, wandering homeless in constant fear and debt, envying others' well-ordered homes. He finally warns the listener not to play with dice but recommends cultivating his land. (*Rig Veda* X:34) Hymn 50 of this most recent last book urges Indra to win riches with valour "in the war for water on their fields." Now the prayer is that "we Gods may quell our Asura foemen." (*Rig Veda* X:53:4) A wedding ceremony is indicated in a hymn of Surya's bridal, the daughter of the sun. (*Rig Veda* X:85)

The first indication of the caste system is outlined in the hymn to Purusha, the embodied human spirit, who is one-fourth creature and three-fourths eternal life in heaven.

The Brahmin was his mouth, of both his arms was the Rajanya made.

His thighs became the Vaisya, from his feet the Sudra was produced.

The Brahmin caste was to be the priests and teachers; the Rajanya represents the king, head of the warrior or Kshatriya caste; Vaishyas are the merchants, craftsmen, and farmers; and the Sudras are the workers. In hymn 109 the *brahmachari* or student is mentioned as engaged in duty as a member of God's own body.

The hymn to liberality is a breath of fresh air:

The riches of the liberal never waste away, while he who will not give finds none to comfort him.

The man with food in store who, when the needy comes in miserable case begging for bread to eat,

Hardens his heart against him - even when of old he did him service - find not one to comfort him.

Yet later we realize that the priests are asking for liberality to support their own services, for the "plowing makes the food that feeds us," and thus a speaking (or paid) Brahmin is better than a silent one.

The power of speech is honored in two hymns.

Where, like men cleansing corn-flour in a cribble, the wise in spirit have created language,

Friends see and recognize the marks of friendship: their speech retains the blessed sign imprinted.

In hymn 125 of the tenth mandala Vak or speech claims to have penetrated earth and heaven, holding together all existence.

A philosophical hymn of creation is found in *Rig Veda* X:129. Beginning from non-being when nothing existed, not even water nor death, that One breathless breathed by itself. At first this All was concealed by darkness and formless chaos, but by heat *(tapas)* that One came into existence. Thus arose desire, the primal seed and germ of Spirit. Sages searching in their hearts discovered kinship with the non-existent. A ray of light extended across the darkness, but what was known above or below? Creative fertility was there with energy and action, but who really knows where this creation came from? For the gods came after the world's creation. Who could know the source of this creation and how it was produced? The one seeing it in the highest heaven only knows, or maybe it does not.

SAMA VEDA

The *Sama Veda* contains the melodies or music for the chants used from the *Rig Veda* for the sacrifices; almost all of its written verses are traceable to the *Rig Veda*, mostly the eighth and ninth books and most to Indra, Agni, or Soma. These are considered the origin of Indian music and probably stimulated great artistry to make the sacrifices worthwhile to their patrons who supported the priests. The *Sama Veda* helped to train the musicians and functioned as a hymnal for the religious rites. The animal sacrifices did not use the *Sama* chants, but they were used extensively in agricultural rites and in the soma rituals for which the plant with inebriating and hallucinogenic qualities was imported from the mountains to the heartland of India. By this time the priests were specializing in different parts of the sacrifices as professional musicians and singers increased. The singing was like the strophe, antistrophe, and epode of the Greek chorus and used the seven tones of the European scale. By the tenth century BC the Aryans had invaded most of northern India, and once again trade resumed with Babylon and others in the near east. As the sacrifices became more complex, the priestly class used them to enhance their role in the society. Many considered this musical portion the most important of the *Vedas*.

YAJUR VEDA

Though also following many of the hymns of the *Rig Veda*, the *Yajur Veda* deviates more from the original text in its collection of the ritual formulas for the priests to use in the sacrifices, which is what *yaja* means. It explains how to construct the altars for new and full-moon sacrifices and other ceremonies. The *Yajur Veda* has two collections or *samhitas* called White and Black, the latter being more obscure in its meanings. By this time (10th century BC and after) the Aryan conquest has proceeded from the northwest and Punjab to cover northern India, especially the Ganges valley. The caste system was in place, and as the warriors settled down to ruling over an agricultural society, the role of the priests and their ceremonies gained influence and justified the Aryan ways to the native workers, who labored for the farmers, merchants, craftsmen, who in turn were governed by their kings and priests. Land and wealth were accumulated in the hands of a few ruling families, and with food scarce the indigenous people were enslaved or had to sell their labour cheap to the ruling classes.

By instituting more elaborate sacrifices for their wealthy patrons, the priests could grow both in numbers and wealth as well. The famous horse sacrifice was not celebrated often but was used by a king to show his lordship over potential adversaries, who were invited to acknowledge this overlordship in the ritual. The parts of the horse symbolize different aspects of the universe so that tremendous power is invoked. The complicated and obscure rituals were presided over by the priests - the three symbols of the lotus leaf, the frog (for rain), and the golden man (for the sun) representing the Aryan dominance over the land and waters of India and the natural powers that sustain agriculture.

The soma sacrifice was the most important and could last up to twelve years. Since the soma plant was imported from distant mountains, it had to be purchased. A ritual drama re-enacted this business and aggressive Aryan history by showing the buyer snatching back the calf, which was paid for the soma plant, after the transaction occurs. The soma plant was then placed in a cart and welcomed as an honored guest and king at the sacrifice. Animals were slain and cut up in the rites before their meat was eaten. After various offerings and other ceremonies the soma juice is poured and toasted to different gods, and finally the text lists the sacrificial fees, usually goats, cows, gold, clothes, and food.

Coronation ceremonies supported the inauguration of kings. The priests tried to keep themselves above the warrior caste though by praising soma as king of the Brahmins. Waters were drawn from various rivers to sprinkle on the king and indicate the area of his kingdom, and he strode in each direction to signify his sovereignty. The king was anointed by the royal priest, giving some water to his son, the designated prince, and ritually enacting a raid against a kinsman's cattle, once again affirming their history of conquest. The booty was taken and divided into three parts for the priest, those who drank, and the original owner. A ritual dice game was played, which the king was allowed to win. The king then rode out in his chariot and was publicly worshiped as a divine ruler.

Agricultural rites were common and regular, and chariot races were no doubt popular at some of the festivals. The Purusha (person) sacrifice symbolized human sacrifice, which may refer back to the time when a hunting and pastoral people did not allow their enemies to live because of the shortage of food. However, in an agricultural society more labour was needed and could produce surplus food. The Purusha sacrifice recognized 184 professional crafts and guilds.

Finally the highest sacrifice was considered to be the Sarvamedha in which the sacrificer offered all of his possessions as the fee at the end of the ceremony. The *Yajur Veda* is actually the *Isha Upanishad,* expressing the mystical view that the supreme spirit pervades everything. This society was highly patriarchal, and the status of women declined, especially as men often married non-Aryan women. Women did not attend public assemblies and could not inherit property on their own. Polyandry was discouraged, but polygamy, adultery, and prostitution were generally accepted except during certain rituals. A sacrificer was not allowed to seek a prostitute on the first day of the sacrificial fire, nor the wife of another on the second day, nor his own wife on the third day.

The priests placed themselves at the top of the caste system as they supervised a religion most of the people could not understand without them. After the *Atharva Veda* was accepted, each sacrifice required at least four priests, one on each side of the fire using the *Rig*, *Sama*, *Yajur*, and *Atharva Vedas*, plus their assistants. After the wars of conquest were completed and the warrior caste settled down to rule, the priests were needed to sustain social stability. Yet in these times the caste system was much more flexible, as it is indicated that one should not ask about the caste of a learned man. The Brahmins, as the priest caste was called, had three obligations or debts to pay back in life: they paid back the seers by studying the *Vedas*, the gods by offering sacrifices, and their fathers by raising a family. Like their European ancestors, the Aryan warriors considered themselves above laboring for food and so organized society that food would be provided for them. One ethical duty later found in the epics was that of taking care of refugees, probably because as marauding raiders they had often been refugees themselves. The priests assured their livelihood by making sure that penance through religious ritual was a prime social value.

ATHARVA VEDA

The latest and fourth *Veda* is in a different category. For a long time many referred to only three *Vedas*, by which complete ceremonies could be conducted with the *Rig hotr* reciting, the *Sama udgatri* singing, and the *Yajur adhvaryu* performing the ritual. Even later the *Atharvan* Brahmin's part was often performed unaccompanied by the other three priests. Also much of it draws from the customs and beliefs of pre-Aryan or pre-Vedic India. The *Atharva Veda* is much longer than the *Sama* and *Yajur* and only about a sixth of it is from the *Rig Veda*.

The *Atharva Veda* is primarily magical spells and incantations. The line between prayer and magic and between white and black magic is usually drawn by ethical considerations. The *bheshajani* are for healing and cures using herbs to treat fever, leprosy, jaundice, dropsy, and other diseases. The Aryans looked down on doctors and medicine, probably because the natives were more skilled in these than they. Other more positive spells were for successful childbirth, romance, fecundity, virility, etc.

The negative or bewitching spells were called *abhichara* and attempted to cause diseases or harm to enemies; often they were aimed at serpents and demons. The sorcery is ascribed to one of the authors, Angiras, whose name is related to Agni (Latin *ignis)*, the divine messenger and possibly a distant cognate of the Greek word for messenger, angel. Another author, Atharvan, derives from the old Iranian root, *atar*, meaning fire. The third author, Bhrigu, was the name of a tribe which opposed Sudas in the battle of ten kings in the *Rig Veda*, and his name has also been related to a Greek word for fire. The fourth author is Brahmin, the name which was given to the *Atharvan* priest, which eventually became so sacred that it was used as a name not only for the priestly caste but even for God the Creator.

In addition to physicians the Vedic Aryans also held in contempt *Atharvan* astrologers as well as magic, but from this came not only astrology but also the beginning of Ayurvedic medicine. Like most ancient peoples, they also believed that the main cause of disease was evil spirits, possession, or what we would call psychological factors. The magical elements, particularly the *abhicara*, and the subjects of healing, herbs, and cooking, which were mostly in the woman's domain, made the *Atharva Veda* obnoxious to many Vedic priests. However, these rituals were very popular, and the Brahmin priest's share of the fees soon became equal to the other three priests' combined. Eventually this shamanic tradition had to be incorporated into the Vedic religion, especially later when it faced the new challenges of Jainism and Buddhism.

The Brahmin caste became even stronger, and their wealth can be seen by the belief that the cow by right belonged exclusively to them. Taxes were collected probably by the warrior Kshatriya caste from the Vaisya artisans, farmers, and merchants. The Sudra workers were too poor to be taxed, and the Brahmins were exempt. One verse (*Atharva Veda* 3:29:3) describes heaven as "where a tax is not paid by a weak man for a stronger."

Marriage ceremonies are included. Here is a brief example:

I am he; you are she.

I am song; you are verse.

I am heaven; you are earth.

Let us two dwell together here;

let us generate children.

According to the *Atharva Veda* (5:17:8-9), a Brahmin could take a wife from the husband of any other caste simply by seizing her hand. Book 18 contains only funeral verses. There are coronation rites for kings, though the prayer is that the people will choose the king, usually already selected by heredity or the council. Philosophy and abstraction are creeping in, as there are two hymns to the deity of time, and *kama* (love, desire, pleasure) is praised as "the first seed of the mind" that generated heaven. (*Atharva Veda* 19:52)

Let us conclude this section on the *Atharva Veda* with some selections from its beautiful hymn to the Earth as a sample of the more positive expression of the *Vedas*:

High Truth, unyielding Order, Consecration,

Ardor and Prayer and Holy Ritual uphold the Earth, may she, the ruling Mistress of what has been and what will come to be, for us spread wide a limitless domain.

Untrammeled in the midst of men, the Earth, adorned with heights and gentle slopes and plains, bears plants and herbs of various healing powers.

May she spread wide for us, afford us joy!

On whom are ocean, river, and all waters, on whom have sprung up food and plowman's crops, on whom moves all that breathes and stirs abroad -

Earth, may she grant to us the long first draught!

To Earth belong the four directions of space.

On her grows food; on her the plowman toils.

She carries likewise all that breathes and stirs.

Earth, may she grant us cattle and food in plenty!

On whom the men of olden days roamed far, on whom the conquering Gods smote the demons, the home of cattle, horses, and of birds, may Earth vouchsafe to us good fortune and glory!

Bearer of all things, hoard of treasures rare, sustaining mother, Earth the golden-breasted who bears the Sacred Universal Fire, whose spouse is Indra - may she grant us wealth!

Limitless Earth, whom the Gods, never sleeping, protect forever with unflagging care, may she exude for us the well-loved honey, shed upon us her splendor copiously!

Earth, who of yore was Water in the oceans, discerned by the Sages' secret powers, whose immortal heart, enwrapped in Truth, abides aloft in the highest firmament, may she procure for us splendor and power, according to her highest royal state!

On whom the flowing Waters, ever the same, course without cease or failure night and day, may she yield milk, this Earth of many streams, and shed on us her splendor copiously!

May Earth, whose measurements the Asvins marked, over whose breadth the foot of Vishnu strode, whom Indra, Lord of power, freed from foes, stream milk for me, as a mother for her son!

Your hills, O Earth, your snow-clad mountain peaks, your forests, may they show us kindliness!

Brown, black, red, multifarious in hue and solid is this vast Earth, guarded by Indra.

Invincible, unconquered, and unharmed,

I have on her established my abode.

Impart to us those vitalizing forces that come, O Earth, from deep within your body, your central point, your navel, purify us wholly.

The Earth is mother; I am son of Earth.

The Rain-giver is my father; may he shower on us blessings!

The Earth on which they circumscribe the altar, on which a band of workmen prepare the oblation, on which the tall bright sacrificial posts are fixed before the start of the oblation - may Earth, herself increasing, grant us increase!

That man, O Earth, who wills us harm, who fights us, who by his thoughts or deadly arms opposes, deliver him to us, forestalling action.

All creatures, born from you, move round upon you.

You carry all that has two legs, three, or four.

To you, O Earth, belong the five human races, those mortals upon whom the rising sun sheds the immortal splendor of his rays.

May the creatures of earth, united together, let flow for me the honey of speech!

Grant to me this boon, O Earth.

Mother of plants and begetter of all things, firm far-flung Earth, sustained by Heavenly Law, kindly and pleasant is she. May we ever dwell on her bosom, passing to and fro!...

Do not thrust us aside from in front or behind, from above or below! Be gracious, O Earth.

Let us not encounter robbers on our path.

Restrain the deadly weapons!

As wide a vista of you as my eye may scan, O Earth, with the kindly help of Sun, so widely may my sight be never dimmed in all the long parade of years to come!

Whether, when I repose on you, O Earth,

I turn upon my Right *side or my left, or whether, extended flat upon my back,*

I meet your pressure from head to foot, be gentle, Earth! You are the couch of all!

Whatever I dig up of you, O Earth, may you of that have quick replenishment!

O purifying One, may my thrust never reach Right *into your vital points, your heart!*

Your circling seasons, nights succeeding days, your summer, O Earth, your splashing rains, your autumn, your winter and frosty season yielding to spring—may each and all produce for us their milk!...

From your numberless tracks by which mankind may travel, your roads on which move both chariots and wagons your paths which are used by the good and the bad, may we choose a way free from foes and robbers!

May you grant us the blessing of all that is wholesome!

She carries in her lap the foolish and also the wise.

She bears the death of the wicked as well as the good.

She lives in friendly collaboration with the boar, offering herself as sanctuary to the wild pig....

Peaceful and fragrant, gracious to the touch, may Earth, swollen with milk, her breasts overflowing, grant me her blessing together with her milk!

The Maker of the world sought her with oblations when she was shrouded in the depth of the ocean.

A vessel of gladness, long cherished in secret, the earth was revealed to mankind for their joy.

Primeval Mother, disperser of men, you, far-flung Earth, fulfill all our desires.

Whatever you lack, may the Lord of creatures, the First-born of Right, supply to you fully!

May your dwellings, O Earth, free from sickness and wasting, flourish for us! Through a long life, watchful, may we always offer to you our tribute!

O Earth, O Mother, dispose my lot in gracious fashion that I be at ease.

In harmony with all the powers of Heaven set me, O Poet, in grace and good fortune!

Brahmanas

Between about 900 and 700 BC the *Brahmanas* were written in prose as sacerdotal commentaries on the four *Vedas* to guide the practices of the sacrifices and give explanations often mythical and fanciful for these customs. However, their limited focus of justifying the priestly actions in the sacrifices restricted the themes of these first attempts at imaginative literature. Nevertheless they do give us information about the social customs of this period and serve as a transition from the *Vedas* to the *Aranyakas* and the mystical *Upanishads*.

The caste system based on colour *(varna)* was now established, though not as rigidly as it became later. The essential difference was between the light-skinned Aryans, who made up the top three castes of the priestly Brahmins, warrior Kshatriyas, and artisan Vaishyas, and the dark-skinned Dasas, who were the servant Sudras. Sudras, like women, could not own property, and only rarely did they rise above service positions. The Vaishyas were the basis of the economic system of trade, crafts, and farming. The Vaishyas were considered inferior by the Brahmins and Kshatriyas, and a female was generally not allowed to marry below her caste, though it was common for a male to do so. Even a Brahmin's daughter was not supposed to marry a Kshatriya.

The rivalry for prestige and power was between the Brahmins and the Kshatriyas or *rajanyas*. Brahmins often held debates on Brahman and other religious issues. Janaka, a *rajanya* gained knowledge and defeated some Brahmins in discussion. So some Brahmins suggested a symposium on Brahman to prove who was superior, but since Brahmins were expected to be superior on these issues, Yajnavalkya prudently replied, "We are Brahmins; he is a *rajanya*. If we win, whom shall we say that we have defeated? But if he defeats us, they will say a *rajanya* has defeated Brahmins; so let us not convene this symposium." Kings were consecrated by Vedic rites and ruled with the help of the assembly *(sabha)* that met in a hall to administer justice; women were excluded. Ordeals were used, such as making a suspected thief touch a hot ax to see if his hand burned, which might be the origin of the saying, "being caught red-handed." Politics and legislation took place in a larger council *(samiti)*. Taxes were collected to support these institutions and the army. Each village was administered by a Gramani, a Vaisya who functioned like a mayor with civil rather than military authority. The Gramani and the royal charioteer *(Suta)* were considered the kingmakers. This latter privileged position was not merely the driver of the king but also his chief advisor and perhaps storyteller as well. The royal priest or *Purohito* was also supposed to advise the king in peace and protect him in war. The season of dew after the monsoons ended was considered the time for "sacking cities," as ambitious kings came into conflict with each other in wars.

In addition to the discussions of sacerdotal matters, the *Brahmanas* do contain some stories meant to explain or rationalize their religious practices. Some of these are quite imaginative, though the usual pattern is for the hero to discover a rite to perform or a chant to intone which miraculously solves whatever problem is pressing to give a happy ending.

Wendy O'Flaherty has translated some stories from the *Jaiminiya Brahmana*, illustrating how they dealt with the fears of death, God, the father, wives, and demonic women; many of these stories are sexually explicit, indicating that these people were not afraid of discussing their sexuality. However, since the usual way of handling these fears was to use a sacrificial ritual, the solutions probably had only limited social and psychological value.

The most famous of these stories, and the best in my opinion, is the tale of Bhrigu's journey in the other world. Bhrigu was the son of Varuna and devoted to learning, and he thought that he was better than the other Brahmins and even better than the gods and his own father. So Varuna decided to teach him something by stopping his life breaths, causing Bhrigu to enter the world beyond, where he saw someone cut another man to pieces and eat him, a second man eating another who was screaming, a third eating a man who was silently screaming, another world where two women were guarding a treasure, a fifth where a stream of blood was guarded by a naked black man with a club and a stream of butter provided all the desires of golden men in golden bowls, and a sixth world where flowed five rivers of blue and white lotuses and flowing honey with wonderful music, celestial nymphs dancing and singing, and a fragrant odor.

When Bhrigu returned, his father Varuna explained to him that the first man represented people who in ignorance destroy trees, which in turn eat them; the second are those who cook animals that cry out and in the other world are eaten by them in return; the third are those who ignorantly cook rice and barley, which scream silently and also eat them in return; the two women are Faith and non-Faith; the river of blood represents those who squeeze the blood out of a Brahmin, and the naked black man guarding is Anger; but the true sacrificers are the golden men, who get the river of butter and the paradise of the five rivers.

To me this myth is a clear warning against the harmful actions of deforestation and meat-eating, and even the eating of living vegetables is to be done in silent respect. It shows an intuitive understanding of the principle of karma or the consequences of action as well as the growing importance of the concept of faith in addition to the usual theme of the sacrifice.

The power of the word is increasing, as the sacrifices were glorified and given power even over the Vedic gods. *Japa* or the practice of chanting a *mantram* like *Aum* practiced ascetically with the sacrifices was believed to produce all one's desires. At the same time knowledge was beginning to be valued. In one exchange mind says that speech merely imitates it, but speech emphasizes the importance of expression and communication; however, Prajapati decides that mind is more important even than the word. This new god, Prajapati, is said to have given birth to both the gods and the demons. The ethical principle of truth appears as the gods are described as being truthful and the demons as being false. However, realizing the ways of the world, many complain that the demons grew strong and rich, just as cattle like salty soil; but by performing the sacrifice the gods attained the whole truth and triumph, as, analogically I might add, people will eventually realize that cattle as well as salt ruins the land.

Prajapati not only was the first to sacrifice but was considered the sacrifice itself. He practiced *tapas* to create by the heat of his own effort, and this heat was also related to cosmic fire and light as well as the warmth of the body and breath. Another concept of energy associated with the breath was *prana*; it also was identified with goodness, as the texts imply that as the life force it cannot be impure or bad. Prajapati not only created but entered into things as form and name, giving them order. Eventually Prajapati would be replaced by Brahman, who was identified with truth and would become the Creator God in the trinity that would include Vishnu, a sun-god who becomes the Preserver, and Shiva, who is derived from the indigenous Rudra, the Destroyer. With all the mental activity going on analysing the rites and their explanation, abstractions were increasing in the religion.

A judgment after death using a scale to weigh good against evil is described in the *Satapatha Brahmana*, an idea which may have been transported from Egypt by merchants. This text recommends that the one who knows this will balance one's deeds in this world so that in the next the good deeds will rise, not the evil ones. Belief in repeated lives through reincarnation is indicated in several passages in the *Brahmanas*. A beef-eater is punished by being born into a strange and sinful creature. As knowledge rivaled the value of ritual, this new problem of how to escape from an endless cycle of rebirth presented itself.

Aranyakas

The larger body of Vedic literature is divided into two parts with the four *Rig, Sama, Yajur*, and *Atharva Samhitas* and their *Brahmanas* making up the Karmakanda on the work of the sacrifices and the *Aranyakas* and the *Upanishads* the section on knowledge called the Jnanakanda. The *Aranyakas* and the *Upanishads* were tacked on to the end of *Brahmanas*, and the only three *Aranyakas* extant share the names of the *Brahmanas* they followed and the *Upanishads* they preceded: *Aitareya*, *Kausitaki*, and the *Taittiriya*; the first two are associated with the *Rig Veda*, the last with the *Yajur Veda*.

The *Aranyakas* are called the forest texts, because ascetics retreated into the forest to study the spiritual doctrines with their students, leading to less emphasis on the sacrificial rites that were still performed in the towns. They were transitional between the *Brahmanas* and the *Upanishads* in that they still discuss rites and have magical content, dull lists of formulas and some hymns from the *Vedas* as well as the early speculations and intellectual discussions that flowered in the *Upanishads*. The sages who took in students in their forest hermitages were not as wealthy as the Brahmins in the towns who served royalty and other wealthy patrons.

The *Taittiriya Aranyaka* tells how when the Vataramsa sages were first approached by other sages, they retreated; but when the sages came back with faith and *tapas* (ardor), they instructed them how to expiate the sin of abortion. Prayers were offered for pregnant women whether they were married or not, even if the father was unknown because of promiscuity. Yet the double standard against women for unchastity was in effect, unless a student seduced the teacher's wife. Truth was the highest value; through truth the right to heaven was retained. Debtors were in fear of punishment in hell, probably because the social punishments in this world were severe—torture and perhaps even death.

The emphasis now was on knowledge, even on wisdom, as they prayed for intelligence. The concept of *prana* as the life energy of the breath is exalted as that which establishes the entire soul. *Prana* is found in trees, animals, and people in ascending order. Human immortality is identified with the soul *(atman)*, not the body. Hell is still feared, but by practicing austerity *(tapas)* to gain knowledge individuals hope to be born into a better world after death or be liberated from rebirth. Non-attachment *(vairagya)* also purifies the body and overcomes death. The essence of the Vedic person was considered Brahman, and the knower or inner person was known as the soul *(atman)*. The guardians of the spiritual treasures of the community were called Brahmavadins (those who discuss Brahman). A son approached his father and asked what was supreme. The father replied, "Truth, *tapas*, self-control, charity, *dharma* (duty), and progeny."

EARLY UPANISHADS

The term *Upanishad* means literally "those who sit near" and implies listening closely to the secret doctrines of a spiritual teacher. Although there are over two hundred *Upanishads*, only fifteen are mentioned by the philosophic commentator Shankara (788-820 CE). These fifteen and the *Maitri* are considered Vedic and the principal *Upanishads*; the rest were written later and are related to the Puranic worship of Shiva, Shakti, and Vishnu. The oldest and longest of the *Upanishads* are the *Brihad-Aranyaka* and the *Chandogya* from about the seventh century BC.

The *Brihad-Aranyaka* has three *Aranyaka* chapters followed by six *Upanishad* chapters. The first chapter of the *Brihad-Aranyaka* Upanishad describes the world as represented by the horse-sacrifice. The primordial battle between the gods and the devils accounts for the evil found in the senses, mind, and speech, but by striking off the evil the divinities were carried beyond death. The priest chants for profound aspiration, one of the most famous verses from the *Upanishads*:

From the unreal lead me to the real!

From darkness lead me to light!

From death lead me to immortality!

The primary message of the *Upanishads* is that this can be done by meditating with the awareness that one's soul *(atman)* is one with all things. Thus whoever knows that one is Brahman (God) becomes this all; even the gods cannot prevent this, since that one becomes their soul *(atman)*. Therefore whoever worships another divinity, thinking it is other than oneself, does not know.

Out of God *(Brahman)* came the Brahmin caste of priests and teachers and the Kshatriyas to rule, development through the Vaishyas and the Sudras. However, a principle was created as justice *(dharma)*, than which nothing is higher, so that a weak person may control one stronger, as if by a king. They say that those who speak the truth speak justice and vice versa, because they are the same. By meditating on the soul *(atman)* alone, one does not perish and can create whatever one wants. Whatever suffering occurs remains with the creatures; only the good goes to the soul, because evil does not go to the gods. The soul is identified with the real, the immortal, and the life-breath *(prana)*, which is veiled by name and form (individuality). By restraining the senses and the mind, one may rest in the space within the heart and become a great Brahmin and like a king may move around within one's body as one pleases. The world of name and form is real, but the soul is the truth or reality of the real. Immortality cannot be obtained through wealth, and all persons and things in the world are dear not for love of them (husband, wife, sons, wealth, gods, etc.); but for the love of the soul, all these are dear. The soul is the overlord of all things, as the spokes of the wheel are held together by the hub.

The principle of action *(karma)* is explained as "one becomes good by good action, bad by bad action." How can one get beyond the duality of seeing, smelling, hearing, speaking to, thinking of, and understanding another? Can one see the seer, smell the smeller, hear the hearer, think the thinker, and understand the understander? It is the soul which is in all things; everything else is wretched. By passing beyond hunger and thirst, sorrow and delusion, old age and death, by overcoming desire for sons, wealth, and worlds, let a Brahmin become disgusted with learning and live as a child; disgusted with that, let one become an ascetic until one transcends both the non-ascetic and the ascetic states. Thus is indicated a spiritual path of learning and discipline that ultimately transcends even learning and discipline in the soul, the inner controller, the immortal, the one dwelling in the mind, whom the mind does not know, who controls the mind from within.

The one departing this world without knowing the imperishable is pitiable, but the one knowing it is a Brahmin. The following refrain is repeated often:

> *That soul is not this, not that.*
>
> *It is incomprehensible, for it is not comprehended.*
>
> *It is indestructible, for it is never destroyed.*
>
> *It is unattached, for it does not attach itself.*
>
> *It is unfettered; it does not suffer; it is not injured.*

The soul is considered intelligent, dear, true, endless, blissful, and stable. As a king prepares a chariot or ship when going on a journey, one should prepare one's soul with the mystic doctrines of the *Upanishads*. The knowledge that is the light in the heart enables one to transcend this world and death while appearing asleep. The evils that are obtained with a body at birth are left behind upon departing at death. One dreams by projecting from oneself, not by sensing actual objects. In sleep the immortal may leave one's nest and go wherever one pleases. In addition to being free from desire the ethical admonition of being without crookedness or sin is also indicated. At death the soul goes out first, then the life, and finally the breaths go out.

The soul is made of everything; as one acts, one becomes. The doer of good becomes good; the doer of evil becomes evil. As is one's desire, such is one's resolve; as is the resolve, such is the action, which one attains for oneself. When one's mind is attached, the inner self goes into the action. Obtaining the consequences of one's actions, whatever one does in this world comes again from the other world to this world of action *(karma)*.

By releasing the desires in one's heart, one may be liberated in immortality, reaching *Brahman* (God). One is the creator of all, one with the world. Whoever knows this becomes immortal, but others go only to sorrow. The knowing is sought through the spiritual practices of repeating the *Vedas*, sacrifices, offerings, penance, and fasting. Eventually one sees everything, as the soul overcomes both the thoughts of having done wrong and having done right. The evil does not burn one; rather one burns the evil. In the soul's being the world-all is known. The student should practice self-restraint, giving, and compassion.

The *Chandogya Upanishad* belongs to the *Sama Veda* and is the last eight chapters of the ten-chapter *Chandogya Brahmana*. The first two chapters of the *Brahmana* discuss sacrifices and other forms of worship. As part of the *Sama Veda*, which is the chants, the *Chandogya Upanishad* emphasizes the importance of chanting the sacred *Aum*. The chanting of *Aum* is associated with the life breath *(prana)*, which is so powerful that when the devils struck it, they fell to pieces. The religious life recommended in the *Chandogya Upanishad* has three parts. The first is sacrifice, study of the *Vedas*, and giving alms; the second is austerity; and the third is studying the sacred knowledge while living in the house of a teacher. One liberal giver, who had many rest-houses built and provided with food, said, "Everywhere people will be eating of my food."

The soul in the heart is identified with *Brahman* (God), and it is the same as the light which shines higher than in heaven. Knowing and reverencing the sacrificial fire is believed to repel evil-doing from oneself. To the one who knows the soul, evil action does not adhere, just as water does not adhere to the leaf of the lotus flower. To know the soul as divine is called the "Loveliness-uniter" because all lovely things come to such.

The doctrine of reincarnation is clearly implied in the *Chandogya Upanishad* as it declares that those whose conduct is pleasant here will enter a pleasant womb of a Brahmin, Kshatriya, or Vaisya; but those of stinking conduct will enter a stinking womb of a dog, swine, or outcast. Thus reincarnation is explained as an ethical consequence of one's actions *(karma)*.

At death the voice goes into the mind, the mind into the breath, the breath into heat, and heat into the highest divinity, the finest essence of truth and soul. Speaking to Svetaketu, the teacher explains that a tree may be struck at the root, the middle, or the top, but it will continue to live if pervaded by the living soul. Yet if the life leaves one branch of it, it dries up; and if it leaves the whole of it, the whole dries up. Then the teacher explains how the soul is the essence of life and does not die, concluding with the repeated refrain that his student thus ought to identify with the soul.

Truly, indeed, when the living soul leaves it,
This body dies; the living soul does not die.
That which is the subtle essence
This whole world has for its soul.
That is reality (truth). That is the soul.
That you are, Svetaketu.

Then the teacher placed salt in water and asked his student to taste different parts of the water. Just so is Being hidden in all of reality, but it is not always perceived. Just as the thief burns his hand on the hot ax when tested, the one who did not steal and is true does not burn his hand, so the whole world has that truth in its soul.

Speech is to be valued, because it makes known right and wrong, true and false, good and bad, pleasant and unpleasant. Mind is revered, because it enables one to do sacred works. Will is valued, because heaven and earth and all things were formed by being willed. Thought is important, because it is better not to be thoughtless. Meditation is revered, because one attains greatness by meditating. Understanding is valued, because by it we can understand everything. Strength maintains everything. Food, water, heat, and space each have their values. Finally also memory, hope, and life *(prana)* are to be revered.

Those, who take delight in the soul, have intercourse with it and find pleasure and bliss in it and freedom; but those, who do not, have perishable worlds and no freedom. The seer does not find death nor sickness nor any distress but sees the all and obtains the all entirely. The soul is free of evil, ageless, deathless, sorrowless, hungerless, and thirstless. For those, who go from here having found the soul here, there is freedom in all worlds. No evil can go into the Brahma-world.

The chaste life of the student of sacred knowledge is the essence of austerity, fasting, and the hermit life, for in that way one finds the reality of the soul. The soul must be searched out and understood. The *Chandogya Upanishad* concludes with the advice that one should learn the *Veda* from the family of a teacher while working for the teacher, then study in one's own home producing sons and pupils, concentrate one's senses upon the soul, be harmless toward all living things except in the sacrifices (The religion has not yet purified itself of animal sacrifices.), so that one may attain the Brahma-world and not return here again. The implication is that one may become free of the cycle of reincarnation.

The *Taittiriya* and *Aitareya Upanishads* were associated with *Aranyakas* of the same name. In the *Taittiriya Upanishad* once again *Aum* is emphasized, as is peace of soul. Prayers often end with *Aum* and the chanting of peace *(shanti)* three times. This may be preceded by the noble sentiment, "May we never hate."17 One teacher says truth is first, another austerity, and a third claims that study and teaching of the *Veda* is first, because it includes austerity and discipline.

The highest goal is to know *Brahman*, for that is truth, knowledge, infinite and found hidden in the heart of being and in the highest heaven, where one may abide with the eternal and intelligent Spirit *(Brahman)*. Words turn away from it, and the mind is baffled by the delight of the eternal; the one who knows this shall not fear anything now or hereafter. Creation becomes a thing of bliss, for who could labour to draw in breath or have the strength to breathe it out if there were not this bliss in the heaven of one's heart?

The *Aitareya Upanishad* begins with the one Spirit creating the universe out of its being. As guardians for the worlds, Spirit made the *Purusha* (person). Out of the cosmic egg came speech, breath, eyes and sight, ears and hearing, skin, hair, and herbs; from the navel and outbreath came death, and from the organ of pleasure seed and waters were born.

In the concluding chapter of this short *Upanishad* the author asked who is this Spirit by whom one sees and hears and smells and speaks and knows? The answer is the following:

That which is heart, this mind—that is,

Consciousness, perception, discernment, intelligence,

Wisdom, insight, persistence, thought, thoughtfulness,

Impulse, memory, conception, purpose, life, desire, will are all names of intelligence.

All things are guided by and based on this intelligence of Spirit *(Brahman)*. Ascending from this world with the intelligent soul, one obtains all desires in the heavenly world, even immortality.

The *Kaushitaki Upanishad* begins by asking if there is an end to the cycle of reincarnation. The teacher answers that one is born again according to one's actions *(karma)*. Ultimately the one who knows Spirit *(Brahman)* transcends even good and evil deeds and all pairs of opposites as a chariot-driver looks down upon two chariot wheels.

A ceremony is described whereby a dying father bequeaths all he has to his son. If he recovers, it is recommended that he live under the lordship of his son or wander as a religious mendicant. This practice of spiritual seeking as a beggar became one of the distinctive characteristics of Indian culture.

A story is told of Pratardana, who by fighting and virility arrives at the beloved home of Indra, who grants him a gift. Pratardana asks Indra to choose for him what would be most beneficial to humanity, but Indra replies that a superior does not choose for an inferior. Pratardana responds that then it is not a gift. After bragging of many violent deeds and saying that anyone who understands him is not injured even after committing the worst crimes such as murdering a parent, Indra identifies himself with the breathing spirit *(prana)* of the intelligent soul *(prajnatman)*. This breathing spirit is the essence of life and thus immortal. It is by intelligence *(prajna)* that one is able to master all of the senses and faculties of the soul. All these faculties are fixed in the intelligence, which is fixed in the breathing spirit, which is in truth the blissful, ageless, immortal soul. One does not become greater by good action nor less by bad action. One's own self *(atman)* causes one to lead up from these worlds by good action or is led downward by bad action. The soul itself *(atman)* is the world-protector and the sovereign of the world. Thus ultimately the soul is responsible for everything it experiences.

It is mentioned in the *Kaushitaki Upanishad* that it is contrary to nature for a Kshatriya to receive a Brahmin as a student. However, the *Upanishads* represent a time when the Kshatriya caste began to compete with Brahmins in spiritual endeavours. Though the Brahmins had control of the formal religion in the villages where the Kshatriyas controlled the government, by tutoring their sons and others in the forest the Kshatriyas developed a less ritualistic and traditional spirituality that is recorded in the mystical *Upanishads*.

Kena, Katha, Isha, and Mundaka

The *Kena Upanishad* consists of an older prose section and some more recent verse with which it begins. The word *Kena* means "by whom" and is the first word in a series of questions asking by whom is the mind projected, by whom does breathing go forth, by whom is speech impelled? What god is behind the eye and ear? The answer to these questions points to a mystical self that is beyond the mind and senses but is that God by which the mind and senses operate.

Those, who think they know it well, know it only slightly. What relates to oneself and the gods needs to be investigated. Beyond thought it is not known by those who think they know it. Beyond understanding it is not known by those who think they understand it, but by those who realize they do not understand it. It is correctly known by an awakening, for the one who knows it finds immortality. It can only be known by the soul. If one does not know it, it is a great loss. The wise see it in all beings and upon leaving this world become immortal.

In the prose section this mystical Spirit *(Brahman)* is shown to transcend the Vedic gods of fire (Agni), wind (Vayu), and even powerful Indra, who being above the other gods at least came nearest to it, realizing that it was Brahman. In summary the *Kena Upanishad* concludes that austerity, restraint, and work are the foundation of the mystical doctrine; the *Vedas* are its limbs, and truth is its home. The one who knows it strikes off evil and becomes established in the most excellent, infinite, heavenly world.

The *Katha Upanishad* utilizes an ancient story from the *Rig Veda* about a father who gives his son Nachiketas to death (Yama) but brings in some of the highest teachings of mystical spirituality, helping us to realize why the *Upanishads* are referred to as the "end of the *Vedas*" in the double sense of completing the Vedic scripture and in explaining the ultimate goals. When Vajashrava was sacrificing all his possessions, faith entered into Nachiketas, his son, who asked his father three times to whom would he give him. Losing patience with these pestering questions, the father finally said, "I give you to Death (Yama)." Nachiketas knew that he was not the first to go to death, nor would he be the last, and like grain one is born again anyway. When he arrived at the house of Death, Yama was not there and only returned after three days. Because Nachiketas had not received the traditional hospitality for three days, Yama granted him three gifts. His first request was that his father would greet him cheerfully when he returned. The second was that he be taught about the sacrificial fire. These were easily granted.

The third request of Nachiketas was that the mystery of what death is be explained to him, for even the gods have had doubts about this. Death tries to make him ask for something else, such as wealth or long life with many pleasures, but Nachiketas firmly insists on his original request, knowing that these other gifts will soon pass away.

So Death begins by explaining that the good is much better than the pleasant, which Nachiketas has just proved that he understands. He wisely wants knowledge not ignorance, and Death describes how those, who think themselves learned but who are ignorant, run around deluded and are like the blind leading the blind. Those, who think this world is the only one, continually come under the control of Death. Death explains that this knowledge cannot be known by reasoning or thought, but it must be declared by another. I interpret this to mean that it must be learned by direct experience or from one who has had the experience.

Death tells how the truth is hard to see, but one must enter into the hidden, secret place in the depth of the heart. By considering this as God, one through *yoga* (union) wisely leaves joy and sorrow behind. One must transcend what is right and not right, what has been done and will be done. The sacred word *Aum* is declared to be the imperishable Spirit *(Brahman)*. The wise realize that they are not born nor die but are unborn, constant, eternal, primeval; this is not slain when the body is slain.

Smaller than the small, greater than the great, the soul is in the heart of every creature here. The one who is not impulsive sees it and is free of sorrow. Through the grace of the creator one sees the greatness of the soul. While sitting one may travel far; while lying down one may go everywhere. Who else but oneself can know the god of joy and sorrow, who is bodiless among bodies and stable among the unstable?

This soul is not obtained by instruction nor by intellect nor by much learning, but is obtained by the one chosen by this; to such the soul reveals itself. However, it is not revealed to those who have not ceased from bad conduct nor to those who are not peaceful. Those, who drink of justice, enter the secret place in the highest heaven. Thus correct ethics is a requirement, and one must also become peaceful.

Psychology is explained in the *Katha Upanishad* by using the analogy of a chariot. The soul is the lord of the chariot, which is the body. The intuition *(buddhi)* is the chariot-driver, the mind the reins, the senses the horses, and the objects of the senses the paths. Those, who do not understand and whose minds are undisciplined with senses out of control, are like the wild horses of a chariot that never reaches its goals; these go on to reincarnate. The wise reach their goal with Vishnu and are not born again. The hierarchy, starting from the bottom, consists of the objects of sense, the senses, the mind, the intuition, the soul, the unmanifest, and the person *(Purusha).*

Though hidden, the soul may be seen by subtle seers with superior intellect. The intelligent restrain speech with the mind, the mind with the knowing soul, the knowing soul with the intuitive soul, and the intuitive soul with the peaceful soul. Yet the spiritual path is as difficult as crossing on the sharpened edge of a razor. By discerning what has no sound nor touch nor form nor decay nor taste nor beginning nor end, one is liberated from the mouth of death.

A wise person, seeking immortality, looked within and saw the soul. The childish go after outward pleasures and walk into the net of widespread death. The wise do not seek stability among the unstable things here. Knowing the experiencer, the living soul is the lord of what has been and what will be. This is the ancient one born from discipline standing in the secret place. This is the truth that all things are one, but those, who see a difference here, go from death to death like water runs to waste among the hills. The soul goes into embodiment according to its actions and according to its knowledge.

The inner soul is in all things yet outside also; it is the one controller which when perceived gives eternal happiness and peace. Its light is greater than the sun, moon, stars, lightning, and fire which do not shine in the world illuminated by this presence. The metaphor of an upside down tree is used to show that heaven is the true root of all life.

The senses may be controlled by the mind, and the mind by the greater self. Through yoga the senses are held back so that one becomes undistracted even by the stirring of the intuition. Thus is found the origin and the end. When all the desires of the heart are cut like knots, then a mortal becomes immortal. There is a channel from the heart to the crown of the head by which one goes up into immortality, but the other channels go in various directions. One should draw out from one's body the inner soul, like an arrow from a reed, to know the pure, the immortal. The *Katha Upanishad* concludes that with this knowledge learned from Death with the entire rule of yoga, Nachiketas attained Brahman and became free from passion and death, and so may any other who knows this concerning the soul.

Greatly respected, the short *Isha Upanishad* is often put at the beginning of the *Upanishads*. *Isha* means "Lord" and marks the trend toward monotheism in the *Upanishads*. The Lord encloses all that moves in the world. The author recommends that enjoyment be found by renouncing the world and not coveting the possessions of others. The One pervades and transcends everything in the world.

> *Whoever sees all beings in the soul and the soul in all beings does not shrink away from this.*
>
> *In whom all beings have become one with the knowing soul what delusion or sorrow is there for the one who sees unity?*
>
> *It is radiant, incorporeal, invulnerable, without tendons, pure, untouched by evil.*
>
> *Wise, intelligent, encompassing, self-existent, it organizes objects throughout eternity.*

The One transcends ignorance and knowledge, non-becoming and becoming. Those, who know these pairs of opposites, pass over death and win immortality. The *Isha Upanishad* concludes with a prayer to the sun and to Agni. The *Mundaka Upanishad* declares Brahman the first of the gods, the creator of all and the protector of the world. Connected to the *Atharva Veda* the *Mundaka Upanishad* has Brahman teaching his eldest son Atharvan. Yet the lower knowledge of the four *Vedas* and the six *Vedangas* (phonetics, ritual, grammar, definition, metrics, and astrology) is differentiated from the higher knowledge of the imperishable source of all things. The ceremonial sacrifices are to be observed; but they are now considered "unsafe boats," and fools, who approve them as better, go again to old age and death.

Like the *Katha*, the *Mundaka Upanishad* warns against the ignorance of thinking oneself learned and going around deluded like the blind leading the blind. Those, who work *(karma)* without understanding because of attachment, when their rewards are exhausted, sink down wretched. "Thinking sacrifices and works of merit are most important, the deluded know nothing better." After enjoying the results of their good works, they enter this world again or even a lower one. The *Mundaka Upanishad* recommends a more mystical path:

> *Those who practice discipline and faith in the forest, the peaceful knowers who live on charity, depart without attachment through the door of the sun, to where lives the immortal Spirit, the imperishable soul.*
>
> *Having tested the worlds won by works, let the seeker of God arrive at detachment.*
>
> *What is not made is not attained by what is done.*

To gain this knowledge the seeker is to go with fuel in hand to a teacher who is learned in the scriptures and established in God. Approaching properly, calming the mind and attaining peace, the knowledge of God may be taught in the truth of reality by which one knows the imperishable Spirit.

The formless that is higher than the imperishable and is the source and goal of all beings may be found in the secret of the heart. The reality of immortal life may be known by using the weapons of the *Upanishads* as a bow, placing an arrow on it sharpened by meditation, stretching it with thought directed to that, and knowing the imperishable as the target. *Aum* is the bow; the soul is the arrow; and God is the target. Thus meditating on the soul and finding peace in the heart, the wise perceive the light of blissful immortality. The knot of the heart is loosened, all doubts vanish, and one's works *(karma)* cease when it is seen. Radiant is the light of lights that illuminates the whole world. God truly is this immortal, in front, behind, to the right and left, below and above; God is all this great universe.

By seeing the brilliant creator, the God-source, being a knower, the seer shakes off good and evil, reaching the supreme identity of life that shines in all beings. Enjoying the soul, doing holy works, such is the best knower of God. The soul can be attained by truth, discipline, correct knowledge, and by studying God. Truth conquers and opens the path to the gods by which sages, whose desires are satisfied, ascend to the supreme home. Vast, divine, subtler than the subtle, it shines out far and close by, resting in the secret place seen by those with vision. It is not grasped by sight nor speech nor angels nor austerity nor work but by the grace of wisdom and the mental purity of meditation which sees the indivisible.

Whatever world a person of pure heart holds clearly in mind is obtained. Yet whoever entertains desires, dwelling on them, is born here and there on account of those desires; but for the one whose desire is satisfied, whose soul is perfected, all desires here on earth vanish away. This soul is not attained by instruction nor intellect nor much learning but by the one whom it chooses, who enters into the all itself. Ascetics with natures purified by renunciation enter the God-worlds and transcend death. As rivers flow into the ocean, the liberated knower reaches the divine Spirit. Whoever knows that supreme God becomes God.

9

Historical Advantages of the Caste System

Historically, the caste system offered several advantages to the population of the Indian subcontinent. While Caste is nowadays seen by instances that render it anachronistic, in its original form the caste system served as an important instrument of order in a society in which mutual consent rather than compulsion ruled; where the ritual rights as well as the economic obligations of members of one caste or sub-caste were strictly circumscribed in relation to those of any other caste or sub-caste; where one was born into one's caste and retained one's station in society for life; where merit was inherited, where equality existed within the caste, but inter-caste relations were unequal and hierarchical.

A well-defined system of mutual interdependence through a division of labour created security within a community.

1. Preservation of order in society through the use of institutional stratification of social groups.
2. Integration of foreigners and invading forces into Indian culture by assigning a caste to them (a process that historian Jawaharlal Nehru referred to as "Indianization"): India has faced repeated invasions from outside the region, dating back to the Macedonian invasion by Alexander the Great. Most invaders were swiftly assimilated into ancient Indian society by assigning them specific castes. Examples include the Kambojas, believed to be of Indo-Scythian descent, who

were retroactively assigned a social position in the Manu Smriti.

3. The Varna system, with its normative interpretation as a division of labour, had and continues to have a heavy bias towards spiritual evolution. The deep religious proclivities and the urge for spiritual uplift had induced the people to search for simpler and effective ways to achieve the spiritual goal which led to innovations like the Bhakti movement which had a powerful impact on the socio-cultural-spiritual life of the people even at mass level without distinctions of caste or class or other social differences. It is these deeply run cultural roots which caused an abiding following for Hinduism even in the face of unrelenting assaults by other religions and had in fact continued to influence the lives of people even after their conversion to other faiths. Thus, the caste system can be said to have preserved ancient cultural values in Indian society.
4. The caste system played an influential role in shaping economic activities. The caste system functioned much like medieval European guilds, ensuring the division of labour, providing for the training of apprentices and, in some cases, allowing manufacturers to achieve narrow specialisation. For instance, in certain regions, producing each variety of cloth was the speciality of a particular sub-caste.
5. Philosophers argue that the majority of people would be comfortable in stratified endogamous groups and have been in ancient times. Membership in a particular caste, with its associated narrative, history and genealogy would instill in its members a sense of group accomplishment and cultural pride. Such sentiments are routinely expressed by the Marathas, for instance.

British Rule

The caste system was first exposed to the modern Western world during the Portuguese occupation and rule of sections of India. The word 'caste' in this context is derived from the Portuguese, 'casta'. Later, other European empires, including the British, occupied parts of the subcontinent.

The earliest use of caste as a basis for interpreting social and demographic data arose from British officials' concern to stamp out female infanticide. Later, the use of caste to classify the population formed a basis for British attempts at social engineering. According to certain British laws (such as the Criminal Tribes Act of 1871), many castes and tribes were described as habitually criminal, and adult male members of such groups forced to report weekly to the local police. The caste-based classification (moneylending, agricultural or martial) was also used for other purposes such as legislation controlling land transfers, the grant of proprietary rights, the regulation of rents, recruitment to the armed forces etc. British anthropologist Herbert Risley's *The Tribes and Castes of Bengal*, published in 1892, was one of the first works on the caste system in India written by a Western scholar.

The earliest forms of classification in the British censuses of India (1865, 1872 and 1881) were based on the varna system, with the population being divided into Brahmins, Kshatriyas, Vaishyas and Shudras. Denzil Ibbetson, in his introduction to the 1881 census of the Punjab, argued that the Indian caste system was more of a social than a religious institution, and that conversion from Hinduism to Islam had not necessarily the slightest effect upon caste. He stated that the varnas had "no present significance". The 1891 census was based primarily on castes as occupational guilds instead of the varnas. Some scholars state that the caste system was broken up greatly during British Raj in India. However, some other historians suggest that the impact of British reforms has been greatly exaggerated.

Initially, the British strengthened the caste system. They gave the Brahmins back special privileges the Muslim rulers had taken away. During the initial days of British East India Company's rules, caste privileges and customs were encouraged in the Bengal Army. But, British law courts disagreed with the discrimination against the lower castes. Many believe that the lack of British respect for sepoys' caste traditions was one of the reasons behind the Indian Rebellion of 1857.

During British rule, the reservation of seats for the "Depressed Classes" was incorporated into the Government of India Act 1935, which went into force in 1937. The Act brought the term "Scheduled castes" into use, which was later clarified in The Government of India (Scheduled Castes) Order, 1936 which contained a list of scheduled castes.

British Census Officers determined caste hierarchy based on the principle, e.g. someone who accepts food and water from another person but the other person does not reciprocate the same way, then the other person is superior to the former. It was contested at many places (a notable example is that the Koeris of UP who said they won't accept water from Brahmins, and so should be placed higher than them). Because it was met with rampant controversies, arbitration was very common during those days. The most notable arbitration stories are:

1. Caste status of Kayastha
2. Caste status of Kurmi.

It raised more questions than it answered and subsequent census records varied radically, making it free for all, after some time.

Varna and Jati

According to the ancient Hindu scriptures, there are four "varnas". The Bhagavad Gita says varnas are decided based on Guna and Karma. Manu Smriti and some other shastras mention four varnas: the Brahmins (teachers, scholars and priests), the Kshatriyas (kings and warriors), the Vaishyas (agriculturists and traders), and Shudras (service providers and artisans). This theoretical system postulated Varna categories as ideals and explained away the reality of thousands of endogamous Jatis actually prevailing in the country as being the result of historical mixing among the "pure" Varnas-*Varna Sankara*. All those, including foreigners, tribals and nomads, who did not subscribe to the norms of the Hindu society were contagious and untouchables. Another group excluded from the main society was called Parjanya or Antyaja. This group of former "untouchables" (self described now as Dalits) i.e. downtrodden, was considered either the lower section of Shudras or outside the Varna system altogether. Passages from scriptures such as Manu Smriti indicate that the varna system was originally non-hereditary.

Several critics of Hinduism state that the caste system is rooted in the varna system mentioned in the ancient Hindu scriptures. However, many groups, such as ISKCON, consider the modern Indian caste system and the varna system as two distinct concepts. Many European scholars from the colonial era regarded the Manu Smriti as the "law book" of the Hindus, and thus concluded that the caste system is a part of Hinduism, an assertion that is rejected by many Hindu scholars, who state that it is an anachronistic social practice, not a religious one.

Although many Hindu scriptures contain passages that can be interpreted to sanction the caste system, they also contain indications that the caste system is not an essential part of Hinduism. The Vedas hardly place any importance on the caste system, mentioning caste only once (in the Purush Sukta) out of tens of thousands of verses. Most vedic scholars believe even this to be a subsequent and artificial insertion. In fact, none other than B. R. Ambedkar concluded after a thorough study that this is a much later interpolation and gave strong scholarly evidence to support his conclusion. In the Vedic period, there was no prohibition against the Shudras listening to the Vedas or participating in any religious rite.

In *Early Evidence for Caste in South India*, George L. Hart stated that "the earliest Tamil texts show the existence of what seems definitely to be caste, but which antedates the Brahmins and the Hindu orthodoxy". He believes that the origins of the caste system can be seen in the "belief system that developed with the agricultural civilization", and was later profoundly influenced by "the Brahmins and the Brahmanical religion". These early Tamil texts also outline the concept of equality. Saint Valluvar has stated "pirapokkum ella uyirkkum", which means "all are equal at birth". Likewise, Saint Auvaiyaar has stated that there are only two castes in the world: those who contribute positively and those who contribute negatively. From these, it can be inferred that the caste system is more of a socio-economic class system.

Caste and Social Status

Traditionally, although the political power lay with the Kshatriyas, historians portrayed that the Brahmins as custodians and interpreters of Dharma enjoyed much prestige and many advantages. Fa Hien, a Buddhist pilgrim from China, visited India around 400 AD. *"Only the lot of the Chandals he found unenviable; outcastes by reason of their degrading work as disposers of dead, they were universally shunned... But no other section of the population were notably disadvantaged, no other caste distinctions attracted comment from the Chinese pilgrim, and no oppressive caste 'system' drew forth his surprised censure.* ". In this period kings of Sudra and Brahmin origin were as common as those of Kshatriya *varna* and caste system was not wholly prohibitive and repressive.

The castes did not constitute a rigid description of the occupation or the social status of a group. Since British society was divided by class, the British attempted to equate the Indian caste system to their own social class system. They saw caste as an indicator of occupation, social standing, and intellectual ability. Intentionally or unintentionally, the caste system became more rigid during the British Raj, when the British started to enumerate castes during the ten year census and codified the system under their rule.

The Harijans, or the people outside the caste system, had the lowest social status. The Harijans, earlier referred to as "untouchables" by some, worked in what were seen as unhealthy, unpleasant or polluting jobs. In the past, the Harijans suffered from social segregation and restrictions, in addition to extreme poverty. They were not allowed temple worship with others, nor water from the same sources. Persons of higher castes would not interact with them. If somehow a member of a higher caste came into physical or social contact with an untouchable, the member of the higher caste was defiled, and had to bathe thoroughly to purge him or herself of the impurity. Social discrimination developed even among the Harijans. Sub-castes among Harijans, like *dhobi*, *nai* etc., would not interact with lower-order Bhangis, who were described as "outcasts even among outcastes".

Sociologists have commented on the historical advantages offered by a rigid social structure, such as the caste system, and its lack of usefulness in the modern world. Historically, the caste system offered several advantages to the population of the Indian subcontinent. While Caste is nowadays seen by instances that render it anachronistic, in its original form, the caste system served as an important instrument of order in a society where mutual consent rather than compulsion ruled;

where the ritual rights as well as the economic obligations of members of one caste or sub-caste were strictly circumscribed in relation to those of any other caste or sub-caste; where one was born into one's caste and retained one's station in society for life; where merit was inherited, where equality existed within the caste, but inter-caste relations were unequal and hierarchical.

A well-defined system of mutual interdependence through a division of labour created security within a community. In addition, the division of labour on the basis of ethnicity allowed immigrants and foreigners to quickly integrate into their own caste niches.

The caste system played an influential role in shaping economic activities. The caste system functioned much like medieval European guilds, ensuring the division of labour, providing for the training of apprentices and, in some cases, allowing manufacturers to achieve narrow specialisation. For instance, in certain regions, producing each variety of cloth was the speciality of a particular sub-caste. Also, philosophers argue that the majority of people would be comfortable in stratified endogamous groups, and have been in ancient times.

Caste Mobility

Some scholars believe that the relative ranking of other castes was fluid or differed from one place to another prior to the arrival of the British. Sociologists such as Bernard Buber and Marriott McKim describe how the perception of the caste system as a static and textual stratification has given way to the perception of the caste system as a more processual, empirical and contextual stratification. Other sociologists such as Y. B Damle have applied theoretical models to explain mobility and flexibility in the caste system in India. According to these scholars, groups of lower-caste individuals could seek to elevate the status of their caste by attempting to emulate the practices of higher castes. Flexibility in caste laws permitted very low-caste religious clerics such as Valmiki to compose the Ramayana, which became a central work of Hindu scripture.

According to some psychologists, mobility across broad caste lines may have been "minimal", though sub-castes (jatis) may change their social status over the generations by fission, relocation, and adoption of new rituals. Sociologist M. N. Srinivas has also debated the question of rigidity in Caste. In an ethnographic study of the Coorgs of Karnataka, he observed considerable flexibility and mobility in their caste hierarchies. He asserts that the caste system is far from a rigid system in which the position of each component caste is fixed for all time. Movement has always been possible, and especially in the middle regions of the hierarchy. It was always possible for groups born into a lower caste to "rise to a higher position by adopting vegetarianism and teetotalism" i.e. adopt the customs of the higher castes. While theoretically "forbidden", the process was not uncommon in practice. The concept of sanskritization, or the adoption of upper-caste norms by the lower castes, addressed the actual complexity and fluidity of caste relations.

Historical examples of mobility in the Indian Caste System among Hindus have been researched. There is also precedent of certain Shudra families within the temples of the Sri Vaishnava sect in South India elevating their caste.

The fact that many of the dynasties were of obscure origin suggests some social mobility: a person of any caste, having once acquired political power, could also acquire a genealogy connecting him with the traditional lineages and conferring Kshatriya status. A number of new castes, such as the Kayasthas (scribes) and Khatris (traders), are mentioned in the sources of this period. According to the Brahmanic sources, they originated from intercaste marriages, but this is clearly an attempt at rationalizing their rank in the hierarchy. Many of these new castes played a major role in society. The hierarchy of castes did not have a uniform distribution throughout the country. Khatri appears to be unquestionably a Prakritised form of the Sanskrit Kshatriya.

Reforms

There have been challenges to the caste system from the time of Buddha, and from the time of Mahavira (Jaina founder) and (still earlier) of Gosala Maskarin (Ajivika founder). Opposition to the system of varna ('caste') is regularly asserted already in the Yoga Upanicads (of early mediaeval date); and is a constant feature of Cina-acara tantrism (Chinese-derived movement in Asom, and also of mediaeval date). The Natha system (likewise mediaeval) founded by Matsya-indra Natha and by Gorakca Natha, and spread throughout India, has likewise been in consistent opposition to the system of varna.

Many Bhakti period saints rejected the caste discriminations and accepted all castes, including untouchables, into their fold. During the British Raj, this sentiment gathered steam, and many Hindu reform movements such as Brahmo Samaj and Arya Samaj renounced caste-based discrimination.

The inclusion of so-called untouchables into the mainstream was argued for by many social reformers. Mahatma Gandhi called them "Harijans" (children of God) although that term is now considered patronizing and the term Dalit ("downtrodden") is the more commonly used. Gandhi's contribution toward the emancipation of the untouchables is still debated, especially in the commentary of his contemporary Dr. B. R. Ambedkar, an untouchable himself, who frequently saw Gandhi's activities as detrimental to the cause of upliftment of his people.

The practice of untouchability was formally outlawed by the Constitution of India in 1950, and has declined significantly since then. K. R. Narayanan, who became the President of India in 1997, and K. G. Balakrishnan (the present Chief Justice of India) have belonged to castes formerly considered untouchable.

British Rule

The fluidity of the caste system was affected by the arrival of the British. Prior to that, the relative ranking of castes differed from one place to another. The castes did not constitute a rigid description of the occupation or the social status of a group. The British attempted to equate the Indian caste system to their own class system. They saw caste as an indicator of occupation, social standing, and intellectual ability. During the initial days of the British East India Company's rule, caste privileges and customs were encouraged, but the British law courts disagreed with the discrimination against the lower castes. However, British policies of divide and rule as well as enumeration of the population into rigid categories during the 10 year census contributed towards the hardening of caste identities.

MODERN STATUS OF THE CASTE SYSTEM

NFHS Survey estimated only Hindu OBC population. Total OBC population derived by assuming Muslim OBC population in same proportion as Hindu OBC population). In some rural areas and small towns, the caste system is still very rigid. Caste is also a factor in the politics of India. The Government of India has officially documented castes and subcastes, primarily to determine those deserving reservation (positive discrimination in education and jobs) through the census. The Indian reservation system, though limited in scope, relies entirely on quotas. The Government lists consist of Scheduled Castes, Scheduled Tribes and Other Backward Classes:

Scheduled Castes (SC)

Scheduled castes generally consist of former "untouchables" (the term "Dalit" is now preferred). The present population is 16% of the total population of India (around 160 million). For example, the Delhi state has 49 castes listed as SC.

Scheduled Castes ("SC"s) and Scheduled Tribes ("ST"s) are Indian population groupings that are explicitly recognized by the Constitution of India, previously called the "depressed classes" by the British. SCs/STs together comprise over 24% of India's population, with SC at over 16% and ST over 8% as per the 2001 Census. The proportion of Scheduled Castes and Scheduled Tribes in the population of India has steadily risen since independence in 1947.

Some Scheduled Castes in India are also known as Dalits Some Scheduled Tribe people are also referred to as Adivasis. Post Independence Scheduled Castes are benefited by reservation policy. With reservations in India, The Constitution laid down 15% and 7. 5% of vacancies to government aided educational institutes and for jobs in the government/public sector, as reserved quota for the SC and ST candidates respectively for a period of five years, after which the situation was to be reviewed. This period was routinely extended by the succeeding governments.

Scheduled castes and scheduled tribes in 2010 Some of the sub-castes of scheduled castes have become relatively better economically. As a benefit of Reservation they have acquired technical and management education as well. Many of them are working in the Government sector, again because of a certain percentage of seats specifically reserved for them in the Government sector. However, the prevailing condition of SCs/STs can not be ascertained in the private sector because of absence of reservation in private sector and due to the absence of any data on the community wise break up of work force in private sector.

History

From the 1850s these communities were loosely referred to as the "Depressed Classes". The early part of the 20th century saw a flurry of activity in the British Raj to assess the feasibility of responsible self-government for India. The Morley-Minto Reforms Report, Montagu-Chelmsford Reforms Report, and the Simon Commission were some of the initiatives that happened in this context. One of the hotly contested issues in the proposed reforms was the topic of reservation of seats for the "Depressed" Classes in provincial and central legislatures.

In 1935 the British passed The Government of India Act 1935, designed to give Indian provinces greater self-rule and set up a national federal structure. Reservation of seats for the Depressed Classes was incorporated into the act, which came into force in 1937.

The Act brought the term "Scheduled Castes" into use, and defined the group as including "such castes, races or tribes or parts of groups within castes, races or tribes, which appear to His Majesty in Council to correspond to the classes of persons formerly known as the 'Depressed Classes', as His Majesty in Council may prefer. " This discretionary definition was clarified in *The Government of India (Scheduled Castes) Order, 1936* which contained a list, or Schedule, of castes throughout the British administered provinces.

After independence, the Constituent Assembly continued the prevailing definition of Scheduled Castes and Tribes, and gave the President of India and Governors of states responsibility to compile a full listing of castes and tribes, and also the power to edit it later as required. The actual complete listing of castes and tribes was made via two orders *The Constitution (Scheduled Castes) Order, 1950*, and *The Constitution (Scheduled Tribes) Order, 1950* respectively.

Constitutional Framework for Safeguarding of Interests

The Constitution provides a framework with a three pronged strategy to improve the situation of SCs and STs.

1. Protective Arrangements-Such measures as are required to enforce equality, to provide punitive measures for transgressions, to eliminate established practices that perpetuate inequities, etc. A number of laws were enacted to operationalize the provisions in the Constitution. Examples of such laws include The Untouchability Practices Act, 1955, Scheduled Caste and Scheduled Tribe (Prevention of Atrocities) Act, 1989, The Employment of Manual scavengers and Construction of Dry Latrines (Prohibition) Act, 1993, etc.
2. Compensatory Discrimination-provide positive preferential treatment in allotment of jobs and access to higher education, as a means to accelerate the integration of the SCs and STs with mainstream society. Compensatory discrimination is also popularly referred to as Reservation.
3. Development-Provide for resources and benefits to bridge the wide gap in social and economic condition between the SCs/STs and other communities.

National Commissions

To effectively implement the various safeguards built into the Constitution and other legislations, the Constitution, under Articles 338 and 338A, provides for two statutory commissions-the National Commission for Scheduled Castes, and National Commission for Scheduled Tribes.

History

In the original Constitution, Article 338 provided for a Special Officer, called the Commissioner for SCs and STs, to have the responsibility of monitoring the effective implementation of various safeguards for SCs/STs in the Constitution as well as other related legislations and to report to the President. To enable efficient discharge of duties, 17 regional offices of the Commissioner were set up all over the country. In the meanwhile there was persistent representation for a replacement of the Commissioner with a multi-member committee. It was proposed that the 48th Amendment to the Constitution be made to alter Article 338 to enable said proposal. While the amendment was being debated, the Ministry of Welfare issued an administrative decision to establish the Commission for SCs/STs as a multi-member committee to discharge the same functions as that of the Commissioner of SCs/STs. The first commission came into being in August 1978. The functions of the commission were modified in September 1987 to advise Government on broad policy issues and levels of development of SCs/STs. In 1990 that the Article 338 was amended to give birth to the statutory National Commission for SCs and STs via the *Constitution (Sixty fifth Amendment) Bill, 1990*. The first Commission under the 65th Amendment was constituted in March 1992 replacing the Commissioner for Scheduled Castes and Scheduled Tribes and the Commission set up under the Ministry of Welfare's Resolution of 1987. In 2002, the Constitution was again amended to split the National Commission for Scheduled Castes and Scheduled Tribes into two separate commissions-the National Commission for Scheduled Castes and the National Commission for Scheduled Tribes

Distribution

Sachar Committee report of 2006 revealed that scheduled castes and tribes of India are not limited to the religion of Hinduism. The 61st Round Survey of the NSSO found that almost nine-tenths of the Buddhists and one-third of the Sikh's in India belonged to the notified scheduled castes of the Constitution while one-third of the Christians belonged to the notified scheduled tribes of the Constitution.

Religion	*Scheduled Caste*	*Scheduled Tribe*
Buddhism	89. 50%	7. 40%
Christianity	9. 00%	32. 80%
Sikhism	37. 0%	0. 90%
Hinduism	22. 20%	9. 10%
Zoroastrianism	-	15. 90%
Jainism	-	2. 60%
Islam	0. 80%	0. 50%

Scheduled Caste Sub-Plan (SCSP)

The strategy of Scheduled Castes Sub-Plan (SCSP) which was evolved in 1979 is one of the most important interventions through the planning process for social, economic and educational development of Scheduled Castes and for improvement in their working and living conditions. It is an umbrella strategy to ensure flow of targeted financial and physical benefits from all the general sectors of development for the benefit of Scheduled Castes.

Under this strategy, population. It entails targeted flow of funds and associated benefits from the annual plan of States/ Union Territories (UTs) at least in proportion to the SC population i.e. 16 % in the total population of the country/the particular state. Presently, 27 States/UTs having sizeable SC populations are implementing Scheduled Castes Sub-Plan. Although the Scheduled Castes population, according to 2001 Census, was 16.66 crores constituting 16.23% of the total population of India, the allocations made through SCSP in recent years have been much lower than the population proportion.

Table below provides the details of total State Plan Outlay, flow to Scheduled Castes Sub-Plan (SCSP) as reported by the State/UT Governments for the last few years especially since the present UPA government is in power at the;

2004-2005	108788. 9	17656	2065. 38	11. 06	68. 3	5591
2005-2006	136234. 5	22111	16422. 63	12. 05	74. 3	5688
2006-2007	152088	24684	21461. 12	14. 11	86. 9	3223
2007-2008*	155013. 2	25159	22939. 99	14. 80	91. 2	2219

Information in respect of 14 States/UTs only and as on 31-12-2007

Source: Network for Social Accountability (NSA) http://nsa. org. in.

Scheduled Castes and Tribes in Indian Army

- Sikh Light Infantry, The Sikh Light Infantry comprises the Mazhabi/Dalit and Ramdasia/Dalit Sikh soldiers; well known for their dountless daring, courage, loyalty and tenacity, is one of the oldest Regiments of the Army.
- Mahar Regiment, The Mahar (Scheduled Caste) Regiment is an Infantry Regiment of the Indian

Army. Although it was originally intended to be a regiment consisting of troops from the Mahars in Maharashtra.

- Naga Regiment, The Naga Regiment is the youngest Regiment of the Indian Army. In 1970, the First Battalion of the Naga Regiment was raised in Ranikhet. This Regiment comprises 50% Nagas tribes and 50% of an equal number of Kumaoni, Garhwali and Gorkhas.

Prominent Members of SC/STs

- B. R. Ambedkar, also known as Babasaheb, was an Indian jurist, political leader, Buddhist activist, thinker, philosopher, historian, anthropologist, orator, prolific writer, economist, editor, scholar, revolutionary and the revivalist of Buddhism in India. He was also the chief architect of the Indian Constitution.
- Birsa Munda, freedom fighters in the Indian struggle for independence against British colonialism
- Jyotirao Phule, was an activist, thinker, social reformer, writer, philosopher, theologist, scholar, editor and revolutionary from Maharashtra, India in the nineteenth century
- K. R. Narayanan, tenth President of India
- K. G. Balakrishnan, Hon'ble Chief Justice of India
- Babu Jagjivan Ram, Former Deputy Prime Minister of India
- G. M. C. Balayogi (1951-2002) (First dalit speaker, Lok Sabha, India)
- Damodaram Sanjivayya (1921-1972) (First dalit Chief Minister of a state in India and first dalit President of Indian National Congress party)
- Kashi Ram, Founder of Bahujan Samaj Party
- Ajit Jogi, first chief minister of the state of Chhattisgarh, India
- Mayavati, Chief Minister of Uttar Pradesh.
- Dr. Faguni Ram, Ph. D (3-Time Member of Parliament and Ex-Minister of State)
- Bangaru Laxman, former President of Bharatiya Janata Party (BJP)

- Sushilkumar Shinde, Current Cabinet Minister for Power
- Shibu Soren, current Chief Minister of Jharkhand state in India
- Meira Kumar, is an Indian politician and a five time Member of Parliament. She was elected unopposed as the first woman Speaker of Lok Sabha on 3 June 2009
- Hon'ble Justice S. Ashok Kumar, Judge Madras High Court and High Court of Andhra Pradesh (Retd)
- K. S. R. Murthy IAS, Retired, Former MP, Lok Sabha
- Ram Vilas Paswan, the president of the Lok Janshakti Party, political party
- Prem Singh (MLA)
- Lala Ram Ken, Member of Parliament (7th and 8th), India
- Divya Bharti, Late Bollywood actress.

Scheduled Tribes (ST)

Scheduled tribes generally consist of tribal groups. The present population is 7% of the total population of India i.e. around 70 million.

Bibliography

Ainapur, L. S.: *Dynamics of Caste Relations in Rural India*, Jaipur, Rawat Publications, 1986.

Baird, Robert: *Religion in Modern India*, New Delhi, Manohar, 1981.

Basham, A.L.: *A Cultural History of India*, Oxford, Clarendon Press, 1975.

Benjamin, Joseph: *Scheduled Castes in Indian Politics and Society*, New Delhi, Ess Ess Publications, 1989.

Brown, Judith M.: *Modern India: The Origins of an Asian Democracy*, New Delhi, Oxford University Press, 1985.

Chaturvedi, M.D.,: *Hinduism, The Eternal Religion,* Bharatiya Vidya Bhavan, Bombay, 1992.

Coomaraswamy, Ananda K.: *Contemporary Indian Philosophy*, Geroge Allen & Unwin, London, 1936.

Dandekar, R.N.: *Some Aspects of the History of Hinduism*, Radhey Shayam Press, Poona. 1967.

Derrett, J. Duncan. *Religion, Law, and the State in India*. London: Faber, 1968.

Dumont, Louis: *The Caste System and Its Implications*, London, Granada Pub. Ltd., 1970.

Farquhar, J.N.: *Modern Religious Movements in India*, Munshiram, New Delhi, 1967.

Gorhe, Neelam: *Social Development and Dalit Women*, Gyan Pub. House, New Delhi, 1995.

Harman, William: *The Sacred Marriage of a Hindu Goddess*, Indiana University Press, Bloomington, 1989.

Hutton, J. H.: *Caste in India: Its Nature, Function and Origins*, London, Cambridge University Press, 1946.

Johnson, S. B.: *Social Mobility Among Untouchables*, Vikas, New Delhi, 1979.

Lakshmanna, C.: *Caste Dynamics in Village India*, Nachiketa Publications, Bombay, 1973.

Mallik, Suneila: *Social Integration of the Scheduled Castes*. Abhinav, New Delhi, 1979.

Mohan, Radhey : *Education and National Development*, Indiana Publications, New Delhi, 1976.

Mohanty, J.: *Indian Education in the Emerging Society*, Sterling Publisher Private Limited, Banglore, 1982.

Paliwal, M.R.: *Social Change and Education: Present and Future*, Uppal Publishing House, New Delhi, 1984.

Rao, M. S. A.: *Social Movement and Social Transformation: A Study of Backward Class Movement*, New Delhi, Macmillian Press, 1978.

Satyamurthy, T.V.: *Region, Religion, Caste, Gender and Culture in Contemporary India*, Delhi, OUP, 1996.

Saxena, Sateshwari: *Educational Planning in India*, Sterling Publishers (pvt.) Ltd., Bombay, 1978.

Sharma, K. L.: *Caste, Class and Social Movements*, Rawat Publications, Jaipur, 1986.

Shukla, P.D.: *Towards New Pattern of Education in India*, Sterling Publishers (Pvt.) Ltd., New Delhi. 1976.

Silverberg, James: *Social Mobility in the Caste System in India*, Mouton Publishers, The Hague, 1968.

Singh, Virendra Prakash: *Caste System and Social Change,* New Delhi, Commonwealth Publishers, 1992.

Thrupp, J. & Willmott. : *Educational Management in Managerialist Times: Beyond the Textual Apologists*, Maidenhead, UK, 2003.

Tiwari, P. O.: *Dimensions of Scheduled Caste Development in India*, Uppal Publishing House, New Delhi, 1991.

Index

□□□